THE
Baseball Research
JOURNAL

Volume 39
Fall 2010
Number 2

Published by
the Society for American Baseball Research

THE BASEBALL RESEARCH JOURNAL
Volume 39, Number 2, Fall 2010

Editor: Nicholas Frankovich
Production and Design Coordinator: Lisa Hochstein
Cover Designer: Lisa Hochstein
Fact Checker: Clifford Blau
Photo Consultant: Mark Fimoff

Front cover: Nolan Ryan. National Baseball Hall of Fame Library, Cooperstown, N.Y.

Published by:
The Society for American Baseball Research, Inc.
812 Huron Road, Suite 719
Cleveland, Ohio 44115-1165

Phone: (216) 575-0500
Fax: (216) 575-0502
Email: info@sabr.org
Web: www.sabr.org

Copyright © 2010
The Society for American Baseball Research
Printed in the United States of America

ISBN 978-1-933599-18-2

Contents

Note from the Editor

The topic of Dan Basco and Michael Davies's article on DIPS, or defense-independent pitching statistics, was suggested to me by an astute sabermetrician. He was finding it hard to identify what the literature was, what the state of the art was, what work in DIPS was built on what earlier work or perhaps even rendered that earlier work obsolete. Why didn't I commission an article that would serve as an overview of the subject to date? I did, and the result is the "The Many Flavors of DIPS," which you can begin reading at page 41.

Basco and Davies do go into more statistical depth than the non-statistician can plumb without sinking, and if you're that kind of reader I propose that you don't plumb it but rather skate over it, take in the scenery, and learn what you can from your tour of the neighborhood. If you're a statistician and it strikes you as nothing you didn't already know, remember, that's a sign that at least it isn't wrong. And then remember that lucidity is not just something we bring to what we read but is also something we've acquired from what we've read over the years. Reference works, handbooks, field guides, textbooks—some of these have shaped our way of thinking so convincingly that we forget that what we learned from them was never in fact innate knowledge.

At some point the tenured physicist stops consulting his college textbooks, but they remain among the foundations on which his expertise stands. It would be a broad jump from your fourth-grade science project to quantum theory. There are intervening steps, and you can't skip any of them. In sabermetrics, a lot of the steps are still missing. Tom Tango in *The Book* (Potomac, 2007) makes an important contribution, but much of the book is still inaccessible to someone who isn't already trained in statistics. Ditto *Curve Ball* (Springer, 2003) by Jim Albert and Jay Bennett. Sabermetric handbooks tend to be like biblical commentaries whose pages are thick with Hebrew and Greek: Of course the committed Bible reader should know the original languages, but to learn them takes years, and in the meantime we'd like not to be locked out of scripture entirely. So we take recourse to translations—and then, to our surprise, sometimes find that the translators were, if not necessarily inspired, let's say insightful.

The King James Version was not completed in a day, and neither is the project of writing the equivalent in sabermetrics. Some good work is being done toward that end—in this issue, by Basco and Davies, and in the previous issue by Basco and his coauthor Jeff Zimmerman, who offered an overview of advanced fielding statistics. Graham MacAree has a nice, 24-part series, "Sabermetrics 101," posted at the site Lookout Landing. There are others. To express sabermetric concepts in the vernacular is a rare talent. But there's a need not just for doing new sabermetrics in plain English but for collecting, organizing, synthesizing, and translating work that's already been done and published in scattershot fashion across the Internet.

This is the first issue of *The Baseball Research Journal* that has been published since John Zajc stepped down as executive director of SABR. His spirit has guided the journal to a degree that he probably hopes you wouldn't guess. He was the GM from whom the field manager would seek advice, which he would never presume to dispense if it wasn't solicited. His policy was to trust in the manager's command of his own clubhouse. Trust is a virtue that can be cultivated, but it helps if it's in the person's DNA. This quality that John brought to his dealings with the editor of *BRJ* was a pleasure to reciprocate, and *BRJ* is better as a result of it. Where it has nodded or fallen short, fault the editor, not him. We welcome John's successor, Marc Appleman, and look forward to all he has to bring to SABR culture.

Someone asked me if I thought that the key to the journal's success was its content. I thought the question was odd. Wasn't it tautological—like asking whether the energy you derive from the food you eat has to do with its caloric content? Only later did I realize that he was probably referring to *BRJ*'s design, which is beautiful in the way graphic design is supposed to be. It's invisible—well, not invisible, but inconspicuous. If you noticed it enough to comment on it, it wouldn't be doing its job, which is to serve the content, not draw attention to itself. Lisa Hochstein, our compositor and designer, has graced recent issues, including this one, with her artist's eye and touch. Let's thank her.

Nick Frankovich

Correspondence

I am grateful for Lee Lowenfish's generous review of my Satchel Paige biography in your summer 2010 issue ("Satchel Paige: Off on His Own, at the Center of the Crowd").

As a lifelong journalist who has written countless book reviews, I also know that authors generally deserve any criticism that accompanies the praise, especially when it comes from an esteemed reviewer like Lee, and I accept most that he offered.

I take exception, however, to several of what he calls my "nagging errors":

Lee took exception when I referred to a 1949 *Sports Illustrated* article, writing that the magazine wasn't founded until 1954. A footnote in my book explains that "this version of *Sports Illustrated*, published by Dell, is unrelated to the current magazine," a fact confirmed by *SI* and Dell.

Lee said the paperback edition of my book failed to correct an error in the hardcover about a world heavyweight bout that took place shortly before Satchel broke into the majors. That fix was made, and paperbacks correctly refer to Joe Louis's 1948 knockout of "Jersey Joe" Walcott.

Lee says I credited the Kansas City Monarchs for playing games under the lights as early as 1930—and that I incorrectly said that white owners didn't follow suit for fifteen years, when it really was five years. I did say that black ballplayers were playing under the lights fifteen years before the major leagues did, but I never said it was the Monarchs who did that or that the year was 1930. As several Negro League historians have confirmed, J. L. Wilkinson's

All-Nations team, which included black and white players, used gas lights for a night game in 1920, which was fifteen years before the Cincinnati Reds hosted the first major-league night game.

Lee also wondered why I spelled Pittsburgh's famous Crawford Grill without an e at the end of grill. I took my spelling from the *Pittsburgh Courier*, the *Pittsburgh Post-Gazette*, Rob Ruck's authoritative writings on the city and its black baseball club, and sources I found when I visited the site of the old restaurant.

Lee wrote that I didn't realize that Moses Fleetwood Walker's nationalism didn't draw many followers. I thought that was implicit in my saying he was a decade too oon, before Marcus Garvey's more successful movement.

I also would like to respond to a couple matters of judgment raised by Lee, although I respect the questions he raised and hesitate to tangle with someone who knows as much as he does.

Lee says I was "largely dismissive" of Bob Feller's role in integrating baseball. I thought that I gave him more than his due when I wrote that his barnstorming tour with Satchel "gave many of the black players their first chance to ride in a plane and play to sell-out crowds of whites as well as blacks. They got to match their skills against a team not just of Major Leaguers but the very best of whiteball. That is what mattered in the end to most of the Negro Leaguers who barnstormed with Feller, including Satchel. By showcasing their skills and those of their teammates, these two traditionalists did as much to advance the racial cause as anyone in baseball."

Lee also took me to task for my "unnecessary denigration" of the roles of integration pioneers Branch Rickey and Jackie Robinson. I

didn't mean to denigrate their roles. But many of the old Negro Leaguers I talked to did resent the way Jackie denigrated the Negro Leagues, in his writings and conversations. And it was they, not me, who first suggested that, if Jackie was the father of equal opportunity in baseball, Satchel was the grandfather.

Last things: I agree with Lee that we need to know more on where "Jewbaby" Floyd got his nickname. (As a Jew who has written extensively on Jewish issues I was especially intrigued, but for the life of me I couldn't find more, despite endless questioning during my visits to Kansas City.) He also is right when he wishes I had said more about Edward Byrd, Satchel's coach in an Alabama reform school. Again, I tried, but a visit to that school, searches by its unofficial historian, and more searches by friends in the Alabama Archives didn't yield anything.

Larry Tye
Lexington, Massachusetts

LEE LOWENFISH RESPONDS

I am glad that Larry Tye did omit in the paperback edition of Satchel the erroneous reference to the second fight of Joe Louis and Max Schmeling as having occurred in 1948. I apologize for the error that perhaps was caused by seeing the same reference to Schmeling in the paperback index.

As for the *Sports Illustrated* of 1949 not being the more famous magazine that began publication in 1954, I believe that fact required citation in the text not buried in an endnote at the back of the book.

On matters of substance Larry Tye shouldn't "hesitate to tangle" with yours truly. That is the only way to explore and ideally reach some useful understanding about the difficult and vital subject of race in baseball and America.

OF PAIGE, LAWRENCE RITTER, AND THE DODGERS IN JERSEY CITY

As a SABR member, I usually read the journals cover to cover. The summer 2010 issue of *The Baseball Research Journal* had several articles that triggered memories I would like to share.

First, "The Brooklyn Dodgers in Jersey City" by John Burbridge. I started out as a Brooklyn fan, mainly because a grandfather, born in 1892, who loved them. Both my parents were from the New York City area, but we were living in Corning, New York, in the 1950s. I had been to my first MLB game in 1954—the Chicago White Sox at the Philadelphia Athletics—with my family, including the grandfather.

For me, however, this was no substitute for the Dodgers or Ebbets Field. I was visiting my aunts and grandmother in Bayonne, New Jersey, in the summer of 1956 when my aunts were willing to take me to nearby Roosevelt Stadium to see the Dodgers host the Pirates on August 6. I experienced great preliminary joy came as we passed the Dodgers' team bus and were close enough to see some of the players.

What do I remember of the game? I do remember the stadium and from the photo can approximate where we sat. I went down to the Dodgers' dugout before the game and got an autograph from coach Jake Pitler. If I am not mistaken, it was the first major-league game for the Pirates' Bill Mazeroski or nearly his first.

I got to my first and only Ebbets Field game the next year (opponent: Phillies), the last one for Ebbets. I should add that, yes, I was a member of Ron Gabriel's Brooklyn Dodgers Fan Club and roomed with Ron at the SABR conferences for a number of years.

Next, the Henry Chadwick Award and Lawrence S. Ritter. I attended NYU as a doctoral student. In 1971, I took a macroeconomics course from Professor Ritter, an excellent teacher, who made the material easy.

Oddly, even though *The Glory of Their Times* was published in 1966 and I'm a baseball fan, my baseball reading at that point had not gotten beyond the Dodgers, Jackie Robinson, and *The Sporting News*. It was not until I joined SABR and my reading got deeper that I got to *Glory*. It is now a part of a fairly good baseball library.

Finally, Lee Lowenfish's review of *Satchel: The Life and Times of an American Legend* by Larry Tye. I read the book, enjoyed it, and noted the same chronological discrepancies as did Lowenfish. I wondered about Satchel's reputation for interacting with fans. I saw him in an exhibition as a Harlem Globetrotter pitcher (versus the House of David) in 1954 in Corning. He was not very cordial to ten-year-old fans.

Those are my comments, for what they're worth.

John Gottko
Corvallis, Oregon

The Day the Phillies Went to Egypt

C. Paul Rogers III

I N THE SPRING OF 1947, a seventeen-year-old south-paw named Curt Simmons was the hottest amateur prospect in the country. Fifteen of the sixteen major league teams were chomping at the bit to sign Simmons as soon as he graduated from high school in June. Phillies general manager Herb Pennock dubbed him "a second Rube Waddell" and sportswriters were touting his curveball as the best since Bob Feller's.

Simmons had earned the title Phenom when he was only sixteen. That summer, 1945, he pitched the Coplay American Legion team to the first of two consecutive Pennsylvania state junior crowns. His mound prowess earned him selection to an American Legion all-star game in Shibe Park in Philadelphia, where he struck out seven of the nine hitters he faced in three innings. That performance led to his selection later in the summer to the East–West American Legion All-Star game in the Polo Grounds in New York City. Babe Ruth managed the East team, for which Curt played, against Ty Cobb, who managed the West. Simmons was probably one of the last to pitch to Ruth. The Babe still liked to get his swings and would jump in during batting practice and take a few cuts against Curt, once hitting a ball onto the roof of the Polo Grounds. During the week leading up to the August 28 contest, Simmons and the other hurlers also came under the tutelage of the great lefty Carl Hubbell.

Simmons was from the small Lehigh Valley burg of Egypt, population well under one thousand. The Legion All-Star game was Simmons's first trip to the Big Apple and his first time even to ride an elevator. When the game arrived, Curt started and pitched four innings before moving to the outfield, his position in high school when he wasn't pitching. He singled in a run and then in the ninth lashed a triple to drive in the run that cut the West's lead to one run, 4–3, and then scored the tying run from third. The East went on to win 5–4 and Simmons was named the game's MVP. Afterward the Babe advised him to switch to the outfield because of how well he hit. (Simmons had in fact batted .465 his senior year in high school, with 20 hits, including two homers, three triples, and six doubles in 43 at-bats.) Ruth, of course, knew something about giving up pitching for full-time outfield play, but Simmons stuck to pitching.

Curt Simmons, who helped lead the 1950 Phillies to the pennant, missed the World Series when his National Guard unit was activated. With the Cardinals in 1964, he finally saw his first World Series action, in two fine starts against the Yankees.

In Simmons's senior year of high school in 1947, he struck out 102 batters and gave up only 12 hits in 43⅓ innings. He threw two no-hitters, three one-hitters, and two four-hitters in leading his Whitehall High School nine to a third straight Lehigh Valley title. In the game against Quakertown on April 8, he whiffed 20 of the 21 batters he retired.

Simmons was in a position to sign for a record bonus, and the neighboring Phillies were hoping to win the bidding war. Long the doormats of the National League, the club was in the midst of a turn-around because of the deep pockets of Bob Carpenter Sr., who had purchased the club during the war for a reported $400,000. Carpenter was a former vice president at DuPont Chemicals who was married to a DuPont. Carpenter named his 28-year-old son Bob Jr. club president, with instructions to spend money to make the Phillies a contender.

Cy Morgan was a Phillies scout from Allentown who had closely followed Simmons throughout his high-school and Legion career. He had become friends with Simmons's parents, and together they hatched a plan to bring the Phillies to Egypt for an exhibition game so that Curt could show his wares against major-league opposition while pitching for the town team. Simmons's father Larry was a cement-mill worker who, in his effort to maximize his son's value, was taking a calculated risk. If Curt pitched well, his stock would rise and so would the bidding war. If he got ripped or was wild, his stock would fall.

In response, the Phillies understood that the price for Simmons might rise or fall but exacted a promise from the elder Simmons that, no matter what, the family would give the Phillies the final opportunity to bid after all the other teams. That is, the Phillies were to have the last shot in exchange for sending their team to Egypt for an in-season exhibition game.

So on Monday, June 2, 1947 the Phillies journeyed to Egypt to play a 5:30 P.M. game against the town's amateur team from the aptly named Twilight League. The Phillies players were not at all happy about playing a game on an off-day in a podunk town against a wild young left-hander at twilight on a field without lights. While the game was billed as a fund-raiser for the town's newly constructed Egypt Memorial Park, it was clear to all that the Phillies would have remained in Philadelphia but for the courting of the young Curt Simmons.

General manager Herb Pennock, president Bob Carpenter, and Cy Morgan also attended, underscoring the importance of the evening. So did scouts from about every other major-league organization. Phillies manager Ben Chapman fielded a lineup made up of about half of his regulars, including outfielders Del Ennis and Johnny Wyrostek, first baseman Howie Schultz, second baseman Lee Handley, and third baseman Jim Tabor. With the exception of Ennis, the Phils' lineup was not exactly Murderers' Row, but they were a big-league ballclub with a 17–23 won–lost record (although they would fade to 62–92 and a seventh-place finish, 32 games behind the pennant-winning Brooklyn Dodgers).

The locals expected a crowd of four thousand. Actual paid attendance was a robust 6,282, as fans from throughout the Lehigh Valley drove to Egypt for the evening. The game turned out to be a corker and it is hard to imagine that anyone went home disappointed. Simmons started with a bang, striking out Jack Albright and Wyrostek in the top of the first. In the second, Tabor touched Simmons for a double. A single

and two costly errors followed, to give the Phillies two unearned runs and a 2–0 lead. The home side came back, however, and got to Phillies starter Dick Mauney for four runs in the bottom of the third to take a 4–2 lead.

The Phillies scored an earned run in the top of the fourth on a double by Schultz and a single by Handley to close to 4–3. There the score stayed until the eighth inning, as Simmons scattered five hits through the first seven. More impressive were his nine strikeouts, better than one an inning—and all this from a youngster only two weeks past his eighteenth birthday.

Del Ennis was the first batter in the eighth. He hoisted to left-center field a high fly that both center fielder Freddie Kimock and left fielder Nat Kemmerer drew a bead on. They didn't draw a bead on each other, however, and collided head-on just as both were about to make the catch. The ball bounced free and Ennis ended up at third with a triple. Kimock was knocked cold while Kemmerer suffered a gash on his forehead from the scary collision. The game was delayed for about ten minutes while medical personnel attended to both players.

When the game resumed, Phillies left fielder Buster Adams rapped a single to center, sending Ennis home with the tying run. Simmons bore down and retired Emil Verban and Hugh Poland on groundballs. With two outs, the go-ahead run was now on third. Sparing no quarter, manager Chapman sent Schoolboy Rowe up to pinch-hit for Howie Schultz. Rowe, a veteran pitcher, was also a decent hitter who would pinch-hit more than a hundred times in his career. The young southpaw proceeded to challenge Rowe, who swung at and missed three consecutive pitches to end the inning.

Neither team could score again, and the authorities determined after nine innings were completed that it was too dark to continue, so the game ended a 4–4 tie. Simmons had fanned 11, walked three, and given up seven hits in his nine-inning complete game. His teammates didn't help much, committing five errors behind him and letting in two unearned runs.

After the game the Phillies were feted to a BBQ dinner before heading back to Philadelphia, where Schoolboy Rowe was to pitch against the Cincinnati Reds the next evening. Simmons, meanwhile, prepared to attend his high-school graduation that Friday, while the bidding for his services increased.

Under baseball's bonus rule at the time, a player who had signed for a bonus of more than $6,000 could play the first year in the minors but after that had to remain on the club's big-league roster unless he

Simmons (third from right), a high-school student and pitcher for the Babe Ruth Eastern team, with team-mates and Carl Hubbell (left) at the American Legion all-star game at the Polo Grounds in 1945. His senior year, Simmons hit .465 with some power but drew even more notice for his pitching performance—he struck out 102 and gave up only 12 hits in 43⅓ innings. After considering bids from the Red Sox and Tigers, he accepted the Phillies' offer of a $65,000 signing bonus, breaking the unofficial record.

cleared waivers before being sent down. So Simmons would, under the bonus rule, be able to pitch in the minor leagues during the 1947 season, but, if he signed for more than $6,000, his team would have to keep him on the big-league roster or risk losing him to a waiver claim in 1948 or thereafter.

After Simmons's performance against the Phillies, the field narrowed to the Phillies, the Red Sox, and the Tigers, all of them presumably willing to spend big money and to carry a skinny teenaged southpaw on their roster. The Red Sox upped the ante to $60,000, and, true to his word, Larry Simmons gave the Phillies the last bid. He told Cy Morgan that Curt would sign for $65,000. Morgan got the go-ahead from Herb Pennock and Bob Carpenter, and the deal was done. Simmons's bonus was the highest ever paid up to then, breaking the unofficial record of the previous year when the New York Yankees paid Bobby Brown, who was in medical school at Tulane, $60,000 to play professional ball.

The Phillies sent Simmons to the Wilmington Blue Rocks of the Class B Interstate League, since he was not tied to the big-league roster until the next season. He made his professional debut on June 20 against the Lancaster Red Roses and won 7–1, striking out 11, walking four, and scattering seven hits. In 18 starts for the Blue Rocks, Simmons won 13 and lost 5, striking out 197 in only 147 innings. He allowed only 107 hits and compiled a 2.69 earned-run average. It was a most impressive beginning, although Simmons was some-times plagued with bouts of wildness, once walking 13 in a game against the Hagerstown Owls.

The Phillies had Simmons join the major-league team after the Interstate League season was com-pleted. They started him in the second game of a doubleheader against the New York Giants at the Polo Grounds on the last day of the 1947 season. The Giants would finish in fourth place but would set a major-league record for home runs with 221. The Phillies lost the first game. The second was played late in the af-ternoon. Giants slugger Johnny Mize was tied with Ralph Kiner for the home-run lead with 51, so Giants manager Mel Ott batted Mize first in the order, to max-imize his number of plate appearances. Simmons kept the home-run tie intact, limiting Mize to a broken-bat single to left in five at-bats.

All told, Simmons struck out nine and scattered five hits, pitching the Phillies to a 3–1 victory. He shut out the Giants for the first eight innings before New York scratched out a run in the ninth. "The shadows were coming in," Simmons recalled, "because it was the second game, so it was a nice set up for a hard-throwing left-hander who was a little wild."

Not surprising, even for a phenom, is that the teenage Simmons struggled in 1948 and 1949 with the Phillies, with wildness often leading to his downfall. In fact, in one start in 1948 he walked 12 Giants. He then came into his own in 1950, helping lead the Whiz Kids to the National League pennant, winning 17 games by August, when his National Guard unit was called to active duty. Simmons was forced to miss the World Series, which had a lot to do with the Yankees' sweep in four tightly fought pitchers' duels.

He would come back from military service in 1952 and, although frequently battling arm trouble, go on to have a distinguished twenty-year career in the major leagues, posting 193 wins against 183 losses. He reemerged on the national scene in 1964 when at the age of 35 he posted an 18–9 won-loss record to help lead the St. Louis Cardinals to the National League pennant (although they got help from the monumental collapse of the Phillies, his old team, in the last ten days of the season—see Bryan Soderholm-DiFatte's article "Beyond Bunning and Rest" at page 25).

Simmons started Game 3 of the World Series and held the slugging New York Yankees at bay for eight innings, surrendering only four hits and a single run before leaving for a pinch-hitter with the score tied 1–1. Unhappily for the Cardinals, Mickey Mantle hit what is now known as a walk-off home run in the bottom of the ninth off Barney Schultz to win it for the Yankees. Simmons also started Game 6 and pitched well, leaving the game in the seventh inning down 3–1 in an eventual 8–3 New York win.

Fourteen years after missing the 1950 World Series, Simmons was able to pitch in one. But it all started in 1947 in the little hamlet of Egypt, Pennsylvania, when the Phillies came to town. ∎

Acknowledgment

The author wishes to thank Gregory Ivy for his cheerful assistance in gathering old microfiche materials in support of this article.

Sources

Allentown Morning Call, 10 April 2008, C2; 15 August 1999; 2 June 1947, 14; 3 June 1947, 16; 4 June 1947, 13.

Bethlehem Globe-Times, 3 June 1947, 14.

Curt Simmons, interview, conducted by author, 1993.

Lieb, Frederick G., and Stan Baumgartner. *The Philadelphia Phillies*. 1953. Reprint, Kent, Ohio: Kent State University Press, 2009.

Marazzi, Rich, and Len Fiorito. *Baseball Players of the 1950s: A Biographical Dictionary of All 1,560 Major Leaguers*. Jefferson, N.C.: McFarland, 2004.

Paxton, Harry. *The Whiz Kids: The Story of the Fightin' Phillies*. New York: David McKay, 1950.

Philadephia Inquirer, 2 June 1947, 22; 3 June 1947, 24.

Porter, David L., ed. *Biographical Dictionary of American Sports—Baseball*. Westport, Conn.: Greenwood Press, 2000.

Roberts, Robin, and C. Paul Rogers III. *The Whiz Kids and the 1950 Pennant*. Philadelphia: Temple Univiversity Press, 1996.

Westcott, Rich, and Frank Bilovsky. *The New Phillies Encyclopedia*. Philadelphia: Temple University Press, 1993.

Who Wore Uniform Number 16 for the Tigers—Before Prince Hal?

Herm Krabbenhoft

SINCE JANUARY 2001, I've been engaged in a baseball-research endeavor that has been fascinating and challenging and sometimes frustrating—the determination of the uniform numbers for Detroit Tigers players, managers, and coaches. In an article in *The National Pastime* in 2006, I described some of my findings for the uniform numbers retired by the Tigers.[1] One of the then unresolved items is the subject of this article.

In my 2006 *TNP* article, in the discussion of uniform-number 16, retired in honor of Hal Newhouser, I wrote the following:

> It is also noted that, according to a number of official 1939 Detroit Tigers scorecards covering the period from June 4 through September 10, a person with the surname Jackym (perhaps former minor league pitcher Joe Jachym?) wore number 16 (perhaps while serving as a batting practice pitcher?). We have not yet been able to find out anything about "Jackym." [Note the spelling difference—the fourth letter in the scorecard surname is *k*, and the fourth letter in Joe's surname is *h*.]

In returning to the Jackym/Jachym situation, I first reexamined *The Sporting News*. Just as I had found four to five years ago, using the Paper of Record (POR) search engine affords no hits for "Jackym." Similarly, using the POR search engine for "Jachym" again yielded four hits:

January 22, 1931, page 22: The final 1930-season batting, fielding, and pitching averages for the Mid-Atlantic League—a Jachym played for Wheeling;

January 26, 1933, page 2: A brief article about the Texas League for the upcoming 1933 season— Joe Jachym was included in a group of players on the reserve list from the homeless Tyler-Shreveport franchise;

February 2, 1933, page 5: A short article about a new investor for the Fort Worth club of the Texas

League—Jachym was included in a list of pitchers who could possibly be added to the team's roster;

October 25, 1934, page 6: The final batting, fielding, and pitching averages for the New York–Pennsylvania League for the 1934 season—a Jachym played for Wilkes-Barre.

There was nothing about a Jachym with the 1939 Detroit Tigers. (I had also gotten no hits on Jackym/Jachym from searches of the ProQuest newspapers.)

Now, however, just to be certain that the POR search engine was comprehensive, I decided to check each of the weekly articles on the Detroit Tigers in *The Sporting News* (usually written by Sam Greene of the *Detroit News*) for the entire 1939 baseball season. That was a tedious process. Essentially I went through each issue of *TSN* page by page. But it was worth the effort. I hit pay dirt: In the June 8 issue (page 14) was the following item in the article on the Tigers:

> The Tigers have a new batting practice pitcher in Joe Jachym of Boston. He joined the team in the East after the trade with the Browns had reduced the mound laborers to a point where extra help was needed for pre-game chores.

That's exactly the information I was seeking. And, just to make sure I hadn't made an error in my POR searches for "Jachym," I repeated it specifically for the *TSN* of June 8, 1939. Again, the POR search engine yielded no hits.

So, there's an important takeaway here: The results from the POR search engine may not be reliable in terms of comprehensiveness. Just because a search does not come up with a hit for what you were searching for, a specific term or person, that does not mean it is not in a given issue of *TSN*; the POR search may have missed it.

Having found out that the wearer of uniform number 16 prior to Newhouser's arrival was indeed Joe Jachym, I wanted to check the Detroit newspapers for any additional information. Accomplishing that would be relatively easy. Since I would be visiting my Mom

In 1939, Joe Jachym joined the Tigers as a batting-practice pitcher, succeeding Charley Eckert, who had been promoted to manage in the minor leagues. Eckert was never listed on the roster. How did it happen that Jachym was issued a uniform number—16, the number Hal Newhouser would later wear? Because it fit. George Gill, who wore 16 immediately before Jachym, was Jachym's height and almost his same weight.

in Michigan for Mother's Day, it would be a snap for me to make a trip to the Detroit Public Library and go through the microfilm versions of the *Detroit News*, the *Detroit Free Press*, and the *Detroit Times*.

While waiting for my plane to take off for Detroit, I had two booklets in my hands—Bobby Plapinger's Baseball Books Catalog number 50 and the spring 2010 issue of *The SABR Bulletin*. The passenger seated next to me asked me if I liked baseball. I replied that I did and that I had done some writing and research on baseball. I also asked him, "What about you; do you follow baseball?" Here's how the conversation between him (John) and me (Herm) proceeded (not verbatim, but reasonably close):

John: Yeah, I love baseball. My Dad used to play baseball.

Herm: Really. Professionally?

John: No, not professionally; just in industrial leagues back in the forties. My uncle played baseball professionally.

Herm: Cool. What's your uncle's name?

John: Joe Jachym.

Herm: What?

John: Joe Jachym: *J-a-c-h-y-m*; pronounced yah-kim.

Herm: This is amazing! You're not going to believe this. [I reached down to my briefcase and pulled out my Jackym/Jachym notes and a copy of my 2006 *TNP* article.] Wait till you see this. This is amazing. Here, please read these couple of sentences about your uncle in this article I wrote a few years ago.

John: Yeah, that's him. Wow!

Herm: This is amazing! Is your uncle Joe still living?

John: No, he died several years ago. But his son, my cousin Jim, is still living. He'll love this.

John then proceeded to tell me some more about Joe Jachym. That he played basketball and baseball at Notre Dame and had some interaction with Knute Rockne, and that he was a longtime high-school coach in Westfield, Massachusetts, and that there's a baseball field named Jachym Field in Joe's honor.

When I got to my Mom's, I did some checking on the Internet and found out that Joe Jachym was captain of the Notre Dame basketball team for the 1927–28 season and cocaptain for the 1928–29 season. He was also a pitcher for the Notre Dame baseball teams from 1927 through 1929, compiling a 14–6 won–lost record.

My trip to the Detroit Public Library was also successful—the *Detroit Free Press* had the following item in the issue of May 25, 1939, in the column "Tiger Notes" by Charles P. Ward (with the dateline New York, May 24):

"The Tiger touring party was increased today by the addition of Joe Jachym, a batting practice pitcher. Jachym succeeds Charley Eckert, who has been promoted to the managership of the Fulton club, of the Kitty League."

Since none of the Detroit Tigers scorecards included Eckert with the list of uniformed personnel, it's strikingly curious that Jachym was issued a uniform with a number.

During this time, Joe's nephew provided me with contact information for Jim Jachym, who, as John had told me on the plane, also had played for a year in the minors in the Houston Astros organization before an arm injury curtailed his career.

A few weeks later I visited Jim Jachym at his home in Westfield, Massachusetts. Jim's sister Ann and his brother Tom were also there to talk about their father's baseball coaching career. Here's a summary of some of the interesting things I learned about Joe Jachym, the person who wore uniform-number 16 for the Detroit Tigers just before Hal Newhouser.

Joe Jachym graduated cum laude from Notre Dame University in June 1929. In the fall, he returned to the Fighting Irish campus to serve as the coach of the freshman basketball and baseball teams. During that time, he interacted with Knute Rockne. In a visit with Rockne at his home, Jachym was asked by the legendary football coach what he intended to do with his life. Jachym replied that he thought he would give professional baseball a try and, if that didn't pan out, he would go into coaching. Rockne wished him well in his quest to become a professional baseball player; he also cautioned him about pursuing a coaching career, pointing out that to be a long-term successful coach is difficult.

As it turned out, Joe's professional baseball career lasted but four seasons: 1930, Wheeling (Class C, Mid-Atlantic League); 1931, Wheeling (again) and also Evansville (Class B, Triple-I League); 1932, both Beaumont and Tyler (Class A, Texas League); and 1934, Wilkes-Barre (Class A, New York–Penn League). Overall, according to Baseball-Reference, Jachym compiled a 43–30 won–lost record (.589) during his minor-league career.[2] However, Baseball-Reference did not include any biographical information for Joe. Fortunately, Joe's kids, Jim, Ann, and Tom, were able to provide me with that, which can now be incorporated into SABR's Minor Leagues Database:

Joe Jachym – Joseph John Jachym (Jake)
Bats: Right
Throws: Right
Height: 6' 1"
Weight: 175 lb.
Born: November 17, 1906, Westfield, Massachusetts
Died: July 19 1991, Westfield, Massachusetts
Buried: St. Mary's Cemetery, Westfield, Massachusetts

Following his stint with the Wilkes-Barre Barons, Jachym returned to his roots in Westfield, Massachusetts, and, after playing in local semipro leagues for a few years, embarked on a coaching and teaching career at Westfield Trade School in the fall of 1939. He coached there for a quarter of a century, through

1964.[3] He continued teaching (general physics, history, and physical education) until he retired in 1972. That Joe Jachym achieved a highly successful coaching career is clearly demonstrated by the following honors he received.

In 1974, Jachym was inducted into the Hall of Fame of the Massachusetts Baseball Coaches Association (MBCA).[4]

On September 1, 1988, the athletic field at Westfield Vocational School was named Joe "Jake" Jachym Field in Joe's honor. A bronze plaque featuring Joe's likeness bears the following inscription:

Athlete—Coach –Teacher
Parent—Spectator—Friend
"His standards and professionalism were exemplary—
He has inspired and left his mark on all of us who have
known him."

In November 1988, Jachym received the Edward J. Hickox Award in recognition of his substantial contributions to amateur athletics.[5]

So, although not to the same degree as Knute Rockne, who achieved legendary status, Joe Jachym did indeed establish a sterling reputation as a long-term successful coach.

OK, so now we've learned some interesting things about Joe Jachym before and after 1939. What about the 1939 season, when he became the Tigers' batting-practice pitcher? How did that come about? And, why did Jachym wear uniform-number 16? Here are the answers.

While hurling for the Beaumont Exporters in 1932, he made a favorable impression on his manager, Del Baker; they became good, lifelong friends. So, when Detroit needed a batting-practice pitcher shortly after the 1939 season began, Baker, now the Tigers' manager, called on his friend to help him out. Jachym joined the Tigers in Boston for their May 21–23 series against the Red Sox.

With respect to why Jachym ended up with uniform-number 16, the likely answer is—"It was available; and it fit." Here are the relevant height and weight numbers to support that hypothesis:

Charley Eckert (the BP pitcher immediately before Jachym) was 5' 10" and weighed 165 pounds.

George Gill (the player who wore number 16 immediately before Jachym) stood 6' 1" and weighed 185 pounds; Gill had been traded to the St. Louis Browns on May 13 (just a week before Jachym joined the Tigers).

Joe Jachym (as indicated above) was around 6' 1" and weighed about 175 pounds.

Hal Newhouser is listed as having been 6' 2" tall and weighing 180 pounds.

So, everything fits.

Finally, to wrap up this story, here's another tidbit about Joe Jachym's time with the 1939 Tigers—he and Hank Greenberg were roommates. Having previously been teammates at both Evansville and Beaumont, they too became good, long-term friends, corresponding with one another from time to time over the ensuing years. In a letter of September 19, 1954, to Jachym, Greenberg, then the general manager of the Cleveland Indians, wrote, "I, too, hope that your boy will be playing with the Indians someday."

CONCLUDING REMARKS

The answer to the question posed in the title of this article has been determined—Joe Jachym, as the Tigers' batting-practice pitcher, wore uniform-number 16 right before Hal Newhouser first donned that flannel jersey on September 9, 1939; Prince Hal kept it for the next fourteen and a half years as he amassed his Hall of Fame credentials. And it was further learned that Joe Jachym, thanks in part to his interactions with Notre Dame's Knute Rockne, also carved out his own hall-of-fame career as a high-school coach. ∎

Acknowledgments
It is a pleasure to thank Joe Jachym's nephew, John, and Joe's kids—Jim, Ann, and Tom—for their kindness and cooperation.

Notes

1. Herm Krabbenhoft, "Fascinating Aspects About the Retired Uniform Numbers of the Detroit Tigers," *The National Pastime* (2006): 77–84.
2. Examination of the statistics, at Baseball-Reference, for the 1932 Texas League reveals that important team-specific information is lacking. Thus, for Beaumont, Joe Jachym is shown with a question mark after his name in both the lists for both team batting and team pitching. Likewise, for Shreveport/Tyler, Joe Jachym is also shown with a question mark after his name in the lists for team batting and team pitching. For each team-batting list, Jachym's full-season statistics are given, as they are for each team-pitching list. In order to separate Jachym's full-season statistics into specific team statistics, I examined the box scores, in *The Sporting News*, for each game played by Beaumont and Shreveport/Tyler in 1932. Here's the pertinent information: For Beaumont, Jachym appeared in 13 games from April 14 through June 14. As a pitcher, he started four games and relieved in nine; his overall won–lost record was 2–1. As a batter, he had seven hits (including one double) in 18 at-bats (for a .389 average). For Shreveport/Tyler, Jachym played only for Tyler (see below). Jachym appeared in 22 games from June 23 through September 11. As a pitcher, he appeared in 20 games, starting 15 and relieving in five; his overall won–lost record was 7–8. As a non-pitcher, he appeared in two games, one as a pinch runner, and one as a pinch-hitter. As a batter, he collected eight hits (including two doubles) in 45 at-bats (for a .178 average).

   Combining his box-score statistics for his tenures with Beaumont and Tyler yields a pitching ledger of 9 wins and 9 losses, which agrees with the full-season statistics at Baseball-Reference. Jachym's combined box-score batting statistics yield 15 hits (including three doubles) in 63 at-bats (for an overall average of .238). These numbers differ from the batting statistics given at Baseball-Reference, which show Jachym with 14 hits (including three doubles) in 59 at-bats (for a .237 average).

   With regard to the Shreveport/Tyler situation, here's the relevant information. From *The Sporting News* (May 19, 1932, page 2): "There will be no more games played by the Sports at Shreveport this summer, as O. L. Biedenharn, owner of the park, has stated he will not rebuild the stands destroyed by fire, May 4. . . . The Caddo Association, owner of the franchise, following Biedenharn's decision, decided to play the remainder of the Sports scheduled home games in Tyler." Again, from *The Sporting News* (May 26, 1932, page 2): "With a new park in a new town and in new uniforms, the Shreveport Sports, now housed at Tyler, Texas, for the rest of the season, will be known as the Tyler Trojans. The same official and player personnel, however, is retained."

   Finally, the following information is provided regarding Jachym's transfer from Beaumont to Tyler. From *The Sporting News* (June 30, 1932, page 7): "Joe Jachym, young right-handed pitcher, was traded by Beaumont to Tyler last week in payment for Rabbit Benton, recently acquired, following the injury of second baseman John Holley. Jachym formerly hurled for Notre Dame University."
3. D. L. Genovese, *The Old Ball Ground* (West Coshocken, Pa.: Infinity Publishing, 2007), 231–44.
4. The MBCA was founded in 1968 with the mission to promote high-school baseball and academics, to foster the highest level of professionalism and ethics among its members, to recognize excellence, and to maintain strong contacts with national, state, and local baseball organizations.
5. The Edward J. Hickox Award is named for Edward J. Hickox, who coached basketball at Springfield College from 1926 to 1941 and later worked for the Basketball Hall of Fame as an executive into the mid-1960s; he was inducted into the Basketball Hall of Fame, as a contributor, in 1959.

The Next Frontier—China

Ryan Hutzler

OPENING DAY

Vendors sold peanuts, popcorn, and hot dogs, but tea and ramen noodles were favorites among the fans in the stands. Tickets ranged in price from $7 to $180 and a 12-ounce beer cost $1.50. Cheerleaders performed in foul territory and elderly fans practiced tai chi near the stadium entrance before the game. During the seventh-inning stretch, the only individual singing "Take Me Out to the Ball Game" was the public-address announcer. The big screen in center field quizzed spectators and, after showing a player cross first base, asked fans if it was (a) a single, (b) a double, or (c) a triple.[1] Baseball had officially arrived—in Beijing.

Saturday, March 15, 2008, marked opening day for Major League Baseball in China. There was no winner that day, as the contest between the Los Angeles Dodgers and San Diego Padres ended in a 3–3 tie, but the score was trivial. Similarly, on Sunday, March 16, when the Padres defeated the Dodgers 6–3 to conclude the two-game series, the result did not concern either the fans or MLB. The sellout crowd of 12,224 at Wukesong Stadium had witnessed history, the first game between major-league teams on Chinese soil.

According to MLB.com reporter Corey Brock, the games appeared less as an actual professional competition than as a novelty, "complete with understandable hiccups and an overall sentiment of newness for the sport."[2] Many of the Chinese fans had never seen professional baseball and found the game complicated during the early innings. "I don't really understand a lot of the rules," one youth baseball coach admitted, "but I've tried to study on the Internet."[3] Yet, by the middle innings of the game, Padres manager Bud Black "could tell that the crowd was following the game. And like all baseball fans, they appreciate a hard-hit ball, a ball that goes a long way."[4]

"To see this . . . takes my breath away," Commissioner Bud Selig said. "If we do as well as I think, people will say this is how it all started."[5] Black agreed with Selig and said, "Hopefully this is the start of more baseball in China. The seeds are planted and we can continue to grow the game. Hopefully the Chinese people will embrace the game and have a passion for it over time like we do in America."[6]

MLB's first-ever journey to China was a mission of goodwill. Members of the Dodgers and Padres met Chinese students and taught them basic fundamentals to increase their understanding of and interest in the sport. The players, coaches, and executives who represented the Padres, Dodgers, and MLB in China were ambassadors for the future development of baseball. In addition to their baseball obligations, they participated in a reciprocal cultural exchange and immersed themselves in Chinese culture and society during the five-day trip. They visited the Great Wall of China and the Forbidden City. Padres vice president Dave Winfield commented on the importance of the trip, explaining, "This isn't like going across the border to Mexico or even the Caribbean. It'll be good for the young guys. I talked to some of them on the way over. It's a new experience for them, something they ordinarily wouldn't get to do."[7] Mets GM and former CEO of the Padres, Sandy Alderson added, "Anytime you get outside the United States and kids get a chance to see a different culture, it's a terrific and broadening experience. I see that kind of thing at the Olympics. I think it helps to mature players a little bit and gives them a better perspective on things."[8]

Although several professional organizations have actively promoted MLB's international expansion in years past, the Padres remain at the forefront of furthering this mission. As early as 1996, the Padres were advancing MLB's international interests by participating in the first regular-season games outside the United States or Canada—a three-game series against the Mets in Monterrey, Mexico. The team's playing regular-season games in foreign nations, Alderson hoped, would increase the Padres' visibility overseas. He explained:

> We want to promote the Padres as an organization and as a brand if you will and anything we can do [that] is of a historic nature adds to that and helps us grow our history. It's easy for the Yankees and Red Sox who already have name recognition and the connotation of excellence and success. For us, we need to keep working at it. This is one of those events that could contribute to our reputation.[9]

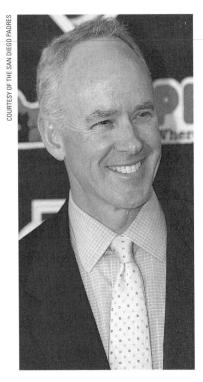

"The key to the growth . . . of baseball in China," said Sandy Alderson, Mets GM and former CEO of the Padres, **"is the introduction of a Chinese player into Major League Baseball. I don't think that anyone can predict how long that will take. But it's important that Major League Baseball and all its clubs are taking the process of finding and developing players who can play in the major leagues."**

The Dodgers have played a similar role in shaping MLB's international development. The franchise was proud to represent MLB in China and build bridges which extend beyond the borders of the United States. Dodgers owner Frank McCourt, who believes that promoting baseball in China is "in the Dodgers' DNA,"[10] spoke about their involvement with MLB's mission of globalization:

> If China puts its mind to it and decides to embrace professional baseball, we know it will be a success. To be part of that and to build a bridge from America to China, I think is very consistent with the history of this ballclub. It's done the same in Japan, in Taiwan, in Latin America.

> Part of what makes the Dodgers a worldwide brand is this organization has always embraced bringing baseball all over the world because of the love of the game. It's a very proud part of our heritage and something that is incumbent upon us to continue.[11]

The China Series indicated MLB's strong commitment to its November 2003 "development agreement"—which was extended for another four years in 2010—with the Chinese Baseball Association (CBA), the governmental organization overseeing baseball events, development, and national team activities in the country. The agreement between MLB and the CBA allowed MLB teams to train and sign players from China,

assigned former MLB players Jim Lefebvre and Bruce Hurst as manager and coach of China's National Team, and sanctioned the establishment of MLB youth and community efforts in China. The China Series cemented MLB's belief that China is a fertile ground for the growth and expansion of baseball in the future. "You need a genesis; you need a starting point," Commissioner Selig explained. "And this is a great way to start."[12] Playing MLB games in China is "quite an experience, to say the least," Selig continued. "I'm thrilled with it. . . . This is history in the making."[13]

A HUNDRED YEARS OF BASEBALL IN CHINA

MLB's China Series was not the first established baseball event played in the country, as baseball has been in China a decade longer than in Japan or any other Asian nation. Dating back to 1863, when American medical missionary Henry William Boone formed the Shanghai Baseball Club, *bangqiu*, or "stickball," flourished in China. National interest in the sport grew rapidly, and in the 1870s the Qing Dynasty sent young scholars to the United States to study America's national pastime in its original setting, as part of the "self-strengthening movement." The students returned to China with a true love for the game. The Chinese proved their baseball talent in 1911 in an exhibition game in San Francisco, where the Chinese Overseas Baseball Club—a team organized in Hawaii—defeated the New York Giants. In 1913, the Chinese competed in their first international baseball tournament, the inaugural Far East Games, and finished third. China placed second to the Philippines in 1915 in a greater-Asia baseball tournament held in Shanghai. Baseball flourished across China for the next half century in Chinese colleges and provincial capitals. In 1934, major-league All-Stars led by Babe Ruth, and Lou Gehrig, having completed a Japan tour, traveled to China to play the Shanghai Pandas.[14]

Baseball became the unofficial sport of the People's Liberation Army during the nation's civil war from 1947 to 1949 and became known as *junqiu*, or "army ball." During the 1950s, baseball helped train soldiers, as it did during Sun Yat-sen's revolution in 1911. Chinese officers believed the sport made better soldiers, who learned to throw a grenade faster, farther, and with curve on it. After the People's Republic was founded in 1949, baseball surged in popularity. The game was recognized as an official sport at the first National Games in 1959, which featured teams from thirty regions across China. The Cultural Revolution, though, soon followed. From 1966 through 1976, Mao Zedong banned baseball and persecuted, tortured, and

Lang Akana, of Hawaiian and Chinese ancestry, was a promising young pitcher in Honolulu in 1914 when Walt McCredie, manager of the Portland Beavers of the Pacific Coast League, tried to recruit him. McCredie's players revolted, threatening to boycott, and he reluctantly declared he would drop Akana. A century later, Major League Baseball appreciates that the success of baseball in China depends to some extent on the development of Chinese players who can compete in the major leagues.

killed coaches, as the sport was viewed as a symbol of Western decadence. This effectively eliminated all interest in baseball, and the sport did not resurface until after Mao's death in 1976, when anti-Western sentiment began to subside and baseball was officially "rehabilitated" by Communist-party leaders. The Chinese government adopted the policy of "friendship first, competition second" with respect to baseball and other sports, including ping-pong, soccer, and basketball. The nation hoped to demonstrate the government's interest in tightening the relationship between sport, politics, and diplomacy. The "friendship first, competition second" policy allowed the Chinese government to preserve the image of the newly developing socialist country while establishing international relationships.[15]

Sensing a growing enthusiasm for baseball in the country, Dodgers owner Peter O'Malley traveled to China in 1986 and began investing in the game's future there to support its reemergence. O'Malley helped construct the first modern baseball stadium in Tianjin, approximately 75 miles southeast of Beijing, and named the venue "Dodger Stadium." In 1988, China hosted its first international baseball tournament, the Beijing International, a Little League championship for 11- and 12-year-olds, which established baseball's future in the nation.[16]

THE CHINESE GET ORGANIZED

Building on O'Malley's success and seeing China's growing interest in baseball, Positive Baseball Limited,

a sports investment company founded by Tom McCarthy, an American, assembled a five-week, trial-run baseball tournament in April and May of 2002. Four teams competed, the Beijing Tigers, Tianjin Lions, Shanghai Golden Eagles, and Guangzhou Leopards, which further generated Chinese interest in baseball. Several months later, a partnership company, Dynamic Sports Marketing, inked a six-year, $5-million deal with the Chinese Baseball Association to own the marketing and advertisement rights of a three-month-long Chinese Baseball League (CBL) season. Further, the deal included advertising the China national baseball team, junior baseball team, and a youth baseball program called "Swing for the Wall."[17]

Since the inaugural season in 2002, during which teams played only 12 games, the CBL has expanded to seven teams, adding the Sichuan Dragons and China Hope Stars, a team of under-21 prospects, in 2005, and the Henan Elephants in 2009. The league features two divisions with 14 game days, and each team hosts the remaining six squads over a three-day weekend, with the top two teams from each division qualifying for the playoffs. The best teams play a maximum of only 11 games.[18] Further, although CBL games are typically free to the public, the average CBL game attracts a few hundred spectators, with the largest crowds approaching 1,000 in Tianjin.[19]

COMPETING AGAINST THE ASIAN POWERHOUSES

With the support of MLB and the signing of the "development agreement" in 2003, the China national team has slowly become more competitive against international competition. The team, which consists of top players from provincial teams, has long been ranked fourth in Asia, but it improved under the tutelage of MLB coaches Jim Lefebvre and Bruce Hurst. While coaching the China national team from 2003 through the 2008 Olympic Games—before becoming the San Diego Padres' hitting coach—Lefebvre witnessed exceptional growth both in the players' skill and in the nation's interest in baseball. Lefebvre explained: "There are some people who are skeptical about what this is all about; I'm not. I've seen it. I've seen what happened in Japan, I've seen what happened in Korea, I've seen what happened in Australia. Look at it now. . . . Just give baseball time."[20] Dodgers manager Joe Torre echoed Lefebvre's opinion: "You don't get instant success in baseball—it's a game you grow into. But if we make sure kids learn to play the game the right way, once they start blossoming we'll see a number of players make an impact in Major League Baseball."[21]

Lefebvre understood how to develop and advance baseball talent and had a rich baseball career both on and off the diamond. In 1965, he was the National League Rookie of the Year with the Los Angeles Dodgers. His eight-year playing career was followed by managerial stints with the Seattle Mariners (1989–91), the Chicago Cubs (1992–93), and the Milwaukee Brewers (1999); he was a coach for the San Diego Padres in 2009. Lefebvre has served as a major-league coach with six different organizations and is experienced in evaluating talent. Of his China national team, he said:

> These are not college-level players . . . they're above that. They are professional-level players right now. Collectively, we might struggle, but we have players on our team right now who are high A, Double-A and possibly Triple-A. We have some guys who, in the right situation, could make it to the big leagues.[22]

Lefebvre emphasized teaching baseball fundamentals to Chinese prospects and witnessed a dramatic improvement in their ability. Many Chinese players lack the upper-body strength of many American and Latino ballplayers—stealing bases is common, as most catchers lack the arm strength needed to throw out advancing runners. Lefebvre worked to develop pitchers' arm strength and hitters' power by putting a bat and ball in their hands at a younger age. Lefebvre said, "These kids are very smart, they're very bright and they have great intuitiveness. They retain it. They have an endless work ethic. What more can you ask for? They see now what they need to do to be successful."[23]

Although the China national team failed to qualify for the 2004 Olympics and in the 2006 World Baseball Classic lost all three games—against Japan, South Korea, and, in a 12–3 blowout loss, rival Chinese Taipei—by a combined score of 40–6, the squad continued to progress. Despite the defeats in the WBC, several scouts saw promise in the Chinese team. "For five or six innings, China held its own," observed Paul Archey, senior vice president of Major League Baseball International. "They just didn't have the depth or the experience. China even [tied the game] against Japan. It gave you a glimpse of what could happen."[24]

Despite MLB's optimism, several factors continue to limit baseball's growth in China, including the International Olympic Committee's (IOC) decision to remove the sport from competition in both the 2012 Summer Olympics in London and the 2016 Games. The IOC's decision has made baseball a low priority in China's Soviet-style system, which funnels promising youngsters into special camps where they are trained specifically to win gold medals and attain national glory. Harvey Schiller, president of the International Baseball Federation (IBAF), had indicated that baseball might be reinstated in the 2016 Summer Olympics if the Europe-dominated IOC voted it back into competition. However, the IOC may ask for the participation of professional players. Dodgers manager Joe Torre echoed the sentiments of most MLB managers when he commented, "I don't want to give any of my players up for the Games, much as I respect them."[25]

Additionally, Wukesong Stadium, which hosted the 2008 Summer Olympics, was demolished in December 2008, as it generated little revenue. The government plans to build a sports and entertainment center and shopping mall at the site.[26] Although construction of a new baseball stadium is expected in Xiamen, Fujian province in 2011, China's capital is without a respectable baseball venue, which may impede the sport's sustained development.[27]

"ASIA-FIED" BASEBALL

As Joseph Reaves, a historian of Asian baseball, observed, the game in China "can look so similar and yet somehow feel so different."[28] Despite Major League Baseball's best efforts to integrate the sport into Chinese culture, baseball will take form in its own, unique manner in China. Regardless of MLB intervention in China, Japan is the keeper and guiding light of baseball in Asia, and China will adapt a Japanese style of baseball, which can coexist with Chinese cultural norms and tendencies. Japanese baseball celebrates "little ball," which is consistent with the Confucian value system and emphasizes team harmony, discipline, and the collective good. Japanese baseball supports sacrifice bunts, sacrifice flies, and slap hits, all of which are assumed to benefit the team as a whole as opposed to boosting personal achievement, whereas American baseball favors "big ball" and mirrors the value Americans place on physicality and individualism. Chinese society not only follows Japanese principles but also takes from Japan its inspiration for playing baseball.[29]

The Chinese word for baseball, bangqiu, translates to "bat ball" or "stick ball," but during World War II the sport was known as yeqiu, or "field ball," a word closely associated to the Japanese and Korean words for baseball, yakyu and yagoo respectively.[30] This parallel is no accident. Baseball's American origins and MLB's involvement in Chinese baseball notwithstanding, the game in China incorporates Asian values. Baseball will conform to the prevailing culture and

Jim Lefebvre, manager of the China national team, with George W. Bush. Lefebvre is credited with developing baseball talent among young Chinese and teaching them fundamentals. "There are some people who are skeptical about what this is all about," he said. "I'm not. I've seen what happened in Japan, I've seen what happened in Korea, I've seen what happened in Australia. Look at it now. . . . Just give baseball time."

societal norms in China, and the sport—the strategy, style of play, and reaction of fans and players—will reflect Chinese values, which are closer to Japanese principles than to American customs. MLB should not interfere with the assimilation process, because Chinese fans and players will reject the sport if it possesses a distinctly American feel. Chinese culture will accept baseball only if it is markedly theirs. It appears MLB understands this notion. "Our goal," according to Jim Small, MLB vice president for Asia, "is not to have a foreign coach; it is [for baseball in China] to be played by the Chinese, coached by the Chinese and umpired by the Chinese."[31]

RELATIONSHIP-BUILDING

After visiting the Great Wall of China before the 2008 China Series, Commissioner Bud Selig passed a local university and noticed Chinese students playing baseball and softball. During his tenure as commissioner of baseball, he has been dedicated to developing baseball globally. As an emerging market of 1.3 billion people, China shows promise as a potential revenue stream of enormous magnitude. MLB has already invested heavily to promote baseball's emergence in China. "We're making inroads," Selig said. He explained:

> We will continue to do what we can to accelerate the process. In fact, I feel so good about it, I have no doubt in my mind that in a decade, baseball will be big in China. We're watching CNN this morning and our series was the lead story on the

sports segment. We're getting positive coverage in a world where there isn't much positive coverage. . . . Given what we've tried to accomplish in this series, it's exceeded anything we could have hoped for.[32]

In sending its product overseas, MLB intends to forge a long-lasting relationship with China, which will help market the sport more effectively and efficiently. Commissioner Selig and MLB officials recognize that China is a growing global economic force and that playing MLB games in China presents an opportunity to take the game's internationalization to a new level.

Selig maintains the China Series was a goodwill mission first and not an economic venture. The commissioner and MLB officials remain steadfast on developing the relationship-building component between MLB and the Chinese people. "The revenue will take care of itself," Dodgers owner Frank McCourt said. "If we focus on revenue first and forget the importance of the relationship, we may be disappointed."[33] Charles Steinberg, executive vice president of marketing for the Dodgers, agreed, saying he hopes to "light a fire that starts burning passion for baseball. If that happens, those that count the money will have their day."[34]

Chinese citizens are only beginning to understand the concepts of leisure, disposable income, and the middle class. China is "a country on the move. The timing for baseball couldn't be better," said McCourt. "We want baseball to be one of the options for entertainment. We want kids to play it in school and for families to be spectators. We are limited only by our imagination."[35] MLB has already established its brand in China and has opened 48 stores across the country. MLB officials were impressed by the enthusiasm Chinese youths already have for baseball. After Game 1 of the China Series, children were throwing baseballs and swinging baseball bats, like children in America. "They were having fun without even knowing all the rules and nuances of the game," McCourt observed. "It is an awesome achievement for everyone involved to pull it off. When the Chinese people become familiar with the game, it will be even better. I think this country will fall in love with baseball."[36] He continued:

> We brought the game of baseball and we can see the joy it brings. We've made an impact here and the Chinese people have made an impact on the American side. They've opened our eyes. We are so impressed with the people here, the history of this country and the architecture of this capital. You can't help but be impressed with the Forbidden City, the Great Wall and now the Bird's Nest stadium [the spectacular venue for opening and closing ceremonies for the 2008 Olympics]. In August, the rest of the world will see what is happening here in China.[37]

Until baseball flourishes in China independent of MLB's guidance and support, MLB must remain patient, help build baseball diamonds, train coaches and players, and provide equipment. Baseball is considered an elite sport in China because, as China's national team captain Zhang Yufeng explained, "It requires special equipment and fields. You pay that much for a bat and you can break it so easy. And the clothes and gloves are also expensive. So it's difficult to get a team together. China's national sport is ping-pong, no doubt. All you need is a ball and a paddle."[38]

Between MLB's desire to sell its products and merchandise and the ability of Chinese citizens to afford them, there is an inherent tension. MLB must determine how to best balance these two sets of competing interests, its own economic interests and those of Chinese citizens. "We need not worry about the money," McCourt explained. "This country grows wealthier by the moment. They don't need our money, they need our help and friendship. We need to be a good partner with the Chinese people and send a clear message that this game can be their game too."[39]

FUTURE PROSPECTS
Baseball remains in its infancy in China. Unlike Japan,

South Korea, and Taiwan, China lacks prominent baseball names, household names like Sadaharu Oh, Ichiro Suzuki, Hideki Matsui, and Daisuke Matsuzaka. Still, MLB continues to invest in the sport in China. Jim Small explained: "The future for baseball in China is very bright. Sports have become increasingly important in Chinese society. As baseball is not only a global sport but also a sport that is hugely popular in Asia, I think it is quite natural for it to take hold in the Chinese sports culture."[40]

MLB hopes to find and develop a prominent Chinese baseball player in the upcoming years to spur national interest in the sport. Yao Ming, the 7-foot-6-inch Chinese center, signed with the Houston Rockets of the National Basketball Association in 2002 and became an all-star-caliber player, stoking China's interest in basketball. China is now the NBA's largest international market. According to Hu Jiashi, vice president of the China Basketball Association, "Basketball used to be behind soccer, but now it's pulling level."[41] To increase its popularity in China, the NBA is supporting the construction of 12 new basketball arenas. The NBA is currently the most popular sports league in China—more than 300 million people play basketball regularly, and 83 percent of males between the ages of 15 and 61 are interested in the game, and the numbers are rising.[42]

MLB believes it can duplicate the NBA's good fortune by signing a standout Chinese ballplayer, hoping he will make it to the big leagues and generate interest back home. "Look what Yao Ming has done to basketball in China," Lefebvre observed. "It is played everywhere. . . . We want to catch lightning in a bottle. We want to create the Yao Ming effect for baseball."[43] Alderson agreed: "The key to the growth and popularity of baseball in China is the introduction of a Chinese player into Major League Baseball. I don't think that anyone can predict how long that will take. But it's important that Major League Baseball and all its clubs are taking the process of finding and developing players who can play in the Major Leagues."[44]

The Chinese are still more familiar with and prefer to participate in soccer, basketball, and ping-pong. Baseball is not yet embedded in China's social fabric. City blocks are devoted to public athletic facilities, artificial-turf soccer fields, and basketball courts but not many baseball diamonds. The scope of the challenge faced by MLB as it strives for brand-name recognition was suggested by Ying Huaong, a construction worker, when he conveyed the common Chinese attitude toward baseball: "I don't know the game, and we don't see it much [on television] but . . . I want to learn more about it. I'm a basketball fan. I like that."[45]

MLB officials are confident baseball's popularity will spread throughout China, and they have 1.3 billion reasons to believe China will be a significant part of baseball's future. The country boasts a huge population and strong athletes in gymnastics and basketball. But baseball is still a new sport here, and MLB officials will not find professional-ready ballplayers in the near future. Regardless, early investment in China's baseball future could prove to be a nice long-term investment for MLB.

MLB's efforts may already be paying dividends. The Chinese Baseball Association claims that more than four million people play baseball in China, and more than 60 Chinese colleges and universities and 1,000 high schools and primary schools support their own teams. A 2008 TNS Sports Asia survey concluded that 16.2 percent of the Chinese population are interested in baseball, although only 1 percent consider themselves true baseball fans. Further, the study reported that approximately 26 percent of Chinese citizens are interested in MLB and its merchandise, a majority of whom are young, highly educated, and earn high incomes.[46]

In addition to MLB, the New York Yankees have actively invested in China's baseball future. In 2007, the team signed a memorandum of understanding with the Chinese Baseball Association. Besides enabling the Yankees to increase their international brand recognition, the agreement, the first of its kind between an MLB club and the CBA, permitted the club to send coaches, scouts, and training personnel to China to help the CBA instruct baseball players and coaches. The partnership will also allow CBA officials to visit the Yankees' facilities in the United States to further their development.[47]

Since 2001, five Chinese players have signed contracts with MLB clubs, and teams believe more Chinese nationals will join MLB in the future. The Seattle Mariners signed the first Chinese player, right-handed pitcher Chao Wang, in 2001. He compiled a record of 0–2 with a 5.14 ERA in 13 games during the 2002 season in the Arizona Rookie League before returning to China. The Mariners also signed catcher Wei Wang and infielder/outfielder Yu Bingjia in 2007. Scouts believe Wang Wei, who hit the first home run in the 2006 WBC, may be the first Chinese star in MLB. However, he has yet to make the Mariners' big-league roster. The Yankees also signed two 19-year-old Chinese prospects, catcher Zhang Zhenwang and left-handed pitcher Liu Kai, to minor-league contracts in 2007.[48]

MLB opened an office in Beijing in 2007 and in 2008 launched a new website to increase its visibility in China. The website, www.major.tv/china, allows baseball fans in China to view highlights, scores, and some games. In 2010, for the first time in its history, MLB televised a regular-season game—the opening-day game between the Red Sox and Yankees—live across China, reaching nearly 300 million fans. Also in 2010, to make games more accessible to viewers across China, MLB signed new agreements with two Chinese broadcast partners, Chongqing TV and Shaanxi TV, to supplement its existing contracts with Guangdong TV, Jiangsu TV, and Shenzhen TV.[49]

Believing grassroots instruction to be vital to baseball's long-term success, MLB has regularly sponsored clinics for Chinese youth. It launched several important initiatives in 2007. In September, MLB established the Play Ball! program in five cities, Beijing, Guangzhou, Shanghai, Tianjin, and Wuxi. Play Ball! has also entered the physical-education curriculum in 120 elementary schools across China, including 30 in Beijing for players from ages 8 through 18. Students learn the rules of the game and receive fundamental instruction to develop baseball skills. Earlier that year, in August, MLB conducted its first China Baseball Academy, a three-week session in Wuxi for 60 of the top-rated 12- through 15-year-olds. Major League Baseball International and the CBA selected the academy's participants from existing provincial baseball organizations in Beijing, Chengdu, Dalian, Guangzhou, Shanghai, Shenzhen, Tianjin, and Wuxi.[50]

MLB hosted the China national baseball team for Spring Training in the United States and provided an opportunity for China's players to train with MLB teams and players. Later that year, Cal Ripken Jr. accompanied MLB officials as part of an envoy for the U.S. Department of State. The delegation visited Beijing, Shanghai, Wuxi, and Guangzhou. In each city, Ripken introduced baseball to Chinese youths in a cross-cultural exchange. He visited schools and youth clubs, ran baseball clinics, and shared personal life stories and experiences to build enthusiasm for the sport. At the outset of the trip, Secretary of State Condoleezza Rice commented on the envoy and Ripken's involvement:

Public diplomacy must be a dialogue with people from around the world and sought out and conducted not only by people like us in government, but by committed Americans from all walks of life. Cal Ripken embodies the best that sports have to offer and we are thrilled that he will be working for our country on this trip and other trips in the future.[51]

In 2009, MLB established its MLB Baseball Park initiative, the first baseball-themed entertainment tour in China. According to MLB sources, 400,000 Chinese citizens attended these programs in Beijing, Shanghai, Guangzhou, Chengdu, and Wuxi. MLB toured ten more cities in 2010, bringing the total to 15. In April 2010, MLB and the CBA signed a contract to promote baseball in China; Chinese officials were quick to point out the paucity of fields and the need for more to be built.[52] Also, in September of 2009, MLB developed its first MLB Baseball Development Center (MBDC) at Dongbeitang high school in Wuxi, Jiangsu province. This baseball academy hosts 16 select school-aged ballplayers and provides standard academic and English-language classes, in addition to exceptional baseball training led by an international team of instructors.[53]

Jeff Brueggemann, who played in the Minnesota Twins organization, is now in his third year of teaching baseball in China, as part of MLB's Play Ball! initiative. "Three years ago,' he said, "I could say bangqiu and people on the street wouldn't know what I was talking about. Now I can talk to anyone and they know what baseball is. They might not know the game, but they know what it is. And they want to learn the game."[54] ∎

Notes

1. Juliet Macur, "Playing in China, Chipping at a Wall," *New York Times*, 16 March 2008.
2. Corey Brock, "Fine China: Dodgers, Padres Shine," MLB.com, 15 March 2008.
3. Mark Magnier, "Baseball Makes a Pitch for China's Masses," *Miami Herald*, 16 March 2008.
4. Corey Brock, "Padres Right at Home in China," MLB.com, 15 March 2008.
5. Corey Brock, "Fine China: Dodgers, Padres Shine," MLB.com, 15 March 2008.
6. Corey Brock, "Second Helpings in Beijing Sweet," MLB.com, 16 March 2008.
7. Mark Zeigler, "Smog in Beijing May Give Dodgers Home-Field Advantage," *San Diego Union-Tribune* 13 March 2008.
8. Ibid.
9. John Schlegel, "NL West Meets Far East in Historic Trip," MLB.com, 12 March 2008.
10. Ken Gurnick, "Torre Sees Bright Future for MLB, China," MLB.com, 14 March 2008.
11. John Schlegel, "NL West Meets Far East in Historic Trip," MLB.com, 12 March 2008.
12. Associated Press, "China Gets Taste of Pastime," *Charlotte Observer*, 16 March 2008.
13. John Schlegel, "NL West Meets Far East in Historic Trip," MLB.com, 12 March 2008.
14. "Baseball Has Deep Roots in China," MLB.com, 12 March 2008, 16 March 2008.
15. Ibid.
16. Ibid.
17. "Organized, Tournament Baseball in China," MLB.com, 12 March 2008.
18. "China Baseball League Facing Obstacles," *USA Today*, 23 May 2009.
19. "Organized, Tournament Baseball in China," MLB.com, 12 March 2008.
20. Corey Brock, "Ready to Play Ball in China," MLB.com, 14 March 2008.
21. Ibid.
22. Corey Brock, "Lefebvre Discusses Baseball in China," MLB.com, 14 March 2008.
23. Ibid.
24. Jim Caple, "Good Showing in '08 Olympics Will Spur Interest," ESPN.com, 1 March 2007.
25. Nick Mulvenney, "Baseball Still Hopeful of Spot at London 2012," Reuters, 16 March 2008.
26. "The Wukesong Baseball Complex Will Be the First Olympic Venue Demolished," Reuters, 14 January 2009.
27. Zhang Hui, "Baseball in China Has a Long Way To Go, Despite MLB Interest," *Global Times*, 2 April 2010.
28. Joseph A. Reaves, *Taking in a Game: A History of Baseball in Asia* (Lincoln: University of Nebraska Press, 2002), 6.
29. Ibid., 3–6.
30. Ibid.
31. Yang Xinwei, "Small Thinks Big About Baseball in China," *China Daily*, 2 April 2010.
32. Ken Gurnick, "Selig: 'This Is Where It Started,'" MLB.com, 16 March 2008.
33. Ibid.
34. Mark Magnier, "Baseball Makes a Pitch for China's Masses," *Miami Herald*, 16 March 2008.
35. Ken Gurnick, "Selig: 'This Is Where It Started,'" MLB.com, 16 March 2008.
36. Ibid.
37. Ibid.
38. Stephen Wade, "Selling Game in China Costly, Rewarding," Associated Press, 11 March 2008.
39. Ken Gurnick, "Selig: 'This Is Where It Started,'" MLB.com, 16 March 2008, 17 March 2008.
40. Eric Green, "First Chinese Baseball Players Signed to Play in United States," USINFO, 26 June 2007.
41. Calum MacLeod, "China Embraces Basketball," *USA Today*, 7 August 2006.
42. Asia Pulse, "NBA to Open First Overseas Store in China," *Asia Times Online*, 1 December 2006.
43. Jack Etkin, "Pro Baseball Takes First Step in Scaling Great Wall in China," *Rocky Mountain News*, 12 March 2008.
44. Corey Brock, "Ready to Play Ball in China," MLB.com, 14 March 2008.
45. Ibid.
46. "MLB Remains Upbeat on China Project," *China Daily*, 27 January 2010.
47. "New York Yankees and Chinese Baseball Association Reach Landmark Agreement," MLB.com, 30 January 2007.
48. Op. cit. 9.
49. Jerry Milani, "MLB Opener to Be Shown in China," *Baseball Digest*, 2 April 2010.
50. "MLB International to Launch Inaugural China Baseball Academy," MLB.com, 7 August 2007.
51. Xinhua, "Envoy Cal Ripken Embarks to Introduce Baseball in China," *People's Daily Online*, 17 October 2007, 21 December 2007.
52. Zhang Hui, "Baseball in China Has a Long Way to Go, Despite MLB Interest," *Global Times*, 2 April 2010.
53. Ibid.
54. Corey Brock, "Ready to Play Ball in China," MLB.com, 14 March 2008.

Beyond Bunning and Short Rest

An Analysis of Managerial Decisions That Led to the Phillies' Epic Collapse of 1964

Bryan Soderholm-Difatte

NEARLY ALL ACCOUNTS OF the 1964 Philadelphia Phillies' epic collapse, which would etch itself deep in the city's historical psyche, focus on the Phillies' 10-game losing streak that started on September 21, when they had a 6½-game lead with only 12 games remaining, and ended with them having lost eight games in the standings in ten days. Half of the Phillies' preferred starting rotation was grappling with injuries—Dennis Bennett was pitching with a sore shoulder, and Ray Culp had not pitched since mid-August because of arm trouble. Even so, manager Gene Mauch is often blamed for starting his two best pitchers, right-handed ace Jim Bunning and left-handed ace Chris Short, twice each on two days' rest, instead of the normal three, during the losing streak. In accounts of the Phillies' implosion—by David Halberstam in *October 1964* and William C. Kashatus in *September Swoon: Richie Allen, the '64 Phillies, and Racial Integration* and in the Baseball Prospectus compilation on great pennant races, *It Ain't Over 'Til It's Over*—Mauch is portrayed as increasingly panicked, lashing out at his players and perhaps over-managing in a desperate attempt to salvage the pennant.[1]

These narratives provide an excellent account of what happened, including key plays along the way—such as with the ever dangerous Frank Robinson at bat, Reds utility infielder Chico Ruiz daringly steals home with two out in the sixth inning, scoring the only run in the game that began the Phillies' 10-game losing streak—and players' perspectives on the unfolding disaster. The authors of these accounts note that Mauch's decision to start Bunning and Short on short rest was ill conceived and probably cost the Phillies some games they might have won had those two been pitching on normal rest. But they do not consider some other decisions made by Mauch that might have cost the Phillies some games during those critical weeks.

After a comprehensive play-by-play analysis from the game logs posted at Baseball-Reference and made available through the painstaking efforts of Retrosheet researchers, I believe there were at least six critical decisions Mauch made, other than those affecting how he used Bunning and Short in the final two weeks, that backfired to upend Philadelphia's pennant dream. Four of them came in the five days *before* the Phillies

Phillies' manager Gene Mauch relied on Chris Short, the best left-hander in the team's rotation and still healthy late in the season. On September 25, starting on two days' rest, he pitched into the eighth inning, allowing only three runs in a game the Braves finally won in the twelfth.

began their 10-game losing streak. To make sure that I fully understood the circumstances of the games, I personally scored each play of each game so I could plainly see how each game developed.

I started with the Phillies' game at Houston on September 16. They went into this game with a comfortable lead of 6 games, with 17 left on the schedule. This was the first of three September starts that Bunning made on only two days' rest. The other two are more understandable, because they're in the midst of the Phillies' 10-game losing streak. But why would manager Mauch start Bunning on short rest on September 16, when at this point the prospect for a tight pennant race down the stretch looked so unlikely? To understand the context, let's begin with a quick look at how the Phillies got to where they were.

HOW THE PHILLIES GOT TO THE THRESHOLD OF A PENNANT

In the article on the 1964 pennant race in *It Ain't Over 'Til It's Over*, the argument is made that what is often overlooked in discussions of the Phillies' collapse is that the team should not have been in contention in the first place, notwithstanding that they exceeded expectations by finishing surprisingly high, fourth place, in 1963.[2] Mauch's daily lineup was much less settled than that of the National League's other putative contenders for 1964—the defending champion Dodgers; the Cardinals, who had finished second the previous year; the Reds; and the Giants—and with many more weaknesses. Mauch had only three players whose names he wrote into the lineup every day—Johnny Callison in right field, Tony Taylor at second base, and rookie sensation Richie Allen, as Dick Allen was then called (against his wishes) at third base. Callison and Allen both had sensational years; Taylor was a steady hand at best.

The only other position player to start as many as 100 games for the Phillies was catcher Clay Dalrymple, a left-handed batter who platooned with the right-handed Gus Triandos. Mauch started the season platooning the rookie left-handed-hitting John Herrnstein at first base with the veteran right-handed-hitting Roy Sievers. Neither hit well, and by midseason Sievers was gone and replaced by veteran right-handed-hitting Frank Thomas (acquired from the Mets in early August), who took over the position full-time until suffering a hand injury in early September that kept him out of the lineup most of the final month of the season. Mauch used a platoon in left field, with the left-handed-hitting Wes Covington paired off first with rookie Danny Cater and later with rookie Alex Johnson, and in center field for most of the second half of the season, with the left-handed-hitting Tony Gonzalez trading off with Cookie Rojas. Mauch started the year with Bobby Wine as his regular shortstop and ended using mostly Ruben Amaro, neither of whom hit well.

Going into the season, the Phillies' pitching was not considered on par with that of the other NL-contending teams. Only Jim Bunning, acquired in a winter trade from Detroit, had an established pedigree. Mauch's starting rotation was right-handers Bunning and Ray Culp and southpaws Chris Short and Dennis Bennett as his core four, with righty Art Mahaffey as a fifth starter. Jack Baldschun was the best of an otherwise suspect bullpen. By September, however, Mauch's starting rotation was in deep trouble. Culp was sidelined with an elbow problem and made his last start on August 15, and Bennett was battling a persistently sore shoulder. Bennett continued to pitch through the pain. Mauch replaced Culp in his four-man rotation with Mahaffey, and 18-year old rookie Rick Wise replaced Mahaffey as the fifth starter, whenever one was needed. Fortunately, Bunning and Short were healthy and pitching well.

The Phillies got off to a fast start, winning 9 of their first 11 games, and never trailed by more than 2 games as they positioned themselves for a pennant chase. On July 16, they moved into a tie for first and gradually built a lead that reached 7½ games on August 20 after a string of 12 wins in 16 games against the three worst teams in the league—the Cubs, the Colts, and the Mets. The Dodgers had imploded, getting off to a 2–9 start, and never recovered. The Giants had spent much of May and June in first place but then went 28–31 in July and August, reaching a nadir of 8½ games behind the Phillies on August 21, amid racial-diversity issues in the San Francisco clubhouse. The Reds had split their first 44 games (actually their first 45, as one was a tie) and then began a steady climb up the standings from sixth to second, which they reached on August 20, although settling in at a distant 7½ games behind the Phillies. And the Cardinals were languishing in eighth place with a 28–31 record on June 15 when they made the trade with the Cubs that brought them Lou Brock. The Cards still trailed by as many as 11 games on August 23, presumably not harboring pennant dreams, but won 13 of their next 16 games—the last in Philadelphia—to close within 5 games of the Phillies, in second place, on September 9.

By mid-September, the question of whether the Phillies were good enough to compete for the pennant was moot. Paced by Allen and Callison on the offensive side, and by Bunning and Short on the mound, Gene Mauch had his Phillies in command of the pennant race. To say that the Phillies had overachieved to get to this point—a 6-game lead with 17 games remaining after Bennett and Baldschun combined for a four-hit, 1–0 shutout in Houston on September 15—and that their subsequent collapse should somehow not diminish the great success they had in 1964 would be disingenuous. Some of the most compelling pennant races in baseball history have involved teams that were not expected to compete but did, and won—the 1914 "Miracle" Braves, the 1969 "Miracle" Mets, anyone?

Of course, some might argue that the 1964 Phillies peaked too early—that eventually their weaknesses caught up with them—while the 1914 Braves and 1969 Mets peaked at just the right time, both coming from far behind to finish first by a decisive margin, their late-season momentum carrying them on to win the World Series before their weaknesses could reassert themselves.

MAUCH'S MAJOR STRATEGIC BLUNDER—LOOKING AHEAD TO THE WORLD SERIES?

And so it was with great expectations that the good citizens of the City of Brotherly Love awoke on the morning of September 16, 1964, for their Phillies had

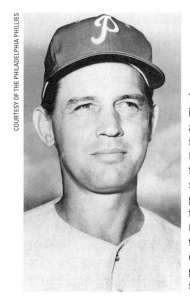

The Phillies' improbable collapse in September 1964 is usually attributed to Gene Mauch's decision to start Jim Bunning and Chris Short on short rest in the final weeks of the season, but several other questionable in-game decisions contributed to their rapid loss of ground to the Cardinals and Reds. He tended to work for one run at a time, calling for sacrifice bunts and giving up too many outs for the sake of advancing a runner.

beaten the Colts out in Houston the night before and held a commanding 6-game lead over second-place St. Louis, with time for the other contenders running out fast. San Francisco was 7½ games back, and Cincinnati, 8½. The Phillies, in fact, had been in first place every day since July 17. It seemed inconceivable that the Phillies would not soon be appearing in the World Series for the third time in franchise history.

It was then that Gene Mauch made perhaps his biggest mistake of the season. He decided to start Bunning, his ace, in Houston on September 16, on only two days' rest. The ninth-place Colts were certainly not contenders. Moreover, in his last start, a 4–1 ten-inning complete game victory in San Francisco, he struck out nine and gave up seven hits. Pitch counts were not much (if at all) in managers' minds back then and were not recorded for posterity, but clearly Bunning threw well over 100 pitches in his 10-inning effort.

In the chapter on the 1964 pennant race in *It Ain't Over 'Til It's Over*, Mauch's decision to start Bunning on this date is called "inexplicable."[3] Kashatus says that Mauch was anxious to extend the Phillies' lead in the standings and that the ninth-place Colts would seem to be perfect patsies for a pitcher of Bunning's caliber even if he was not fully rested.[4] Halberstam says Mauch wanted Bunning to pitch in every series the Phillies played down the stretch.[5] Both Kashatus and Halberstam say Mauch wanted Bunning to pitch in Los Angeles, but he would have anyway, if he had not started in Houston.[6] He would have opened the series in L.A. for the Phillies the very next day—and would have been in to start the opening game in the next series against the Reds, who still had some hope for the pennant, while the Dodgers had none. By starting in

Houston, however, Bunning was indeed available to pitch the final game of the LA series, but that meant he would miss the Cincinnati series entirely, unless Mauch intended to use him again on short rest.

Those explanations might be true, but they don't make sense, at least not to me. Why start Bunning on short rest? When we consider the calendar and that the Phillies were beginning to print World Series tickets, what emerges as the most plausible reason for this decision is that Mauch was trying to set up his best pitcher, Jim Bunning, to start the first game of the World Series—scheduled to begin on Wednesday, October 7—on suitable rest. (See table 1.) Ironically, had there been a game scheduled between the Phillies and Reds on Saturday, October 3, Bunning would have been perfectly lined up to start the World Series by making his last five regular-season starts on normal rest. But a quirk in the scheduling had the Phillies and Reds concluding the season with games on Friday, October 2, and Sunday, October 4, but *with a day off on Saturday* between the two games.

Table 1. Bunning's Projected Starts on Normal Rest After Sept. 13

Sept 13 at Giants	Sept 14 at Colts	Sept 15 at Colts	Sept 16 at Colts	**Sept 17 at Dodgers**	Sept 18 at Dodgers	Sept 19 at Dodgers
Sept 20 at Dodgers	**Sept 21 at Reds**	Sept 22 at Reds	Sept 23 at Reds	Sept 24 at Braves	**Sept 25 at Braves**	Sept 26 at Braves
Sept 27 at Braves	Sept 28 at Cardinals	**Sept 29 at Cardinals**	Sept 30 at Cardinals	Oct 1	Oct 2 at Reds	**Oct 3**
Oct 4 at Reds	Oct 5	Oct 6	**Oct 7 World Series Game 1**	Oct 8	Oct 9	Oct 10

If this analysis is correct, Mauch faced a dilemma. If Bunning continued to pitch on his normal schedule, his last start before the World Series—assuming he was to start the first game, which of course was a given—would have been on September 29, giving him a full week off before the World Series began. (See table 1.) Starting pitchers especially establish a rhythm for pitching during the season, and Mauch probably assumed that seven days between starts was too long for a workhorse like Bunning, who might lose his edge with so much downtime.

Mauch could have decided to give his ace four days' rest between his remaining starts, which would have had Bunning making his final start of the regular season on Friday, October 2, giving him another four days' rest before the start of the World Series. But this would not have been a viable solution for Mauch even if he were willing to buck the then conventional practice of the top starting pitcher taking the mound every four days and to start Bunning every fifth day. With Culp out, Bennett hurting, and no depth in his rotation, Mauch really had no option to go to a five-man rotation until the World Series. Instead, he appears to have decided that keeping to the rhythm of three days' rest between starts was preferable and took the gamble of starting Bunning—presumably just this once—on short rest against the woeful Houston Colts, in order to set him up to have proper rest before his final regular-season start on October 2. That would have given Bunning an extra fourth day before pitching in Game 1 of the World Series. (See table 2.)

Table 2. Mauch's Intention for Bunning's Starts After Sept.13?

Sept 13 at Giants	Sept 14 at Colts	Sept 15 at Colts	Sept 16 at Colts	Sept 17 at Dodgers	Sept 18 at Dodgers	Sept 19 at Dodgers
Sept 20 at Dodgers	Sept 21 at Reds	Sept 22 at Reds	Sept 23 at Reds	Sept 24 at Braves	Sept 25 at Braves	Sept 26 at Braves
Sept 27 at Braves	Sept 28 at Cardinals	Sept 29 at Cardinals	Sept 30 at Cardinals	Oct 1	Oct 2 at Reds	Oct 3
Oct 4 at Reds	Oct 5	Oct 6	Oct 7 World Series Game 1	Oct 8	Oct 9	Oct 10

In his Houston start on short rest, Bunning gave up six runs in 4⅓ innings, leaving the game after giving up three hits and two walks to the six batters he faced in the fifth. At the time, it was a loss that had no bearing on the standings, and in fact the Phillies won the next day in the first of four games in Los Angeles, beating Don Drysdale, against whom Bunning would have pitched on normal rest, to increase their lead to 6½ games with 15 remaining. All seemed right with the world in Philadelphia, but Gene Mauch had made what in hindsight proved to be a disastrous decision: starting Jim Bunning on two days' rest.

QUICK HOOK OF YOUNG STARTER HAS CONSEQUENCES

Although the Phillies did win 4–3 that next day, September 17, in Los Angeles, Mauch made another decision that would have unanticipated consequences down the road. He started right-hander Rick Wise, a rookie teen, instead of Art Mahaffey, whose previous two starts apparently had caused Mauch to lose confidence in him, according to several accounts, including Kashatus's.[7] Mahaffey had given up three runs in only two-thirds of an inning on September 8 in a 3–2 loss to

the Dodgers in Philadelphia, and then two runs in two innings on September 12 in a 9–1 loss in San Francisco.

Wise was making only the eighth start of his career, however. Back in August, he did have back-to-back victories in which he pitched effectively into the eighth inning, but in his two starts immediately before this one on September 17 he did not pitch well. He gave up five runs in four innings to the Braves on August 25 and was removed by Mauch in the first inning of his next start on September 7 against the Dodgers after facing only three batters—giving up two walks and a single—all of whom scored. He got no one out.

Here was Wise starting against the Dodgers again, ten days later, and he already had a 3–0 lead from the top of the first, but this game began much the same way as his last start had. Wise had given up two singles, a walk, and a groundout resulting in two runs when Mauch decided that—even with a 6-game lead and a depleted starting rotation—he had seen enough for the day of young rookie Wise, who had turned 19 only days before. With left-handed batters Johnny Roseboro and Ron Fairly next up for Dodgers, Mauch called on veteran southpaw Bobby Shantz rather than let Wise try to work his way out of trouble and see if he might settle down.

At the time, it seemed like a brilliant move. Shantz pitched into the eighth inning and gave up only one run of his own to earn the 4–3 win that put the Phillies up by 6½ games. However, with Bunning and Short his only two healthy starting pitchers, Mauch had no pitchers to spare. Instead of showing commitment to his decision to start a young rookie in a late-season game during a pennant drive, Mauch replaced him in the first inning. In effect, he used two pitchers in one "starting role" that day. An unintended consequence was that Bobby Shantz, who faced 25 batters in relief of Wise, was unavailable to pitch in dire circumstances two days later.

The Phillies' unraveling began the next two days with consecutive 4–3 losses in Los Angeles. Chris Short, starting on normal rest, took a 3–0 lead into the last of the seventh on September 18, having given up only two hits. Three batters later, the score was tied on a three-run home run by Frank Howard. The Dodgers won on a two-out single off Phillies' relief ace Jack Baldschun with two outs in the ninth. The next day, September 19, the two teams battled into the sixteenth inning, tied 3-3, when Baldschun—having already worked two innings in this game and six innings in the previous four days—gave up a single to Willie Davis, intentionally walked Tommy Davis after Willie stole second, and then surrendered a wild pitch that advanced Willie to third with left-handed batter Ron Fairly at the plate.

Gene Mauch chose this moment to replace his relief ace with rookie southpaw Morrie Steevens, who was appearing in his first major-league game of the season and had only 12 appearances in the major leagues before this. Mauch had only one other left-handed option available, the crafty veteran Bobby Shantz, but Shantz had pitched 7⅓ innings just two days before in relief of Wise and was not sufficiently rested—apparently not even to face one batter, although getting the out would have meant going into the seventeenth inning. Instead of staying with Baldschun to get one more out to escape the inning, Mauch went with Steevens. There were two out, and the possible winning run on third. As a left-hander, whether pitching from the stretch or from a full windup, Steevens on his delivery would have had his back to the runner at third. Steevens apparently was so focused on Fairly, as well he should have been, that he was inattentive to Willie Davis, which he should not have been; Willie Davis took advantage and stole home, scoring the winning run.

BUNTING DICK ALLEN

Mauch had an opportunity to win this game in the fourteenth inning, when Johnny Callison led off with a single. Dick Allen, the cleanup hitter, strolled to the plate. After Allen was the pitcher's spot (the result of an earlier double switch) but, this being a long game in which he had already used seven position players off the bench, Mauch had limited options for a pinch-hitter. Specifically, he had the light-hitting Bobby Wine, who was batting .209, with only 4 home runs and 33 RBI, and hadn't played in five days—except as a defensive substitute who did not get a chance to bat.

Allen, coming to bat with nobody out and Callison on first in the fourteenth inning of a tie game, was the Phillies' most dangerous hitter. He already had 26 home runs for the year and was third in the league in slugging percentage. In his three previous plate appearances, he had two singles and been intentionally walked by the Dodgers. Even though he knew that Wine was to bat next, Mauch opted to play for one run rather than letting his cleanup batter hit with the possibility of driving in the run. He had Allen—his best and most feared hitter—lay down a sacrifice bunt. Allen did so successfully, but that left Mauch with only two outs to work with and two weak hitters—Wine, followed by .238-hitting catcher Clay Dalrymple—to try to drive in Callison from second. Callison was picked off, Wine flied out, and the Phillies failed to score, ultimately setting up Willie Davis's game-winning steal of home. The loss still seemed relatively inconsequential, however, as Bunning came back on September 20, on his normal rest, to win his eighteenth game of the season, 3–2, both runs unearned in the ninth.

WITH 12 GAMES LEFT, THE PHILLIES FACE THE PERFECT STORM

We are now at where most accounts of the Phillies' 1964 collapse begin. When the Phillies returned to Philadelphia on September 21 for their final homestand of seven games, they once again had a 6½-game lead over both the Reds and the Cardinals and were 7 games ahead of the Giants. Even if the Reds or Cardinals won all of their remaining games, the Phillies needed to win only 7 of their remaining 12 games to win the pennant outright. If the Cardinals or Reds won 10 of their last 13 games—which, in fact, St. Louis did—the Phillies could have finished the season 4–8 and still gone to the World Series. It would take nearly a perfect storm for Philadelphia to *not* win the pennant.

And, as fate would have it, the remaining schedule conspired to make that perfect storm plausible. (See table 3.) The Reds had five of their 13 games remaining against the Phillies, and the Cardinals had three games left with the Phillies, giving both teams the opportunity to make up significant ground against

Table 3. Remaining Games for National League Contenders as of Sept. 21
(won–lost records before games of Sept. 21)

Philadelphia Phillies 1st, 90–60, + 6½	St. Louis Cardinals 2nd, 83–66, -6½	Cincinnati Reds 2nd, 83–66, -6½	San Francisco Giants 4th, 83–67, -7
3 vs. Cincinnati Reds (83–66)	2 at New York Mets (50–99)	3 at Philadelphia (90–60)	3 at Houston Colts (63–88)
4 vs Milwaukee Braves (77–72)	5 at Pittsburgh Pirates (76–72)	5 at NewYork Mets (50–99)	3 at Chicago Cubs (67–82)
3 at St. Louis Cardinals (83–66)	3 vs Philadelphia (90–60)	3 vs Pittsburgh Pirates (76–72)	3 vs Houston Colts (63–88)
2 at Cincinnati Reds (83–66)	3 vs New York Mets (50–99)	2 vs Philadelphia (90–60)	3 vs Chicago Cubs (67–82)

the first-place team they had to overtake. But the Reds also had five games against the awful Mets and three against the struggling Pirates, who were in sixth place at the close of play on September 20. And the Cardinals had five against those awful Mets and five against those struggling Pirates. The Giants, who really shouldn't have been in the discussion at this point, as any combination of six Phillies' wins or six losses of their own would eliminate them from contention, had the advantage of playing their final 12 games against the eighth-place Cubs and ninth-place Colts.

The Phillies, however, did not have any of the National League's worst teams on their remaining schedule. In eight of their final 12 games, they had to contend against their two closest competitors, the Reds and Cardinals—meaning they would lose ground in any game they lost. And the Phillies' other four games were with the fifth-place Milwaukee Braves, whose potent lineup was well able to do serious damage to Mauch's worn-out pitching staff, especially with his regular third starter, Culp, disabled with an elbow problem; his fourth regular starter, Bennett, enduring a sore shoulder; and both Mahaffey and Wise deemed less than reliable by their manager. The Phillies were scheduled to close the season with three games in St. Louis and two in Cincinnati. At this point, at the start of play on September 21, both the Cardinals and the Reds still had a dim chance, but Mauch had reason to hope they would no longer be a pennant threat by then.

To put their remaining schedules in a different perspective: The Reds and the Cardinals were playing teams (including the Phillies) with a combined winning percentage of .483 on the morning of September 21, while the Phillies were going against teams (the Reds, Braves, and Cardinals) with a combined winning percentage of .544—a significant difference. Philadelphia had a tougher schedule, but still, a 6½-game lead with only 12 remaining should have been safe, almost impossible to lose.

The Phillies seemed to have an advantage in that seven of their final 12 games were at home. With a 46–28 record at Connie Mack Stadium, the Phillies at this point had the best home record in the National League. Their first three games were against the Reds, who really needed to sweep the series to have a realistic chance of catching the Phillies. While there was nothing at the moment the Phillies could do about the Cardinals and the Giants, just one win in the three games would leave the Reds 5½ games back, a gap that would be virtually impossible to close with only 10 games left. How important would just one win have

been? Even if the Cardinals swept their upcoming two-game series with the Mets in New York, one Phillies win against the Reds would have left St. Louis five games behind with 11 remaining, and with not very much hope.

BUNTING DICK ALLEN AGAIN AS THE LOSING STREAK BEGINS

The Phillies lost the first game of their series with the Reds in dramatic fashion, 1–0, when Chico Ruiz stole home with two outs in the sixth inning. On his delivery, Mahaffey, back in the starting rotation, would have been facing the third-base line. Of course, with Frank Robinson, one of baseball's most accomplished and feared batters, at the plate, the Phillies (including their manager) could be excused for assuming that an attempt to steal home in this situation was highly improbable. But steal home Ruiz did. Reds pitcher John Tsitouris was in command the whole game, pitching a six-hit shutout, and Philadelphia's lead was down to 5½ games.

All accounts of this game mention that both Mauch and Reds manager Dick Sisler were shocked that Ruiz had the gall to try to steal home with Frank Robinson at bat. What they don't mention is that the Phillies' best chance for a run came when Tony Gonzalez led off the home first with a single, bringing up Dick Allen—whom Mauch had batting second in the lineup, rather than in a power slot, and whom he once again asked to sacrifice the runner to second rather than hit away with the possibility of setting up a big first inning. The Phillies had all 27 outs remaining, so why give up Philadelphia's best, most effective hitter at this point in the game? If Allen got out and the runner was still on first, Mauch would have still had two outs in the inning and eight more innings to go. The sacrifice turned out to be good, but the runner ended up stranded on third.

This was the second time in three days that Mauch called for Allen to lay down a sacrifice bunt. The first time, as we have already seen, in the September 19 game in Los Angeles, Mauch had Allen bunt with a runner on first and nobody out in the 14th inning in an effort to break a 3–3 tie, despite knowing that none of the batters following Allen in the order were notable run-producing hitters. This time, in the first inning with nobody out, Mauch was hoping to set up an early run. With Dick Allen on his way to 201 hits, 29 of them home runs, an OPS of .939 (fifth in the league), and more total bases, 352, than anyone else in the league (Willie Mays had 351), Mauch's decision to have Allen sacrifice-bunt is open to legitimate question, especially as most other managers did not use their most power-

Dick Allen, the NL Rookie of the Year for 1964, played in all 162 games and was one of only two players—the others were second baseman Tony Taylor and right fielder Johnny Callison—whom Mauch wrote into the lineup nearly every day. Twice over the course of three games, with the score tied, Mauch had Allen lay down a sacrifice bunt. Allen did so successfully both times, but neither effort led to a run, and it was by one run that the Phillies lost both games.

ful hitters to lay one down for lesser lights to try to drive the runner home.

Allen batted .542 with runners on base during the 17 days that forever shocked Philadelphia. (See sidebar.) Had he been allowed to swing away in either of those plate appearances against the Dodgers and Reds, the outcome of either game, or of both games, might have been different. One more win at that point in the season, with so few games remaining, might have been all it would have taken to permanently deflate the hopes of the Reds and Cardinals before they began their surge upward.

Gene Mauch's reputation as manager was that he tended to call for plays—the sacrifice, the hit-and-run—to work for one run at a time, even from the very beginning of the game, in order to score first if at all possible. The problem is that sacrificing an out to help set up a run is precisely that—giving up an out, and there are only three outs an inning and 27 a game. While this strategy made sense for managers of teams (Walter Alston, for example, with his mid-1960s Dodgers) that had difficulty scoring runs, Mauch had a lineup with much more ability to score runs. Even so, he often chose to sacrifice for one run—even with his best hitters at the plate—instead of trusting in his firepower.

The two best hitters in the Phillies' lineup, Allen and Callison, who hit a combined total of 60 home runs in 1964, both, in the course of the season, laid down six sacrifice bunts to move a base runner up with nobody out. In calling for them to do so, Mauch,

WHERE SHOULD DICK ALLEN HAVE HIT?

It seems Gene Mauch never decided where the appropriate place in the batting order was for his rookie phenom, Dick Allen, in 1964; he changed his mind about that at least three times. In the first part of the season—64 games from opening day through June 12, during which the Phillies went 29–21 (.580)—the powerful Allen most often batted second, a lineup spot usually used to help set up runs for the third, fourth, and fifth hitters. Allen batted cleanup only three times in the first two months of the season—understandable, given that he was still an unproven rookie. By this point in the season, June 12, he was batting .294 and had 12 home runs and 32 RBIs, leading the Phillies in all three triple-crown categories. Allen also had an .895 OPS. Aside from his power numbers suggesting that the third or fourth slots in the batting order would have been a more logical fit for him, he also had a propensity to strike out a lot—not a good thing for a number-two batter. Allen led the league in strikeouts in 1964 with 138, averaging one strikeout every five at-bats when he batted second in the order.

Seeing what his emerging young slugger could do, Mauch put Allen into the cleanup spot on June 13, where he stayed for 53 of the Phillies' next 55 games, during which they went 33–22 (.600). By August 6, Allen was batting .311 and had a .913 OPS, with 19 home runs and 56 RBIs. On August 7, however, right-handed power-hitting Frank Thomas joined the Phillies to fill their glaring weakness at first base. From then until September 17, Mauch alternated Thomas with the left-handed Wes Covington in the cleanup spot. Of the 42 games played in that time, Allen batted fourth only twice and once again was used most frequently (23 times) in the number-two spot of the lineup, although Mauch also often had him batting third (17 times), with the usual number-three hitter, Johnny Callison, second in the order in those games. From looking at who the opposing starting pitcher was, it is not apparent that Mauch's shifting of Allen and Callison between second and third in the order had anything to do with whether the pitcher threw left-handed or right-handed. The Phillies were 27–15 (.643) in their best stretch of the season, at the end of which Allen was batting a team-high .307 and had a team-best .913 OPS, with 26 home runs and 79 RBI.

Mauch, however, still had not settled on a permanent spot in the batting order for his most dangerous hitter. In the final 15 games, Allen batted fourth eight times, second five times, and third twice. He finished the season batting .318 (fifth in the league), with 29 home runs and 91 RBIs.

Would it have made a difference had Mauch stayed with Allen in the second or third slot in the final weeks, particularly when the games became desperate as Philadelphia's lead evaporated? There is much to be said for lineup stability. There is also much to be said for a hitter batting cleanup who was as much of a power threat as Dick Allen was. In the final 15 games of the season, Allen continued to hit well even as the rest of the Phillies did not. While the Phillies as a team were terrible in the clutch with runners on base, especially in scoring position, Allen was . . . well, clutch. He went 13-for-26 with runners on base in those 15 games—a .500 batting average—and walked or was intentionally walked several times. He also had those two sacrifice bunts.

in the interest of playing for one run, gave up as outs the two batters most likely to drive in runs. Of the league's other premier hitters who also hit for power, Willie Mays had one sacrifice bunt for the Giants in 1964, Orlando Cepeda and Willie McCovey none; Frank Robinson did not have a sacrifice all year for the Reds; neither did Ken Boyer for the Cardinals; nor did Hank Aaron or Eddie Mathews for the Braves. Milwaukee, in fact, had five players who hit 20 or more home runs, only one of whom had any sacrifice hits—Denis Menke, not otherwise known as a power guy, with four.

LOSING BUILDS MOMENTUM

After the Phillies' dispiriting 1–0 loss on September 21, Chris Short was roughed up the following day in a 9–2 loss to Cincinnati, victimized by yet another steal of home (by Pete Rose, as part of a double-steal in the third) and by a two-run homer by Frank Robinson. And on September 23, in the final game of the series, Vada Pinson's second home run of the day broke a 3–3 tie in the seventh as Cincinnati went on to a 6–4 win to sweep the series. Bunning, whose regular turn in the rotation would have had him starting the first game of this series if not for his short-rest start in Houston, did not pitch against Cincinnati.

The failure to take even one game from the Reds cost the Phillies three games in the standings in three days, but with a 3½-game lead and now only nine games remaining, it still seemed time was on their side. Moreover, the Cardinals and Giants were both five games back, presumably no longer in the picture. But for Philadelphia, the losing had become contagious. Bunning, pitching for the second time on his normal rest after his September 16 start in Houston, threw six strong innings on September 24 in the first of four games against the Braves, but the Phillies were held scoreless until the eighth in a 5–3 loss. But the Phillies had a three-game lead at the end of the day.

No need yet to be desperate, but Gene Mauch, feeling that the sure-thing pennant was slipping away, acted in desperation On September 25 he started Short, on only two days' rest, instead of Mahaffey, whose turn it was in the rotation and who had pitched so well in his previous start (the one where he neglected to check Chico Ruiz at third). Kashatus suggests that Mauch did not start Mahaffey in this game because he felt that the pitcher had cracked under pressure when he allowed Ruiz to steal home.[8] Short pitched effectively into the eighth inning, giving up only three runs on seven hits, but left trailing in the game. Callison tied the score in the eighth with a two-run home run, and the game went into extra innings. In the tenth, Joe Torre's two-run home run for the Braves was matched in the bottom of the inning by Dick Allen's two-run inside-the-park home run, which tied the game at 5–5. Milwaukee won in the twelfth, however, 7–5. As had been the case too often in recent games, Mauch's Phillies were abysmal with runners in scoring position. In eight such at-bats in this game, they were hitless.

STAYING WITH SHANTZ TOO LONG

But things looked brighter the next day, September 26, when the Phillies took an early 4–0 lead behind Mahaffey against the Braves, only to once again go cold at the plate when there were opportunities to score runs. The game went into the ninth inning, the Phillies' lead in the game whittled down to 4–3. Due up for the Braves in the ninth were two of baseball's best hitters, the right-handed Hank Aaron followed by the left-handed cleanup hitter Eddie Mathews. The Braves' pitcher, batting fifth in the order as a result of earlier maneuvers by Milwaukee manager Bobby Bragan, was scheduled to bat third in the inning. Fourth up in the inning, however, would be another dangerous right-handed batter, Rico Carty.

Despite this formidable array of mostly right-handed batters, beginning with perennial home-run threat Aaron, Mauch allowed southpaw Bobby Shantz to take the mound in the ninth. Shantz had gotten the final two outs of the eighth, coming into the game in a bases-loaded situation with one out. The Braves' third run of the game was scored on a passed ball. The Phillies' right-handed relief ace, Baldschun, was no longer available, having relieved starter Mahaffey in the eighth, and was followed by Shantz. With Aaron leading off the ninth, capable of tying the game on one swing, Mauch could have turned to right-hander Ed Roebuck, warming up in the bullpen. Instead, he stayed with Shantz.

He stayed with Shantz after Aaron started the ninth with a single. This made sense, since Mathews was a left-handed power hitter. He stayed with Shantz after Mathews singled even after the right-handed Frank Bolling was announced as a pinch-hitter. This maybe also made sense, since Bolling, the Braves' mostly regular second baseman, was hardly a dangerous hitter, his average hovering slightly above .200. Bolling reached on an error, loading the bases. The Phillies had a one-run lead but had yet to secure an out in the ninth. Coming up to bat was the right-handed Carty. He had come into the game batting .325, with 20 home runs and 80 RBIs. Still, Mauch stayed with southpaw

Bobby Shantz, when he had right-hander Ed Roebuck waiting in the bullpen.

Why not turn to Roebuck? In a month when Mauch's bullpen was stressed—relief ace Baldschun had lost four games already in September and allowed 37 of the 106 batters he had faced so far in the month to reach base, including one of two in this game before Shantz replaced him in the eighth—Roebuck had been pitching well. (See table 4.) In fact, Roebuck had allowed only four earned runs in his previous 14 appearances dating back to August 18. Two of those came on the three-run home run he surrendered to Vada Pinson that made him the losing pitcher in the final game of the series with Cincinnati. (See table 4.) That was three days ago. Presumably, Mauch no longer had much trust in Roebuck because he stayed with Shantz in a situation where he desperately needed an out. Carty tripled, the Phillies' lead was gone, Shantz was removed from the game, and Mauch finally brought in Roebuck. The Phillies went down quietly in their half of the ninth.

Gene Mauch had now watched his team lose six straight games, eight of their last nine dating to September 18, and nine of eleven dating to when he decided to start Bunning on short rest against Houston. With the Reds having extended their winning streak to seven straight games, the Phillies' lead was down to half a game. Meanwhile, the Cardinals, having won five of their last six, had closed to within a game and a half.

BUNNING AND SHORT IN DESPERATION STARTS

Now was truly desperation time for Mauch and the Phillies. Bunning told Halberstam he volunteered to pitch the final game of the Milwaukee series with only two days' rest. With Bennett suffering through a sore shoulder, Mauch probably felt he had no other choice—certainly not 19-year old Rick Wise, who pitched to only four batters, giving up two runs, in his last start on September 17 and to only three batters in his start before that. Following a script similar to that of his short stint against Houston, Bunning gave up five consecutive hits before departing in the fourth without getting an out. All five hits led to runs in a 14–8 Milwaukee blowout in Philadelphia's final home game of the season. Ironically, given that they lost, this was the Phillies' first real offensive outburst since they beat the Giants, 9–3, way back on September 5 in Philadelphia. The Reds beat the Mets in a double-header, and for the first time since July 16 the Phillies were no longer in first place. Philadelphia was now down a game to Cincinnati and just barely ahead—by half-a-game—of the surging third-place Cardinals of St. Louis, the Phillies' next destination.

The unintended consequence of his having started Short and Bunning out of turn against Milwaukee was that Mauch was now forced to use his two best pitchers on only two days' rest between starts against the Cardinals—which were now a team *they* (the Phillies) had to beat to keep from falling behind yet another suddenly emergent pennant contender, let alone to keep pace with the Reds, against whom they would

Table 4. Phillies' Right-Handed Relievers Jack Baldschun and Ed Roebuck, Sept. 1–Sept. 25 (before Sept. 26 game vs Milwaukee)

| | Jack Baldschun | | | | | | | Ed Roebuck | | | | | |
	IP	H	R	ER	BB	SO		IP	H	R	ER	BB	SO
Sept 3 vs. Houston (loss)	1	2	1	1	1	2		1.1	1	0	0	1	2
Sept 4 vs. San Francisco (win)	2	1	0	0	2	2	W						
Sept 6 vs San Francisco (loss)	3	3	1	0	1	4	L						
Sept 7 vs Los Angeles (loss)								2	0	0	0	0	0
Sept 8 vs Los Angeles (loss)	2	0	0	0	0	0							
Sept 9 vs St. Louis (loss)	4	8	5	4	0	1	L	1	2	2	0	1	0
Sept 15 at Houston (win)	3	1	0	0	2	4	SV						
Sept 16 at Houston (loss)								2	0	0	0	0	1
Sept 17 at L. A. (win)	1	0	0	0	0	0	SV						
Sept 18 at Los Angeles (loss)	1.2	2	1	0	2	1	L						
Sept 19 at Los Angeles (loss)	2.2	3	1	1	2	2	L	5	5	0	0	1	2
Sept 22 vs Cincinnati (loss)								1.2	0	0	0	1	2
Sept 23 vs Cincinnati (loss)	1	1	0	0	0	0		1	2	2	2	0	0
Sept 24 vs Milwaukee (loss)	1.2	3	2	2	1	0							
Sept 25 vs Milwaukee (loss)	0.1	1	0	0	0	0							
Totals, Sept 1 through Sept 25	23.1	25	11	8	11	16		14	10	4	2	4	7
	1–4, 2 SV							0–0, 0 SV					
	3.09 ERA, 1.54 WHIP							1.29 ERA, 1.0 WHIP					

COURTESY OF THE PHILADELPHIA PHILLIES

Jim Bunning, who finished the 1964 season at 19–8, went 2–4 during the stretch from September 16 through October 4. Three times in the final three weeks of the season he started on only two days' rest.

play their final two games of the season. Had they pitched in turn in the rotation, Short and Bunning would have been available to pitch on normal rest in the season series that now mattered the most—against the Cardinals, with the pennant at stake. Both did start in St. Louis, but on short rest, and both lost.

In the first of the three-game series, Mauch had Short making his third start in seven days. It was his second consecutive start on two days' rest. Short pitched into the sixth inning, leaving the game trailing 3–0. His mound opponent was Bob Gibson, who was making 1964 the year that established him as almost impossible to beat when the Cardinals needed a win—as they did on this day—and Gibson delivered a 5–1 victory. As had become all too commonplace in their now-eight game losing streak, the Phillies had great difficulty with runners in scoring position, going 0-for-7 in this game. (See table 5.) Philadelphia was now in third place, 1½ games behind idle Cincinnati.

The next day, September 29, the Phillies got only one hit in nine at-bats with runners in scoring position—a two-run single with the bases loaded by pinch-hitter Gus Triandos—as they lost for the ninth

straight time, 4–2. Bennett, starting with five days' rest for his sore pitching shoulder, was much less effective than in his previous start. He got out of the first inning giving up only one run before being saved by a line-drive double play, but he gave up three consecutive hits and a sacrifice in the second before he could go no further. The Phillies lost no ground in the standings as the Reds lost to the Pirates; the Cardinals were now tied for first.

Table 5. Phillies' Clutch Hitting, Sept. 16 to End of Season

	Final Score	Batting RISP	Runners LOB
16 September at Houston	Lost, 6–5	3 for 10	8
17 September at Los Angeles	Won, 4–3	3 for 11	8
18 September at Los Angeles	Lost, 4–3	2 for 9	11
19 September at Los Angeles	Lost, 4–3 (16)	3 for 14	16
20 September at Los Angeles	Won, 3–2	2 for 6	5
25 September vs Milwaukee	Lost, 7–5 (12)	0 for 8	8
26 September vs Milwaukee	Lost, 6–4	1 for 7	8
27 September vs Milwaukee	Lost, 14–8	4 for 8	5
28 September at St. Louis	Lost, 5–1	0 for 7	7
29 September at St. Louis	Lost, 4–2	1 for 9	8
30 September at St. Louis	Lost, 8–5	1 for 3	3
2 October at Cincinnati	Won, 4–3	3 for 6	6
4 October at Cincinnati	Won, 10–0	5 for 10	5

With only three games left and a game and a half back, the final game in St. Louis was critical for the Phillies. Once again, Gene Mauch asked Bunning, his ace, to pitch on two days' rest. His only other option was Art Mahaffey, who had pitched into the eighth inning four days before, giving up only three runs against the power-hitting Braves. And the game before that, Mahaffey had given up only one run in 6.2 innings against Cincinnati, the game he lost, 1–0, because he failed to pay attention to the remote possibility (which became reality) that Chico Ruiz might try to steal home with two outs and Frank Robinson (Frank Robinson!) batting. Mahaffey was rested and he was pitching well, but for whatever reason Mauch did not trust him and chose to go with the worn-out Bunning, now making his fifth start in 15 days.

As was becoming predictable when he pitched on short rest, Bunning was battered around, giving up a two-run home run in the second, allowing five consecutive batters to reach base (one on an error) to start the third though only surrendering two runs, and leaving with one out in the fourth after consecutive singles. Both baserunners scored. After four innings, the Cardinals had an 8–0 lead on their way to an 8–5 win. They took a one-game lead over the Reds, who lost for the second straight time to the Pirates.

Then, blessedly for the Philadelphia Phillies, came their first day of rest since August 31. They had played 31 games in the first 30 days of September.

TOO LATE FOR A HAPPY ENDING

The day off on October 1 and another offday scheduled for October 3 meant that, in the final two games of the season, in Cincinnati, Mauch could start his two best pitchers, Short and Bunning, on their normal three days' rest. Now in third place, trailing St. Louis by 2½ games and Cincinnati by two, Philadelphia could still finish the 162-game schedule tied for first if they won both their games against the Reds, *and* the Cardinals lost all three of theirs against the lowly Mets, which would create a three-way tie. Their only possibility of making the World Series, which ten consecutive losses ago seemed such a sure thing, would be to win a never-before three-way playoff series with the Reds and Cardinals to determine the pennant winner. It could have even been a four-way tie for first at the end of the scheduled 162-game regular season, but only if the Giants, who were now three games back, won all three of their remaining games against the Cubs in San Francisco *and* if the Cardinals were swept by the Mets *and* if the Phillies won both of their games against the Reds.

None of those things happened, except for the Phillies ending their 10-game losing streak by winning their final two games of the regular season against the Reds. In the first game, Short left in the seventh, trailing 3–0, but Dick Allen tied the socre with an eighth-inning triple and then scored what proved to be the winning run. The Cardinals, meanwhile, lost two games to the Mets, setting up a final-day scenario for a three-way tie (the Giants having already been eliminated by losing on Saturday to the Cubs). Pitching on normal rest, Jim Bunning hurled a six-hit masterpiece to shut out the Reds, 10-0, never allowing a runner past second base. Allen hit two home runs.

The Phillies were now tied with the Reds, both teams awaiting the outcome of the Cardinals game with the Mets in St. Louis. The Mets had a 3–2 lead in the fifth, but the score proved deceiving, as the Cardinals brought in Gibson in relief to shut down the Mets and scored three times in the fifth, the sixth, and the eighth on their way to an 11–5 victory and the 1964 National League pennant. For good measure, St. Louis went on to win the World Series that Philadelphia had seemed sure was theirs to play.

WAS GENE MAUCH GUILTY OF OVER-MANAGING?

Certainly Mauch's strategic miscalculation in starting Bunning and Short on short rest against Milwaukee—before, arguably, he needed to resort to that, even if his starting rotation was in disarray because of the injuries to Culp and Bennett—and his hitters' inability to take advantage of scoring opportunities contributed to the Phillies' colossal collapse, which haunts Philadelphia to this day. But the question remains whether the manager may have cost his team the pennant by his penchant for *overmanaging* in game situations. Baseball can be unforgiving, quick to smack down those who think they can master the flow of the game. Mauch was an intense baseball man who prided himself on his intimate knowledge of the game. As a manager, he tended to be very hands-on.

Managerial brilliance can be a tricky thing. Managers are both strategists and tacticians in the dugout. They must navigate a delicate line between managing too much and managing too little. At the game level, managing too little could mean not anticipating how the game might play out given the current situation. Or it could mean not trying to force the action when the game situation might suggest that it should be forced. Managing too much, on the other hand, could mean trying so hard to force the action that the natural flow and rhythm of the game for the players is interrupted. The one managerial style could convey a lack of urgency, with the result that players lose focus and fail to execute or to exercise subtle skills. The other style, over-managing, could convey too much urgency, even panic, with the result that players play tight and do not follow, or in some cases even develop, their instincts for the game. This was a criticism that Dick Allen in particular made, according to Halberstam, Kashatus, and, in his autobiography, Allen himself. Over-managing is not necessarily indicative of managerial brilliance in game situations. It can, rather, indicate a manager's overwhelming desire to maintain tight control over each game, perhaps for fear of the second-guessing that comes with losing. Or it can indicate that he does not fully trust his players' instincts and ability or even (dare we say?) that he has some wish to prove his relevance to the outcome of games when it's the players' performance that is the obvious determinant.

Managers must understand what is most appropriate for their team and make adjustments to their styles and strategies when necessary. The 1964 Phillies probably would not have been in a position to win the pennant without Mauch as their manager, but his intensity (often manifested as sarcasm and the belittling of his players when things didn't work out) and constant maneuvers to try to wrest the advantage in games may have caught up with him in the final weeks of the season. When it was all over, Mauch blamed himself for the debacle. This was telling not so much because he attempted to remove the stigma of the collapse from his players but because, in the final weeks, he may have put on himself too much of the burden to win games instead of allowing the games to play out with less urgency.

Table 6. Bunning's Starts During the Phillies' Sept. Debacle

Sept 13 Bunning **Win** at Giants +6	Sept 14 **Win** at Colts +6½	Sept 15 **Win** at Colts +6½	Sept 16 Bunning Loss at Colts +6	Sept 17 **Win** at Dodgers +6½	Sept 18 Loss at Dodgers +6	Sept 19 Loss at Dodgers +5½
Sept 20 Bunning **Win** at Dodgers +6½	Sept 21 Loss vs Reds +5½	Sept 22 Loss vs Reds +4½	Sept 23 Loss vs Reds +3½	Sept 24 Bunning Loss vs Braves +3	Sept 25 Loss vs Braves +1½	Sept 26 Loss vs Braves +½
Sept 27 Bunning Loss vs Braves 2nd, -1	Sept 28 Loss vs Cardinals 3rd, -1½	Sept 29 Loss vs Cardinals 3rd, -1½	Sept 30 Bunning Loss vs Cardinals 3rd, -2½	Oct 1 3rd, -2½	Oct 2 **Win** at Reds 3rd, -1½	Oct 3 3rd, -1
Oct 4 Bunning **Win** at Reds 2nd tied, -1	Oct 5	Oct 6	Oct 7 **World Series Game 1 Yankees at Cardinals**	Oct 8	Oct 9	Oct 10

First he was in a rush to clinch the pennant, and he quite likely began preparing for the World Series prematurely when, with a 6-game lead, he started Bunning in Houston on short rest, probably so he would be aligned for Game 1 of the World Series. Then he overreacted to a string of defeats, especially to the Reds, that still left the Phillies in control of the pennant race with fewer than ten games remaining—if no longer in commanding control. Then, as the defeats piled on, he panicked as he tried desperately to pick up wins by starting his two best pitchers twice consecutively on short rest, wearing them down, when they, and especially Bunning, would have been more effective with normal rest.

The Phillies lost the pennant by one game. Even if Mauch had lost all of those games where he had no obvious starting pitcher (with Culp unable to pitch because of his elbow and Bennett badly hampered with a bum shoulder), Bunning and Short would have been more likely to pitch effectively and gain a victory on normal rest, as Bunning proved in both of his stretch-drive victories. Just one additional win by both, or two by either, could have changed the outcome of the pennant race. In effect, it may be that Mauch turned possible wins into losses by panicking rather than simply accepting losses for the sake of maximizing the odds of winning when his two best pitchers started.

If Mauch made his decision to start his ace on September 16 in Houston on only two days' rest in order to line Bunning's remaining starts up with Game 1 of the World Series—this appears to be the only plausible explanation, if you study the calendar—it suggests that at that point he took the pennant for granted. Joe McCarthy, by contrast, when he was managing the Yankees in the 1930s and 1940s, led pennant-winning teams that typically finished strong and with a huge lead at the end of September.

Mauch apparently was willing to risk a loss by Bunning on short rest, for the purpose of setting him up for the World Series. But the National League pennant had not yet been clinched. Perhaps Mauch should have waited for his Phillies to officially clinch the pennant before trying to arrange the rotation so that Jim Bunning would be able to start Game 1 of the World Series with the appropriate rest between his final regular-season starts. There likely would have been time enough for that.

While one could argue that the impact of his starting Bunning in Houston on September 16 could have been mitigated had Mauch thereafter kept Bunning on a normal schedule, this decision of his had a devastating cascading effect as the Phillies went into their 10-game losing streak, because Bunning turned out not to be available to pitch against one of the remaining contending clubs, the Reds. In trying to prepare for the World Series, Mauch forgot the importance of starting his best pitchers in their appropriate turn. Baseball has a way of punishing hubris. ■

Notes

1. David Halberstam, *October 1964* (New York: Villard Books, 1994); William C. Kashatus, *September Swoon: Richie Allen, the '64 Phillies, and Racial Integration* (University Park: Pennsylvania State University Press, 2004); Steven Goldman, ed., *It Ain't Over 'Til It's Over: The Baseball Prospectus Pennant Race Book* (New York: Basic Books, 2007).
2. Clifford Corcoran, "There Is No Expedient to Which a Man Should Not Avoid to Avoid the Real Labor of Thinking," in *It Ain't Over 'Til It's Over*, ed. Goldman, 134.
3. Ibid., 141.
4. Kashatus, *September Swoon*, 118.
5. Halberstam, *October 1964*, 303.
6. Kashatus, *September Swoon*, 119; Halberstam, *October 1964*, 303.
7. Kashatus, *September Swoon*, 119.
8. Ibid., 124.

Home Run Derby Curse

Fact or Fiction?

Joseph McCollum and Marcus Jaiclin

A VARIETY OF SOURCES have indicated the existence of a Home Run Derby curse. For example, Alex Rodriguez has been quoted as saying about the Derby, "I try to stay away from that" and "My responsibility is to the New York Yankees. I need my swing to be at its best."[1] The implication is that participation in the Derby would leave his swing somewhere other than at its best. In the *Wall Street Journal*, we read that "for each of the past four years, one player who has hit at least 10 home runs in the Derby has seen his power disappear once play resumed for the second half of the season."[2] We also see on mlb.com that the curse is real "at least since 1999" and that "43 out of 74 players saw a decrease in their production after the Derby."[3]

Hardball Times came out with the opposite perspective: "No matter how long a hitter lasts or how many home runs he hits, we still don't see any signs of a second-half decline."[4] However, the list of caveats to their analysis was almost as long as their analysis, which might lead to some skepticism.

We hope to put this subject to rest with some clear assumptions and a careful consideration from multiple perspectives.

WHAT IS A HOME RUN DERBY CURSE?

The goal of this analysis is to determine if the claim of a Home Run Derby curse is borne out by the performance of the players who participated. In order to do so, we need to determine how the idea of a Home Run Derby Curse should be interpreted statistically.

Interpretation 1

A player who participates in the Home Run Derby experiences a decrease in offensive and power hitting statistics in the second half, *as compared to the first half of that season.*

Interpretation 2

A player who participates in the Home Run Derby experiences a decrease in offensive and power hitting statistics in the second half, *as compared to his usual production.*

Behind the first interpretation is the assumption that a player would have continued to perform at the same level for the rest of the season had he not participated in the Derby. There is certainly some reason to believe that this is true—the player is clearly capable of performing at this level, having done so for half of a season. However, if this level is substantially above his typical level, it may be unreasonable to expect this to continue for the full 162 games. So it seems that this interpretation would tend to predict for the second half a level of performance that is higher than one should reasonably expect.

Behind the second interpretation is the assumption that a player's career statistics are more indicative of his likely performance than is his first half of the season. Players selected to participate in the Derby are those leading the league in power hitting in the first half of the season and so are, for all except the best of players, performing at a level above their average statistics. Similarly, participants in the Derby are often having an excellent season at the peak of their careers, so a somewhat higher level of performance is to be expected again in the second half of the season. So it seems that this interpretation would tend to predict a level of performance in the second half that is lower than one should reasonably expect.

Neither interpretation is perfect, so we will consider both comparisons, looking at the difference between the post-Derby statistics and pre-Derby statistics, and then at the post-Derby statistics and the players' usual statistics. In addition, we will consider a third comparison, where we will build a comparable dataset to estimate the expected regression to the mean and to see if a similar effect can be found in a dataset where the actual participation in the Derby is not present as a variable.

ANALYSIS 1: ON ALL PARTICIPANTS IN THE HOME RUN DERBY

In our first pass through the data, for each player who ever participated in the Home Run Derby, we collected all of his statistics for all seasons, separating any seasons where he participated in the Home Run Derby from any seasons where he did not participate. We restricted the seasons to those where the player reached a total of 502 plate appearances, in order to exclude any unusual averages for a player. The total number of player-seasons in the data is 1,111 (up to and including the 2009 season), 192 of which were

The Baseball Research Journal, Fall 2010

seasons where a player participated in the Derby. There were six player-seasons where a player participated in the Derby and did not reach 502 plate appearances, and so those were excluded. This number is small enough to give some indication that participation in the Derby may not be linked to injury in the second half, though the number of occurrences of this is too small to allow us to perform any statistical inference process.

In order to simplify the analysis, we have focused on two offensive statistics: OPS and the percentage of plate appearances that were home runs. We found similar results with other statistics, so the analysis does not depend substantially on this choice. Note that these players averaged 10 to 15 fewer games played after the All-Star Break than before (due to its timing in the schedule more than their own playing time), so only statistics that are computed per at-bat, per plate appearance, or per game would make sense in these comparisons.

Comparison 1.1: Pre-Derby to Post-Derby, for Seasons Where Player Did Participate

Pre-Derby		Post-Derby	
OPS	HR %	OPS	HR %
.969	6.061	.926	5.346

Clearly, there is a significant overall drop-off in production for those players who participated in the Derby; both decreases are statistically significant (OPS, $P < 10^{-5}$, HR %, $P < 10^{-6}$). This difference, essentially, is the origin of the idea of a Home Run Derby curse; however, some decrease should be expected, as noted above.

Comparison 1.2: First Half to Second Half, for Seasons Where Player Did Not Participate

First Half		Second Half	
OPS	HR %	OPS	HR %
.851	4.201	.858	4.288

Both of these differences are not statistically significant, so, in a typical season, these players perform at about the same level after the All-Star Break as they do before. However, these levels are substantially lower than the level they perform at in seasons where they are selected to the Derby, which is also to be expected, since they were not among the league leaders in power hitting when the Derby participants were invited.

Comparison 1.3: First Half to Second Half, All Seasons

First Half		Second Half	
OPS	HR %	OPS	HR %
.871	4.522	.870	4.471

Joe Carter participated in the Home Run Derby in 1991, 1992, and 1996—seasons whose first half were his best, fifth-best, and second-best. To answer their question whether a Home Run Derby curse exists, McCollum and Jaiclin looked at his three seasons whose second half were Carter's best, fifth-best, and second-best. See pages 35–36.

Again, we see essentially no change; the overall levels are slightly higher since they include more of these players' best seasons. However, the important comparison to make here is between the performance after the Home Run Derby and these two half-seasons: post-Derby performance is closer to pre-Derby performance than it is to these same players' average performance:

Comparison 1.4: Post-Derby Participation versus Pre-Derby and versus Typical Season

	Post-Derby vs.Pre-	vs. Avg. First Half	vs. Avg. Second Half
Change in OPS	− .043	+.055	+.056
Change in HR %	− .716	+0.824	+0.875

Note: It may appear that differences do not add up exactly due to round-off effects.

The differences in the second and third columns are clearly statistically significant (versus first-half OPS: $P < 10^{-8}$ and HR %: $P < 10^{-10}$; versus second-half OPS: $P < 10^{-5}$ and HR %: $P < 10^{-7}$; first column is from comparison 1.1), so the players' performance has declined somewhat from pre-Derby performance but is still superior to their own average performance. This leads us to believe that the "second-half slump" could be simply due to a regression to their mean.

In order to test this, it makes sense to restrict the dataset to players whose performance in seasons where they participate in the Derby is closer to their average performance—that is, to restrict the dataset to the top players. If there is less of a drop-off among the top players, then regression to the mean is a likely explanation. So we considered the same comparisons with players who participated in the Derby more than once; players selected more than once have higher average statistics, and so we would expect a smaller drop-off if regression to the mean is the best explanation.

38

ANALYSIS 2: ON REPEAT PARTICIPANTS IN THE HOME RUN DERBY

Here, we make the same comparisons using the same statistics on the smaller data set of players who participated in the Home Run Derby more than once.

Comparison 2.1: *Pre-Derby to Post-Derby, for Seasons Where Player Did Participate*

Pre-Derby		Post-Derby	
OPS	HR %	OPS	HR %
.993	6.176	.961	5.787

Again, these differences are statistically significant (OPS: $P < .01$, and HR %: $P < .03$), but the differences are much smaller than in the full dataset. The post-Derby values are statistically significantly better than the values for all participants, and pre-Derby OPS is nearly so (OPS, pre: $.05 < P < .06$; HR %, pre: $0.25 < P < 0.30$; OPS, post: $P < .001$; HR %, post: $P < .04$), so the assumption that repeat participation picks out the better players is generally supported by these values.

Comparison 2.2: *Pre-Derby to Post-Derby, for Seasons Where Player Did Not Participate*

Pre-Derby		Post-Derby	
OPS	HR %	OPS	HR %
.869	4.424	.880	4.584

As in the first section, these differences are not statistically significant, so their performance is similar from first half to second half in seasons where they did not participate.

Comparison 2.3: *Pre-Derby to Post-Derby, All Seasons*

Pre-Derby		Post-Derby	
OPS	HR %	OPS	HR %
.901	4.874	.901	4.893

Again, these differences are not statistically significant; in fact, they are almost indistinguishable.

Comparison 2.4: *Post-Derby Participation versus Pre-Derby and versus Typical Season*

	vs. Pre-Derby	vs. Avg. Pre-Derby	vs. Avg. Post-Derby
Change in OPS:	−.032	+.060	+.060
Change in HR %:	−.389	+0.914	+0.894

Note: It may appear that differences do not add up exactly due to round-off effects.

Here we see, as anticipated, a smaller difference between the pre-Derby and post-Derby statistics than we saw in the full data set, and a difference that is very similar to what we saw in the full data set when compared to their typical season statistics. All of these differences are statistically significant (versus first-half OPS: $P < .001$ and HR %: $P < .0001$; versus second-half OPS: $P < .001$ and HR %: $P < .0001$; 1st column is from comparison 2.1).

In this dataset, however, there was one other statistical measure that provided an additional insight. Here, we consider the BABIP (batting average on balls in play). Most hitters, and most pitchers (measured against) have a long-term batting average of about .300 on balls put in play (that is. excluding strikeouts and home runs), and any significant deviation from this is most likely an indication of good or bad luck. In comparison 2.1, there was a notable decrease in BABIP (from .308 to .301) in this dataset, so almost half of the drop-off in OPS from the first half to the second half can be attributed to a decrease in luck at the plate (.014 of the .032—the .007 difference is doubled because BABIP will contribute to both OPS and SLG). If we remove the entire .014 from the OPS, the difference in OPS in comparison 1.1 is no longer statistically significant. The difference in HR percentage remains, however, since home runs do not contribute in any way to BABIP. None of the other data sets have a BABIP difference bigger than .003.

This second analysis provides some indication that the differences we saw in the first analysis are a simple regression to a mean: In players whose mean is closer to the league lead, we have noticeably less decline from the first half to the second half in years when they participated in the Home Run Derby.

ANALYSIS 3: ON COMPARABLE SECOND-HALF STATISTICS

A third approach would be to try to build a dataset that removes the variable of actually participating in the Home Run Derby. Participation in the Home Run Derby is based on first-half statistics, so we decided to start with seasons with comparable second-half statistics and then compare these to the first half of the same season. If a drop-off occurs from the second half of these seasons to the first half, it cannot be due to any kind of curse, since the effect comes before the supposed cause.

To build this dataset, we looked at each player who participated in a Derby. We replaced the seasons that the player participated in the Derby with comparable seasons as follows:

If a player was selected to participate in the Derby in a season which had his best first-half OPS and HR-percentage statistics, then we replaced that season with the season where he had his best second-half OPS and HR-percentage statistics. For example, Danny

NATIONAL BASEBALL HALL OF FAME LIBRARY, COOPERSTOWN, N.Y.

In 1991, when Danny Tartabull participated in the Home Run Derby, his first-half home-run rate was 50 percent above the average of his first-half numbers in nine professional seasons up to that point. In the second half, his home-run average was actually below average by 11.4 percent. But one example does not a Home Run Derby curse make. The authors found that on the whole the trajectory of a player's offensive numbers over the course of a season are the same regardless of his participation in the Derby.

Tartabull was selected to the Derby in 1991, in a season where his OPS was 14.0 percent above the average of his OPS values in the first half of his nine full seasons in professional baseball through 1990, and his HR percentage was 50.2 percent above his average, which we added to get a total "first-half score" of 64.2 for this season. This was the best first half score of his career. However, his second-half statistics in 1991 were not as good: He was 11.5 percent above his second-half average in OPS but 11.4 percent below average in HR percentage for a second-half score of 0.1. In 1987, he had a second half that was 11.8 percent above average in OPS and 29.2 percent above in HR percentage, giving a second-half score of 41.0, which was the best second-half score of his career, so we replaced his 1991 season with his 1987 season in this new dataset.

Similarly, Joe Carter participated in 1991, 1992 and 1996, which had his best, fifth-best, and second-best first-half scores respectively, and so we replaced these with 1989, 1994, and 1986, which were his best, second-best, and fifth-best second-half scores. In this process, we did not consider any seasons before 1985, since that was the first season the Derby took place, and again we only considered seasons where the player had a minimum of 450 plate appearances. In some cases, the season selected was the same as the one where the player participated in the Derby, if the rankings were the same.

This dataset should give us an effective estimate of the amount of regression to the mean we should expect after the Home Run Derby.

Comparison 3.1: Second Half to First Half, for Seasons Comparable to Those Where Player Did Participate, Using All Derby Participants

Second Half		First Half	
OPS	HR %	OPS	HR %
.960	6.032	.916	5.351

Comparison 3.2: Home Run Derby Curse versus Estimated Regression to the Mean

	Derby Curse	Estimated Regression to the Mean
Change in OPS	−.043	−.043
Change in HR %	−.716	−.680

Note: It may appear that differences do not add up exactly due to round-off effects.

The differences here are essentially identical to those we saw in comparison 1.1—in fact, the averages in comparison 3.1 are almost identical to those we saw in comparison 1.1. In other words, *the statistics we saw in the Home Run Derby curse are essentially the same as when there was no Home Run Derby played.* This provides very strong evidence that the Home Run Derby curse is simply an expected statistical variation.

The comparisons to their typical season will also be essentially identical, since the values in comparison 3.1 are so close to those in comparison 1.1.

CONCLUSION

Home Run Derby curse, fact or fiction? We have no choice but to conclude that it's fiction. If we consider all the ways that the statistics should behave if there is no curse, we find that they consistently match that model. Certainly, some players will have a decline in power-hitting statistics from the first half of the season to the second after participating in the Derby, but it is clear from the analysis that this would have occurred for those players regardless of whether they chose to participate or not. ∎

Notes

1. Mark Feinsand, "A-Rod to Skip HR Derby, Claims It Tampers with Swing," *New York Daily News*, 30 June 2008.
2. Dave Cameron, "The Mysterious Curse of the Home Run Derby," *Wall Street Journal*, 13 July 2009.
3. "The HR Derby Curse Is Real!" mlb.com, fantasy411.mlblogs.com/archives/2008/07/the_hr_derby_curse_is_real.html
4. Derek Carty, "Do Hitters Decline After the Home Run Derby?" Hardball Times, 13 July 2009.

The Many Flavors of DIPS

A History and an Overview

Dan Basco and Michael Davies

HOW MUCH CONTROL, if any, does a pitcher have over whether a batted ball in play fails in for a hit? What if something that had traditionally been regarded as the pitcher's responsibility was simply the residue of luck?

Asking himself these questions,[1] Voros McCracken, a paralegal who participated in a Rotisserie league in his spare time, went on to develop the concept of DIPS, defense-independent pitching statistics. Posting to the Usenet group rec.sports.baseball on November 18, 1999, almost eleven years ago to the day we are writing this, he described the "pitching evaluation tool" he was kicking around in his head and asked for some feedback. "I call it 'Defensive Independent Pitching' and what it does is evaluate a pitcher base[d] strictly on the statistics his defense has no ability to affect."[2]

EARLY PITCHING STATISTICS

The early history of pitching and pitching statistics has been told often. Alan Schwarz in *The Numbers Game* does the job well.[3] Originally, the pitcher's job was to serve the ball over the plate so the batter could hit it. The idea that his job was to make the ball hard to hit was slow to take hold. In his biographical article on Jim Creighton, "the greatest pitcher of his day," John Thorn notes that

> the 1850s did produce some pitchers who tried to deceive batters with "headwork"—which meant

changing arcs and speeds, and sometimes bowling wide ones until the frustrated batter lunged at a pitch. (The latter tactic produced such incredible, documented pitch totals as that in the second Atlantic–Excelsior game of 1860, when the Atlantics' Matty O'Brien threw 325 pitches in nine innings, Creighton 280 in seven.) On balance, however, the pioneer pitcher and batter were collaborators in putting the ball in play rather than the mortal adversaries they have been ever since. Creighton added an illegal but imperceptible wrist snap to his swooping low release.[4]

In 1912, when the practice of pulling starting pitchers had begun to grow more common, John Heydler, National League president, dropped "earned runs per game" in favor of a new statistic, "earned-run average," which joined G, IP, W, L, win percentage, SO, BB, and H in the list of pitching stats that, a century later, are still the most familiar and mainstream, the ones most likely to appear next to a pitcher's name on the scoreboard.

WINS, LOSSES, AND ERA QUESTIONED

When wins, losses, and ERA became the primary measuring stick for pitchers, observers started to notice how much variation from year to year there was in the top-ten lists in wins and ERA.

As early as 1944, Ted Oliver, in his self-published *Kings of the Mound: A Pitcher's Rating Manual*, described a formula, Weighted Pitcher's Rating, used to assess the pitcher's wins and losses relative to his team's wins and losses.[5]

In the late 1970s, Bill James started tracking pitcher run support.

In 1992, Michael Wolverton, a Stanford computer-science graduate, developed SNWL, support-neutral won–lost. SNWL assigns to a pitcher a number, a fraction of a win or a loss, that's calculated from his innings pitched and runs allowed. Around this time, in the 1990s, Keith Woolner, then a software developer with Oracle, invented Composite Opponent Pitcher rating, which tracked a pitcher's "strength of schedule," or the difficulty of his opponents.[6]

Jim Creighton, the greatest pitcher of his day, had a few stellar seasons (1860–62) for the Brooklyn Excelsiors before dying of a baseball-related injury in October 1862 at age 21. Creighton was exceptional in his effort to actually frustrate batters, who, in John Thorn's description, tended to be "collaborators" with pitchers "in putting the ball in play rather than the mortal adversaries they have been ever since."

In November 1999, Voros McCracken, a paralegal who participated in a Rotisserie league in his spare time, posted to the Usenet group rec.sports.baseball, describing the "pitching evaluation tool" he was kicking around in his head. "I call it 'Defensive Independent Pitching,'" he wrote, "and what it does is evaluate a pitcher base[d] strictly on the statistics his defense has no ability to affect."

But none of these metrics addressed the real issue involved in the effort to evaluate pitchers solely on their wins and losses. The outcome of the game is the product of runs scored as well as of runs prevented. Let's assume that 50 percent of a game's outcome is run prevention. How much of that is the pitcher's responsibility?

Doesn't ERA solve all the problems that this question poses? Not entirely. Here's Michael Wolverton, writing at Baseball Prospectus, on the limitations of ERA:[7]

I've done it! I've solved the problem of removing the corrupting influence of fielding on pitchers' runs allowed. We simply pay a sportswriter to sit in the press box, munch Cheetos, and decide which safeties would have been outs with normal fielding effort. Whenever one of these "errors" occurs, we reconstruct the inning—not the game, mind you, just the inning—pretending as if the error never happened. Count up the runs that would have scored in this hypothetical reconstructed inning, and you have a revised run total for the pitcher. Things get a lot more complicated for relievers and team totals, and we'll broaden the 'plays that should have been made' definition a little bit, but you get the idea.

The problem is that the distinction between an earned run and an unearned run is based on errors and passed balls, which are largely subjective decisions made by official scorers. Moreover, if an error is made when there are two outs and then the pitcher goes on to put runners on base and give up runs, all the runs are counted as unearned. Then there are routine double plays not turned and missed plays that an average fielder might have made but that aren't scored as errors—even though the fielders are at fault, all the runs the fielders give up are charged to the pitcher. Consider also that, after a pitcher has left a game, his ERA will still rise if a reliever allows the inherited runners to score, while the reliever's ERA remains unscathed.

OTHER STATISTICS

In the original Rotisserie league of the 1980s, batters were tracked for batting average, home runs, RBIs, and stolen bases. Pitchers were tracked by wins, ERA, saves, and—the innovation of Dan Okrent, the godfather of fantasy baseball—a baserunners-allowed ratio, which we now know as WHIP (walks plus hits per inning pitched).[8]

Component ERA (ERC) was invented by Bill James and introduced in 2000 in *Stats All-Time Major League Handbook*.[9] To get ERC, first you have to calculate a Pitcher's Total Base Estimate (PTB), which reflects a pitcher's hits allowed, home runs allowed, unintentional walks, and hit batsmen. The PTB is then figured into a formula that includes walks, hits, hit batsmen, batters faced, and innings pitched.[10]

WHIP and ERC for individual pitchers are more consistent—they vary less from year to year—than do ERA or winning percentage but still have built into them the assumption that hits are entirely the pitcher's responsibility.

VOROS McCRACKEN

Voros McCracken joined a Rotisserie league in 1999 and began following sabermetric websites, where it was generally recognized that ERA was not a pure measure of pitching but reflected to some extent the fielding behind the pitcher. McCracken was frustrated that sabermetricians mostly threw up their hands at the prospect of trying to distinguish pitching effectiveness from fielding. "This seemed like a stupid approach to the problem, to give up," McCracken said, and he set out to solve the problem logically.

He divided pitching stats into two categories: events (singles, doubles, triples, sacrifice flies, groundball and fly-ball outs) that the defense behind him contributed to and those events (strikeouts, walks, home runs, hit by pitches) that it did not. Using Excel software and applying some of what he learned in a statistics course at Butler, he went to work analyzing the data.[11]

Stripping the pitcher's performance down into its component parts—strikeouts, walks, home runs, and hits—McCracken discovered that there was a high year-to-year correlation between a pitcher's strikeout rates ($r = 0.792$) and walk rates ($r = 0.681$), medium correlation for home-run rates ($r = 0.505$), and very low correlation (r = 0.153) in BABIP (batting average on balls in play). (McCracken was using the symbol $H instead of BABIP; what we now call BABIP has been known as HPBP [hits per ball in play] and in-play average [IPAvg] as well as $H. In this article we will use the acronym BABIP.)

Individual pitchers might jump from top to bottom of the league in BABIP in consecutive years, or from bottom to top. The graph below illustrates the volatility of BABIP for individual pitchers. While for the whole league BABIP remained close to constant, rising and falling only gently over the course of Nolan Ryan's career, his personal BABIP was constantly spiking and plummeting. On the whole, his BABIP was below league average—some years, dramatically below it—but in eight different seasons, distributed widely across his 27-year MLB career, he was either at or above (though, when above, usually only slightly) the league average.

The seasons McCracken looked at specifically for pitcher performance were 1998 and 1999. In broad terms: McCracken's DIPS calculations were designed to determine what a pitcher's stats would have been if he pitched in an average ballpark with an average defense and, most important, had average luck when it came to balls in play.[12] The original formulas McCracken used for balls kept out of play and hits per ball in play were

Balls kept out of play = (HR + BB + HBP + SO) / TBF

Hits per ball in play = (H − HR) / (Outs + H − SO − HR)

He found the pitcher had control over the balls kept out of play but not over the hits per ball in play.[13] He concluded that "you can better predict a pitcher's hits per balls in play from the rate of the rest of the pitcher's team than from the pitcher's own rate," which suggests that the hits surrendered by a pitcher may be more a reflection of team defense and park than of pitching ability.[14]

McCracken posted his query on this subject to the Usenet group in 1999 and fourteen months later, in January 2001, found a receptive audience for his article "Pitchers and Defense: How Much Control Do Hurlers Have?" which was posted online at Baseball Prospectus.[15] Shortly thereafter, Rob Neyer of ESPN briefly discussed it.[16] According to McCracken, "All hell broke loose," as he received 1,700 e-mails in two days,[17] from sabermetricians who took varying degrees of exception to McCracken's assertion that "there is little if any difference among major league pitchers in their ability to prevent hits on balls in play."[18] Craig R. Wright and Bill James wrote in to Neyer with reservations about McCracken's theory,[19] beginning the long and ongoing discussion within the sabermetric community over whether pitchers have control over hits on balls in play and, if they do, how much. James changed his mind after further research. From the 2001 edition of *The New Bill James Historical Abstract*:

1. Like most things, McCracken's argument can be taken too literally. A pitcher does have some input into the hits/innings ratio behind him, other than that which is reflected in the homerun and strikeout column.

Graph 1. Nolan Ryan's BABIP versus MLB BABIP

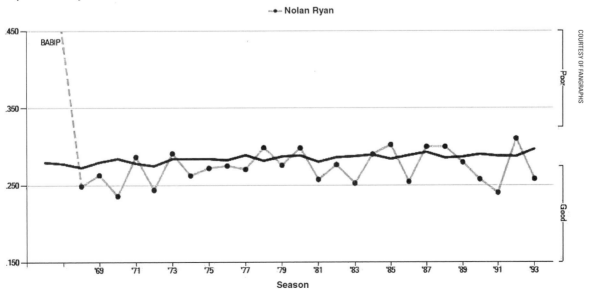

2. With that qualification, I am quite certain that McCracken is correct.

3. This knowledge is significant, very useful.

4. I feel stupid for not having realized it 30 years ago.[20]

McCracken's work caught the attention of Paul De-Podesta, assistant general manager of the Oakland A's. After reading the article, "the first thing I thought of," he said, "was Chad Bradford." Bradford, a submarine-style right-handed pitcher, was posting ERAs below 2.00 for the AAA affiliate for the Chicago White Sox. His unorthodox delivery led traditional scouts to believe he was never going to be an effective big-league pitcher. Bradford's walk rate, strikeout rate, and home runs allowed made his statistics look even better than his microscopic ERAs. General manager Billy Beane pulled off a steal of a trade to acquire Bradford, who would become one of the most dominant setup men for the A's in the period 2001–4.[21]

Meanwhile, McCracken, who finished in first place in his fantasy league for three years, was sifting through his inbox in August 2002 when he noticed a message from the Boston Red Sox. "Would you be interested in working for us?"[22]

STUDIES PROVING McCRACKEN WRONG

McCracken's work got people thinking about pitching performance with fielding factored out. The thinking manifested itself in forms ranging from insults directed at McCracken's work and sanity to thoughtful and thorough research by those looking to prove or disprove his idea. The two leading responses to McCracken's work came in July 2003 from Tom Tippett at Diamond Mind Baseball and in February 2004 from Mitchel Lichtman at Baseball Think Factory.

Part of what most made Tom Tippett's work compelling was that he drew his data from a much longer period, 1913 through 2002, than did McCracken, who initially looked at only two seasons, 1998 and 1999.

Tippett drew three main conclusions.

Pitchers do influence BABIP.

A pitcher shows statistically significant BABIP consistency across the length of his career.

Small influence over BABIP (much smaller than influence over strikeouts and walks) is still significant because such a large percentage of balls are put into play.

Tippett observed that McCracken may have been mis-led by the bad BABIP numbers that Greg Maddux, Randy Johnson, and Pedro Martinez had in the 1999 season. Most seasons they posted BABIP numbers lower (better) than the league average. Also of note: Six of the top 35 pitchers in career BABIP were knuck-leballers (Charlie Hough was the best overall), and soft-tossing lefties like Jamie Moyer had low BABIPs despite low strikeout rates. (In Moyer's case, he made up for the low strikeout rate with an exceptionally low walk rate.) Successful pitchers with low strikeout rates and high BABIPs—Tommy John is an example—led Tippett to suggest further research on the ability of pitchers to induce double-play groundballs.[23]

Mitchel Lichtman's sample was from the twelve-year period 1992–2003. In his article on DIPS at Baseball Think Factory, he analyzed different kinds of BIP (balls in play) and defined six categories:

infield line drives
outfield line drives
infield pop flies
outfield pop flies
outfield fly balls
non-bunt groundballs

He calculated the percentage of BIP that each of these categories represented, the BABIP for each category,

Drawing on data from 1913 through 2002, Tom Tippett of Diamond Mind Baseball found that six of the top 35 pitchers in BABIP were knuckleballers. He observed that soft-tossing lefties such as Jamie Moyer (right) had low BABIPs despite low strikeout rates. In Moyer's case, he made up for it with an exceptionally low walk rate. Successful pitchers with low strikeout rates and high BABIPs—Tommy John, for example—led Tippett to suggest further research on the ability of pitchers to induce double-play groundballs.

and the year-to-year correlations for each of those. Lichtman found that, while McCracken was correct in that a pitcher does not have much control over his *overall* BABIP, he does have considerable control over individual components such as groundball and fly-ball rates. Additionally, he found that park factor and defense exert considerable influence over year-to-year correlations.[24]

Further work by various writers at Baseball Prospectus led to additional conclusions:[25]

Major league pitchers have a better BABIP than minor league pitchers who never made it to the big leagues.

The ability to induce infield pop-ups is a repeatable skill by major league pitchers.

Pitchers have considerable control over whether the ball is hit on the ground or in the air. Groundballs are significantly less likely to go for extra-base hits but do go through more often for singles.

Pitchers have less control (as opposed to no control) over hits than over walks, strikeouts, and home runs.

Run average (RA), simply RA = R/IP * 9, has a greater year-to-year correlation than ERA.

Additionally, Erik Allen, Arvin Hsu, and Tom Tango used regression analysis to break down the responsibility of what determines the outcome of a batted ball:[26]

Luck	44 percent
Pitcher	28 percent
Fielding	17 percent
Park	11 percent

Tom Tango further elaborated this on his website, where he discussed the concept of DRS, the defensive responsibility spectrum, which lists the categories of recorded events in a baseball game.[27] The events on the far left are 100 percent the responsibility of the pitcher. Events on the far right are 100 percent the responsibility of the fielders. Everything else is listed in between.

Defensive Responsibility Spectrum
HBP, balk, pickoff, SO, BB, HR, WP, SB, CS, 2B, 3B, 1B, batting outs, PB, running outs

Bill James too has begun to look at pitching in a new light. At one time he was resigned to thinking that the predictability of pitching performance was low. In *The Bill James Handbook 2010*, his revised view of the matter involves the difference between what he calls elemental stats and summary stats. Elemental stats for pitchers include strikeouts, innings, and walks. These are the components that make up summary stats such as ERA. Because it's complex, reflecting several elemental stats as well as fielding and park factor, ERA is, like a pitcher's won–lost record, hard to predict. Accurate prediction of a pitcher's elemental stats increases the accuracy of his predicted summary stats.[28]

The Hardball Times has run several studies using batted-ball data from Baseball Info Solutions. Several important conclusions were drawn by David Gassko in "Do Players Control Batted Balls? (Part Two)" in *The Hardball Times 2007 Annual*. Gassko concluded that pitchers show some consistency, though not much, in home runs allowed per outfield fly ball allowed. THT studies suggested that outfield fly balls allowed are more consistent year to year than are home runs allowed per outfield fly balls allowed.[29]

NEW METRICS

Since McCracken's article in 2001, many metrics have been developed in an effort to better evaluate a pitcher's performance and to project his future performance. How is an earned run truly "earned" against a pitcher? The thought process of sabermetricians on this subject had changed. Runs, Dayn Perry explains, "are more like molecules than atoms. They're compounds made up of singles, doubles, triples, home runs, walks, errors, stolen bases, baserunning, sacrifices, balks, hit batsmen, strikes, balls, fouls into the stands, and so on. To evaluate how a pitcher is doing his job, we need to focus on how well he masters the game at an atomic level."[30]

Defense-independent pitching statistics can be divided into two basic categories: those that use only what are widely considered to be entirely defense-independent statistics (strikeouts, walks, hit batters, balks) and those that include batted-ball data (groundball and fly-ball rates, and so on.). The second group claims a preponderance of the newer metrics, because sabermetricians increasingly agree that pitchers have some control over BABIP, although how much is still a point of contention.

Batted-Ball Data Not Required

McCracken's DIPS formulas and FIP (fielding-independent pitching), a stat based on Bill James's Component ERA, are the only widely used DIPS statistics that do not require batted-ball data (groundballs, fly balls, and line drives).

McCracken's DIPS ERA (Version 1.0). The only individual-player stats that McCracken used to calculate DIPS ERA were batters faced, home runs, walks, intentional walks, strikeouts, and hit batsmen. His methodology for arriving at DIPS ERA was long and complicated. He took the raw total of walks and divided it by BFP – HBP – IBB to get a new walk total. He took the strikeouts and divided them by BFP – HBP – BB. The home-run total was divided by BFP – HBP – TBB – SO. McCracken then used park factor and league (American or National) adjustments to arrive at new (DIPS) walk, strikeout, and home-run totals. He used league average rates for singles, doubles, triples, and innings pitched. Again, McCracken assumes that the pitcher had average luck, pitched in an average park, and had an average defense. Using Jim Furtado's Extrapolated Runs formula shown below, which applies certain values to specific events, a number of expected runs (XR) is calculated from the adjusted values for 1B, 2B, 3B, HR, TBB, HBP, and total hits and from the unchanged values for batters faced:

$$(1B * .50) + (2B * .72) + (3B * 1.04) + (HR * 1.44) +$$
$$((TBB + HBP) * .33) - ((BFP - H - TBB - HBP) * .098)$$

This XR total is multiplied by 0.9297 (because, in McCracken's data, 92.97 percent of all runs were earned) to obtain DIPS ER. Like the standard ERA formula, DIPS ER is divided by the DIPS IP and multiplied by 9 to obtain ERA—in this case, DIPS ERA.[31]

DIPS ERA, Version 2.0. In January 2002, Hardball Times ran McCracken's article "DIPS Version 2.0."[32] He made some improvements to his original formula, slightly simplifying it and accounting for the small differences he found in pitcher BABIP among specific groups of pitchers: knuckleballers and left-handers. The revised formula required the same elemental stats—batters faced, home runs, walks, intentional walks, strikeouts, and hit batsmen. It also required park factors but not league averages; McCracken simply took the league-average values and replaced them with constants. In addition to adjusting for strikeouts and home runs, he made BABIP adjustments for knuckleball pitchers and left-handers—he discovered that knuckleball pitchers had a lower BABIP by .010 and that the average BABIP of left-handed pitchers was lower than that of right-handers by .002.[33] The difference in pitcher handedness was statistically significant, but McCracken was not sure why it was important.[34] He used a different formula to arrive at DIPS ER (dER), dropping the XR formula entirely and creating his own new formula:[35]

$$dER = (dH - dHR) * .49674 + dHR * 1.294375 + (dBB -$$
$$dIBB) * .3325 + dIBB * .0864336 + dSO * (- .084691) + dHP$$
$$* .3077 + (BFP - dHP - dBB - dSO - dH) * (- .082927)$$

DIPS 2.0 is the main McCracken formula that is still used to compare the effectiveness of DIPS against other pitching metrics that will be discussed later in this article. The formula is still posted on ESPN.com, without the adjustments for parks, knuckleball pitchers, and left-handed pitchers.[36] McCracken also investigated the ratio of groundballs to fly balls, worried that the distinction between a fly ball and a line drive is imprecise and subjective, and expressed the hope that more data on batted-ball types would become readily available.[37]

DICE (Defense-Independent Component ERA) and Fielding-Independent Pitching (FIP). After DIPS ERA, the first improvement on ERA in the defense-independent direction was DICE, or defense-independent component ERA, introduced by Clay Dreslough at Baseball Mogul in 2000. It was based on Bill James's ERC (component ERA) but was modified to leave out hits. The formula

$$3 + (3 * (BB + HBP) + 13 * HR - 2 * K) / IP$$

was designed for ease of use and at the time was one of the best predictors of next-year performance available.[38] For whatever reason, this formula never caught on and would be reintroduced a couple of years later.

Currently, the most widely used metric that involves exclusively defense-independent statistics is FIP, fielding-independent pitching. Popularized by Tom Tango, FIP is similar to DICE but has taken hold in the sabermetric community and is more widely used.[39] Formulas for FIP vary slightly. The version

$$C + (13 * HR + 3 * BB - 2 * K) / IP$$

is common. (Sometimes HBP are added to walks, and sometimes intentional walks are subtracted from walks.) The constant C, usually in the vicinity of 3.20, is used to adjust FIP to the league average ERA, making the final number more recognizable and accessible at a glance. In some cases, the constant is adjusted differently; for instance, at some websites the constant is higher for AL pitchers than for NL pitchers, since AL pitchers, who face designated hitters, typically have higher ERAs. Some versions of FIP are scaled in context with RA as opposed to ERA.

Batted-Ball Data Required

Batted-ball type has been found to have even more

predictive value than FIP. Further research has suggested that, although a pitcher has significant control over walks, hit batsmen, and strikeouts, his control over home runs is more volatile and is highly influenced by his home-park factor.

xFIP, Expected Fielding-Independent Pitching. Created by Dave Studeman of Hardball Times, xFIP, or expected fielding-independent pitching, is nearly identical to FIP, the only difference being the substitution of .106 * FB for HR. The idea is that a pitcher really has no control over whether a fly ball turns into a home run or not, so, for every fly ball that he allows, he is debited the league frequency of home runs per fly ball.[40]

tRA. Like DIPS ERA, tRA requires not just one single formula but a lengthy step-by-step process. Created by Matthew Carruth and Graham MacAree at Stat-Corner.com, tRA involves every action a pitcher is responsible for—groundballs, popups, outfield fly balls, line drives, home runs, strikeouts, walks, and hit by pitches. The idea is that, for every one of these events, there is an expected-out value and an expected-run value. Here are expected-run and expected-out values for 2008:[41]

Table 1.

Event	Out value	Run value
Strikeout	1.000	−0.105
Walk	0.000	0.329
Hit by pitch	0.000	0.345
Line drive	0.305	0.384
Groundball	0.812	0.053
Outfield fly ball	0.830	0.046
Infield fly ball	0.985	−0.096
Home run	0.000	1.394

What do the numbers in table 1 mean? The out value is the probability of an out occurring in a given situation. On a walk, hit by pitch, or home run, the out value is zero because an out never occurs. On a strikeout, the out value is 1, because a strikeout always results in an out (except in those rare cases when the runner takes first when strike three is a passed ball). Obviously, the probability of getting out on an infield fly ball is high, and the batted ball that it's hardest to make an out on is the line drive.

The run value is based on the run expectancy matrix, or 24-states matrix. The run expectancy matrix is a chart, 8-by-3, that shows the expected (average) number of runs that are scored in an inning during a given state (e.g., runners on first and second, one out).

The given state is made up of two parts: the number of outs, and which bases are occupied.[42]

Table 2.

Runners	Run value 0 out	Run value 1 out	Run value 2 outs
None on	0.555	0.297	0.117
First base	0.953	0.573	0.251
Second base	1.189	0.725	0.344
Third base	1.482	0.983	0.387
First and second	1.573	0.971	0.466
First and third	1.904	1.243	0.538
Second and third	2.052	1.467	0.634
Bases loaded	2.417	1.650	0.815

After this matrix is generated, the difference in runs can be applied using this formula:

play_run_value = runs_scored + (run_expectancy_after − run_expectancy_before)

The run value in the chart would be plugged in for "play_run_value" in the formula. Strikeouts and infield fly balls actually have a negative run value, since they decrease a team's chances of scoring. Conversely, home runs have an expected run value greater than 1, not only because a home run will drive in any runners on base but also because, even on a solo home run, it is still possible that more runs can score in the inning, as the batter who hit the home run didn't make an out.

After park factors are applied, each of these numbers will be multiplied by the pitcher's individual frequencies of each statistic in table 1 (strikeouts, walks, hit by pitch, line drives, groundballs, outfield fly balls, infield fly balls, home runs) and by the number of total batters he faced, and the result will be expected runs (in a neutral park with an average defense). From the outs table above, his expected outs can also be determined. These two numbers are then entered into the following formula to get tRA:[43]

tRA = expected_runs / expected_outs * 27

The tRA stat is by far the most complicated pitching stat to compute. It requires examination of play-by-play data for every single player and constant assessment of the 24-states matrix. Its value should not be ignored, however, as an in-season prediction tool, as tRA has proven to help predict ERA in-season. In its classical form, the tRA value is keyed to the runs-allowed scale, although it is often converted to the ERA scale.[44]

LIPS, Luck-Independent Pitching Statistics. David Gassko in 2005 introduced LIPS, or luck-independent pitching statistics, as DIPS 3.0. Year to year, LIPS correlates better with ERA than FIP does. Gassko uses walks, strikeouts, hit batsmen, infield flies, outfield flies, and ground balls, as opposed to McCracken's walks, strikeouts, hit batsmen, and home runs.[45]

Since then, Gassko has refined the metric in an effort to make it entirely independent of defense, park, and luck. He replaces a pitcher's line-drive rate (known to be random) with the league-average line-drive rate and adjusts the pitcher's other batted-ball rates (known to be consistent for an individual pitcher) accordingly. These transformed batted-ball rates get multiplied by the league-average outcome rates for each possible outcome (single, double, etc.). "If an average NL pitcher allows 0.21 singles per ground ball," Gassko writes, "we calculate that [a pitcher who is expected to give up 42 groundballs] will allow 0.21*42 = 8.8 ground ball singles." This process is repeated for each batted-ball type and each pitching outcome to fill a complete line of result-based statistics (single, double, triple, home run, base on error).

All these numbers, along with strikeouts, walks, and hit by pitches, get park-adjusted, and the resulting values get inputted into David Smyth's BaseRuns formula,[46] outputting an expected runs-allowed value. This number is then adjusted *back* to the original biased park factors in order to have the final number represent the pitcher's luck-independent ERA at his own park. Finally, Gassko uses groundball rates to estimate unearned runs, subtracting those from total LIPS runs allowed to give a true ERA.[47]

QERA, QuikERA. QERA, or QuikERA, was developed by Nate Silver, the inventor of the PECOTA preseason projections, at Baseball Prospectus in 2006. The formula

$$(2.69 - .66 * (GB / BIP) + 3.88 * (BB / PA) - 3.4 * (K / PA))\;^\wedge\; 2$$

was designed to account for interdependent relationships between a pitcher's groundball rate, walk rate, and strikeout rate. QuikERA, according to Silver,

> estimates what a pitcher's ERA should be based solely on his strikeout rate, walk rate, and GB/FB ratio. These three components—K rate, BB rate, GB/FB—stabilize very quickly, and they have the strongest predictive relationship with a pitcher's ERA going forward. What's more, they are not very dependent on park effects, allowing us to make reasonable comparisons of pitchers across

different teams. . . . note that everything ends up expressed in terms of percentages: strikeouts per opponent plate appearance, walks per opponent plate appearance, and groundballs as a percentage of all balls hit into play.[48]

The intent of this formula was to adjust for the issues prevalent in FIP and xFIP. Another important feature of this formula is that it takes the ratio of walks and strikeouts per plate appearance instead of per inning. Why is this important? Think about it this way. The number of innings a pitcher pitches is equal to the number of outs times three. The innings a pitcher pitches might be longer innings because of poor defense. QERA allows us to see a pitcher's true rates of strikeouts and walks. McCracken understood this as well, but Silver, with QERA, spells out this concept more clearly than he did.

SIERA, Skill Interactive ERA. In a five-part series at Baseball Prospectus in February 2010, Matt Swartz and Eric Seidman introduced SIERA as an improvement over QERA. The formula for SIERA is

$6.145 - 16.986 * (SO / PA) + 11.434 * (BB / PA) - 1.858 * ((GB - FB - PU) / PA) + 7.653 * ((SO / PA) \wedge 2) +/- 6.664 * (((GB - FB - PU) / PA) \wedge 2) + 10.130 * (SO/PA) * ((GB - FB - PU) / PA) - 5.195 * (BB / PA) * ((GB - FB - PU) / PA)$, where +/- is a negative sign when $(GB - FB - PU) / PA$ is positive, and where +/- is a positive sign when $(GB - FB - PU) / PA$ is negative.[49]

Why such a long formula? When they algebraically factored out all of the individual components of Silver's QERA formula and analyzed the effect of each component, Swartz and Seidman discovered that, while there is an interdependent relationship between strikeout and groundball rates and between walk and groundball rates, there is no real interdependency between walks and strikeouts. They also changed all instances of GB/BIP to (GB − FB − PU) / PA, since GB/BIP was not considered a repeatable pitcher skill. When doing regression analysis to predict the next season's ERA, they found that SIERA predicted the next season's park-adjusted ERA better than did QERA, tRA, FIP, xFIP, or ERA. However, SIERA was not as strong as FIP or tRA at predicting in-season ERA changes, but it did better than QERA or xFIP. Also, the adjustments in SIERA proved to be much better estimates for some pitchers with extremely high rates of groundballs to total balls in play, such as Brandon Webb and Joel Pineiro, and for pitchers, such as Johan Santana, who strike out a lot of batters.[50]

LIMITATIONS

The biggest issue with DIPS statistics is the subjectivity in the batted-ball data. This is also a problem with some of the defensive metrics, such as UZR and Defensive Runs Saved, that rely on batted-ball metrics from either MLBAM or Baseball Info Solutions (BIS). What is the issue?

As Colin Wyers pointed out on Hardball Times and Baseball Prospectus, for the scorers who from their seats in the press box chart batted-ball data, he found "a modest correlation between the height of the press box and the line-drive rate reported." This leads to some discrepancies, as Baseball Prospectus and Retrosheet use Gameday/MLBAM data, and FanGraphs uses BIS data. As of now, it is difficult to objectively define the difference between a fly ball and line drive or even between either of those and what BIS designates as "fliners."[51] BIS has tried to minimize the bias by randomly assigning their video scouts to different parks. At least two video scouts view the same ball. In 2009, they improved on their accuracy on all balls in play by adding objective batted-ball timer data, which is a measure of the interval between the time the ball leaves the bat and when it lands on the ground or in a fielder's glove. The time intervals help the analyst make the distinctions between a fly ball, a fliner, and a line drive more objective.[52]

USES OF DIPS

The most widespread use of DIPS today is in the fantasy-league community, where in articles on sites such as FanGraphs.com pitchers are analyzed in terms of FIP, xFIP, and tRA more often than in terms of the more conventional metrics—ERA, wins, WHIP, and so on. DIPS tend to give fantasy-leaguers an edge over their competitors.

Zack Greinke says his favorite stat, "besides facing individual batters, is FIP, which is kind of like walks to strikeouts and home runs given up. So I try to get ahead of the count without leaving it run down the middle in a person's power zone, get ahead in the count. That helps me not walk guys, and then, when I get two strikes, I try to strike guys out. And that's how I try to pitch, to keep my FIP as low as possible."

DIPS have caught on with some MLB players, including Zack Greinke and Brian Bannister of the Kansas City Royals. "My favorite [stat]," Greinke says, "besides facing individual batters, is FIP, which is kind of like walks to strikeouts and home runs given up. So I try to get ahead of the count without leaving it run down the middle in a person's power zone, get ahead in the count. That helps me not walk guys, and then, when I get two strikes, I try to strike guys out. And that's how I try to pitch, to keep my FIP as low as possible."[53]

Bannister knew that his BABIP of .264 in 2007 was unusually low. "It's tough," he said,

because I'm a student of it, and all last year [2007] I was well aware I was among the league leaders in it. But what do you do? Just because you're continuing to get outs, do you say, 'Oh, this shouldn't be happening'? I realize very well that I could regress to the mean. . . . One thing sabermetrics and statistics have allowed me to do is relax. I know the odds. I know percentages. I know that three out of every 10 batted balls should go for hits, and I deal with it. It's helped me be a better player.[54]

ANALYSIS

DIPS are designed to separate out defense and, more important, luck from measures of pitching performance. Beyond the obvious, "luck" includes timing and the order of events in an inning. For example, if a pitcher's results in one inning occur in this order—walk, strikeout, groundout, home run, strikeout—his runs allowed in the inning are different from an inning where the order is home run, strikeout, walk, strikeout, groundout. Even though the pitcher tallied the same results, the sequence changes his runs allowed from two in the first case to one in the second.[55]

Some of these metrics are simple and so user-friendly, like FIP and xFIP, which require only a few numbers and no park adjustments. QERA and SIERA are slightly more complicated but easy enough to calculate with a formula on an Excel sheet (and then making a park adjustment at the end for SIERA). Other metrics are more involved.

Some metrics paint a clearer picture of what is truly happening within a season, such as FIP, xFIP, and tRA. These are widely accepted for forecasting future ERA within a season and are frequently used by writers at such sites as Hardball Times and FanGraphs. LIPS and SIERA are more useful for preseason player predictions, for forecasting ERA for the upcoming season.

When McCracken released DIPS 2.0, he was "hoping this is the beginning of a discussion and not the end of it."[56] His most important achievement to the sabermetric community was to get fans and front offices to think differently about how to separate pitching from defense. It was not that he had a PhD in mathematics and could perform complex statistical analysis or that he was smarter than everyone else in the sabermetric community. It was that he calmly sought to answer a question that was important but deemed unanswerable. For what he was trying to do (gain an edge in his fantasy baseball league), he didn't feel it was worthwhile to come up with another metric to reevaluate pitcher won–lost record. In the process, he surprised even himself by discovering the lack of year-to-year correlation in hits. "I did everything," he wrote, "within my power to come to a different conclusion than the one I did."[57]

We don't know what dimension of the game will be significantly elucidated by innovative statistical analysis next. Defense? Baserunning? Relief pitching? Clutch hitting? Who will discover it? Somebody trying to answer an "unanswerable" question, crunching numbers and perusing the likes of Hardball Times, Fangraphs, Baseball Prospectus, and, yes, even *The Baseball Research Journal*, looking to build on whatever work has already been done. ∎

Notes

1. Michael Lewis, *Moneyball* (New York: Norton, 2003), 237–38.
2. Alan Schwarz, *The Numbers Game: Baseball's Lifelong Fascination with Statistics* (New York: Thomas Dunne Books, 2004), 201–11; rec.sports.baseball, 18 November 1999, http://groups.google.com/group/ rec.sport.baseball.analysis/msg/b450fe58c05a5a82
3. Schwarz, *The Numbers Game*, 14–18, 25–31.
4. John Thorn, "Jim Creighton," Baseball Biography Project, http://bioproj.sabr.org/.
5. Gabriel B. Costa, Michael R. Huber, and John T. Saccoman, *Practicing Sabermetrics: Putting the Science of Baseball Statistics to Work* (Jefferson, N.C.: McFarland, 2009), 101–2.
6. Schwarz, *The Numbers Game*, 212.
7. Jonah Keri, ed., *Baseball Between the Numbers: Why Everything You Know About the Game is Wrong* (New York: Basic Books, 2006), 88.
8. Schwarz, *The Numbers Game*, 174–76.
9. Bill James, Don Zminda, and Neil Munro, *Stats All-Time Major League Handbook* (Skokie, Ill.: STATS Publishing, 2000).
10. Baseball Info Solutions and Bill James, *Bill James Handbook 2010* (Skokie, Ill.: ACTA Sports, 2009), 498.
11. Schwarz, *The Numbers Game*, 210–11.
12. Voros McCracken, "Defense Independent Pitching Stats," www.futilityinfielder.com/dips.html.
13. Schwarz, *The Numbers Game*, 211–12.
14. Voros McCracken, "Pitching and Defense: How Much Control Do Hurlers Have?" 23 January 2001, www.baseballprospectus.com/article.php?articleid=878.
15. Ibid.
16. Rob Neyer, ESPN.com, 31 January 2001, http://a.espncdn.com/mlb/s/2001/0115/1017090.html.
17. Schwarz, *The Numbers Game*, 213.
18. McCracken, "Pitching and Defense: How Much Control Do Hurlers Have?"
19. Neyer, ESPN.com, 31 January 2001.
20. Quoted by Lewis in *Moneyball*, 239–40.
21. Ibid., 241–43.
22. Schwarz, *The Numbers Game*, 213.
23. Tom Tippett. "Can Pitchers Prevent Hits on Balls in Play?" 21 July 2003, Diamond Mind, http://www.diamond-mind.com/.
24. Mitchel Lichtman, "DIPS Revisited," 29 February 2004, Baseball Think Factory.
25. Keri, ed., *Baseball Between the Numbers*, 57, 91–94.
26. Ibid., 92.
27. Tom Tango, "Defensive Responsibility Spectrum (DRS): Breaking Up the Fielders from the Pitchers," http://www.tangotiger.net/drspectrum.html.
28. Baseball Info Solutions and Bill James, *The Bill James Handbook*, 2010, 477–83.
29. David Gassko, "Do Players Control Batted Balls? (Part Two)," *The Hardball Times Baseball Annual, 2007* (Skokie, Ill.: ACTA Sports, 2006), 158–60.
30. Dayn Perry, "When Does a Pitcher Earn an Earned Run," in *Baseball Between the Numbers*, ed. Jonah Keri (New York: Basic Books, 2007), 90.
31. McCracken, "Defense Independent Pitching Stats."
32. Voros McCracken, "DIPS Version 2.0," Baseball Think Factory, 25 January 2002.
33. Voros McCracken, "Defense Independent Pitching Stats, Version 2.0 Formula," 17 January 2002, Baseball Think Factory.
34. McCracken, "DIPS Version 2.0."
35. McCracken, "Defense Independent Pitching Stats, Version 2.0 Formula."
36. MLB Statistics Glossary, 1 June 2007, ESPN.com.
37. McCracken, "Defense Independent Pitching Stats, Version 2.0 Formula."
38. "DICE: A new pitching statistic. Defense Independent Component ERA," 19 July 2000, http://www.sportsmogul.com/content/dice.htm.
39. Tom Tango, "Defensive Responsibility Spectrum (DRS): Breaking Up the Fielders from the Pitchers," http://www.tangotiger.net/drspectrum.html.
40. Dave Studeman, "I'm Batty for Baseball Stats," 10 May 2005, Hardball Times.
41. Graham MacAree, StatCorner—About tRA, 2009, http://www.statcorner.com/tRAabout.html.
42. Tom M. Tango, Mitchel G. Lichtman, and Andrew E. Dolphin, *The Book: Playing the Percentages in Baseball* (Washington, D.C.: Potomac Books, 2007), 19.
43. MacAree, StatCorner—About tRA."
44. Matt Swartz and Eric Seidman, "Introducing SIERA, Part 4," 11 February 2010, Baseball Prospectus.
45. David Gassko, "Batted Balls and DIPS," 30 August 2005, Hardball Times.
46. Brandon Heipp, "A Promising New Run Estimator: Base Runs," http://gosu02.tripod.com/id8.html.
47. David Gassko, "Explaining LIPS," 16 June 2009, Hardball Times.
48. Nate Silver, "Lies, Damned Lies: Playoff Hurlers," 27 September 2006, Baseball Prospectus.
49. Matt Swartz and Eric Seidman, "Introducing SIERA, Part 5," 12 February 2010, Baseball Prospectus.
50. Matt Swartz and Eric Seidman, "Introducing SIERA, Part 1," 8 February 2010, Baseball Prospectus.
51. Colin Wyers, "Manufactured Runs: Thawing Out Frozen Ropes," 13 April 2010, Baseball Prospectus.
52. The Fielding Bible Awards / Plus/Minus / Frequently Asked Questions about Plus/Minus and Runs Saved, www.fieldingbible.com/.
53. Dick Kaegel, "Subtle Tweaks Elevate Greinke's Game: Improved Changeup, Focus Lead to Cy Young Season," 18 November 2009, MLB.com.
54. Jeff Passan "Royals' Bannister Unafraid to Do the Math," 8 March 2010, http://sports.yahoo.com/.
55. Colin Wyers, "How Well Can We Predict ERA?" 18 June 2009, Hardball Times.
56. McCracken, "DIPS Version 2.0."
57. McCracken, "Pitching and Defense: How Much Control Do Hurlers Have?"

Does a Pitcher's Height Matter?

Glenn P. Greenberg

I N 1993 THE LOS ANGELES DODGERS traded a setup man for a very good second baseman on the Montreal Expos. It may have seemed like the Dodgers had just ripped off their trading partner. The setup man had a great arm but, according to Tommy Lasorda, he was too small to handle the rigors of starting and therefore had limited potential. The pitcher was Pedro Martinez.

There are many baseball theories. Some theories—for example, that control is the most important part of pitching—have merit. But some are wrong. Case in point: Players used to say that Bob Feller's fastball rose, but physics has proven that it couldn't, that it was physically impossible.

One common baseball theory is that taller pitchers are more durable and just intrinsically better than shorter pitchers. In this article I investigate whether that notion is true. I examined this theory by using a number of statistical techniques, including linear regressions and chi-square tests. For all linear regressions, transformations and nonlinear regressions were done but failed to substantially improve the r-squares. For an explanation of how the statistics were analyzed you can read the appendix at the end of the article.

In my analysis, I examined only players who were good enough to be drafted. As a result, the most this paper can say is that, when it comes to players who are good enough to be drafted in the Rule 4 amateur draft, the correlation between height and a player's effectiveness or durability is not statistically significant. It is possible, regardless of the findings of this article, that there is a correlation between height and a player's effectiveness or durability at lower levels, but I do not address the issue here, because of insufficient data and confounding variables, such as social pressures that convince shorter people to play positions other than pitcher.

The idea that taller pitchers are more effective and durable is ingrained in baseball. For example, Whitey Ford signed with the Yankees after they offered him more than the Dodgers did, who "told me they thought I was too small anyway," Ford recalled many years later.[1] At first glance, the theory makes intuitive sense. Taller pitchers are more intimidating, throw on a greater downhill plane, and release the ball closer to the plate. You would think that someone taller would be able to throw harder since they have longer arms and their greater size should enable them to be better able to withstand the punishment of pitching.

However, if you start to think about these assumptions, many of them just don't hold up. While Randy Johnson was incredibly intimidating at 6-foot-10, the same can be said for Pedro Martinez at 5-foot-11. While longer arms, acting as levers, are certainly helpful in throwing hard, having a quick arm is just as important, if not more so. When it comes to durability, each pitcher is throwing his hardest, so his muscles are working at their hardest. Jon Rauch is not trying less hard to throw his 92-mph fastball than Francisco Rodriguez is trying when he throws his fastball at 92 mph. "We're not selling jeans here," as Billy Beane, responding to scouts who said that Jeremy Brown had a bad body, is quoted in *Moneyball*. Under this thinking height should not have a significant impact on a pitcher's effectiveness or durability.

PITCHING EFFECTIVENESS

The first question to be studied is whether height has an effect on major-league pitchers' effectiveness. Taking the years 1990 through 2007, I looked at starting pitchers who qualified for the earned-run-average title for one season or more and at relief pitchers who pitched in 45 or more games (or the equivalent in a strike-shortened season) while starting fewer than ten games.

As you can see in table 1, the data show no evidence of a statistically significant correlation, for starting pitchers, between height (in inches) and any of the customary measures of pitching effectiveness. These include strikeouts per nine innings, walks per nine innings, strikeouts per walk, home runs per nine innings, WHIP (walks plus hits divided by innings pitched), and earned run average. The highest r-square was .5 percent for a nonlinear regression for strikeouts per nine innings pitched. An r-square of .5 percent is extraordinarily small. It means that height has little ability to predict the number of strikeouts per nine innings a pitcher would throw. In addition, the p-values are all very high, the lowest being .14—almost three times greater than the maximum p-value indicating statistical significance.

Table 2 shows that there is also no correlation between height and effectiveness for relief pitchers. The highest r-square is .3 percent, which is simply too small for the line to have predictive powers. The p-values are also well above the .05 limit, too high to be statistically significant. As a result, it can be said that the statistics do not show a correlation between pitching height and effectiveness for an established major-league pitcher.

In sum, the data indicate that height is essentially irrelevant when a pitcher is good enough to become an established major-league pitcher.

At this point we can say out loud what our eyes say when we watch Tim Lincecum or Greg Maddux. Height does not matter for major-league pitchers because only the truly talented make it to the major leagues in the first place.

MAKING IT TO THE MAJORS

What should be important to major-league franchises is finding players who have the talent to become major-league pitchers. If taller minor-league pitchers are more effective, then it makes sense to scout taller pitchers. There is the belief that taller, leaner young pitchers are more "projectable"—more likely to throw harder as they get older—than their shorter counter-parts. For example, Joel Zumaya was drafted in the eleventh round in 2002 despite topping out only in the upper 80s, because he had a "projectable" body. If the theories about pitchers' heights are correct, one would expect drafted pitchers who are taller, both starters and relievers, to be more likely to make it to higher levels in the minor leagues and to become established major-league pitchers. Looking at the Rule 4 amateur draft from 1985 through 2002, we actually find no correlation between the two variables (table 3). The p-value of .21 is well above the maximum of .05 for showing a statistically significant correlation between height and professional advancement. The evidence, therefore, said that there is no correlation between height and making it to the majors—or to Triple A, or to Double A, and so on—as a pitcher.

The data for three subcategories were then examined for the likelihood of becoming

an established major-league pitcher,

an established major-league starting pitcher,

an established major-league relief pitcher.

The study applied the same criteria as were used for evaluating pitching effectiveness. The p-values were .61 for an established pitcher, .52 for an established relief pitcher, and .005 for an established starting pitcher. As a result, it can be said that there was insufficient

Table 1. Established Major-League Starting Pitchers, 1990–2007

Dependent Variable	Linear Regression R-Squared	P-Value of Data	Sign of the Effect (If there is one)
Walks / 9 innings pitched	.0001	.82	N/A
Earned-run average	.00001	.94	N/A
Home runs / 9 innings pitched	.003	.29	N/A
Strikeouts / 9 innings pitched	.005	.14	N/A
Strikeouts / walk	.0006	.61	N/A
WHIP (Walks plus hits divided by innings pitched)	.0003	.73	N/A

Table 2. Established Major-League Relief Pitchers, 1990–2007

Dependent Variable	Regression R-Squared	P-Value of Data	Sign of the Effect (If there is one)
Walks / 9 innings pitched	.0007	.48	N/A
Earned-run average	.0026	.19	N/A
Home runs / 9 innings pitched	.0008	.46	N/A
Strikeouts / 9 innings pitched	.003	.13	N/A
Strikeouts / walk	.00003	.89	N/A
WHIP	.001	.42	N/A

Table 3. Rule 4 Amateur Draft, 1985–2002

Dependent Variable	P-Value of Chi-Square Test	Sign of the Effect (If there is one)
Round drafted	0	Positive *
Highest level got to in professional baseball (majors, AAA, etc.)	.21	N/A
Becoming established major-league pitcher	.61	N/A
Becoming established major-league starting pitcher	.005	Positive**
Becoming established major-league relief pitcher	.52	N/A

* The taller he is, the higher the round he would be drafted
** The taller he is, the more likely he would become an established major league starting pitcher

evidence to show a correlation between height and becoming an established major-league pitcher in general (whether a starter or a reliever) but that there was enough evidence to show a correlation between height and becoming *specifically* an established major-league starting pitcher. While drafted shorter players are just as likely to become established major-league relief pitchers and established major-league pitchers in general, taller pitchers are more likely to become established major-league starting pitchers.

The explanation for these results is uncertain. Brad Steil, director of baseball operations for the Minnesota Twins, writes that it is possible that "perhaps there are just more taller pitchers who are able to meet the minimum standard of performance that allows a pitcher to be a major league starter."[2] On the other hand, I speculate that shorter pitchers are given fewer opportunities to make it as an established major-league starting pitcher because of the preconceptions that are embodied in the theory being tested here. In effect, then, as with Pedro Martinez, the commonly held belief becomes a self-fulfilling prophecy.

If shorter pitchers have the same ability as do taller pitchers to advance through the minor-league system and to get major-league hitters out, then the quality of their pitches should be equal. Also, shorter pitchers walk the same number of players per nine innings, pitch the same number of innings, and get injured at the same rate (as will be shown later) as taller pitchers. Given this information shorter pitchers should be just as durable as taller pitchers in any given game, as well as throughout the season. As a result, the conclusion that makes the most sense is that the reason for the statistically significant correlation between height and becoming an established major-league starting pitcher is opportunity rather than any difference due to genetics.

DURABILITY

Another reason shorter pitchers are drafted later is durability. The theory is that shorter pitchers are less durable than taller ones. David Cameron stated the prevailing theory about durability in an article in Baseball Prospectus: "There is validity to the belief that

shorter pitchers have a smaller margin for error. In order to generate the same power as a pitcher with more natural strength, they can tend to put more pressure on their arms, thus leading to poor mechanics and eventual injuries."[3]

The first question when it comes to durability is, for starting pitchers, whether a short pitcher can throw as many innings as a tall pitcher can or, for relievers, whether a short pitcher can throw as many innings and appear in as many games. As table 4 reflects, the r-squares never got above even .003, or .3 percent, no matter what was done to the data. The p-values also were well above .05, the maximum level of statistical significance. These data show insufficient evidence of a correlation between height and a pitcher's use during a season.

The second question is how likely a pitcher is to pitch year after year without getting injured. One way of measuring that is to see how many years an established major-league starting pitcher was able to qualify for the ERA title and how many years an established major-league relief pitcher was able to throw in more than 45 games. The p-value for the starting pitchers was .98, and for relief pitchers it was .45—which essentially means that the chances that there is a correlation between height and years as an established major league starting pitcher or relief pitchers are about as great as the chances that Switzerland will start World War III.

Height was not correlated to durability in seasons in which players were healthy, but that fact does not end the analysis. For us to be able to say that height does not correlate to durability at all, short pitchers would have to throw as much and stay off the disabled list as much as taller pitchers. The data for players on the disabled list at any time during 1994 through 2007 can be seen in table 5. There is no statistically significant correlation for games started or innings pitched; the highest r-square being .002 and the lowest p-value being .096. However, there is a correlation between height and games—a negative one: greater height correlates to fewer games pitched.

The evidence on a correlation between height and disabling injuries tends to confirm these data. Dr. Robert

Table 4. Durability Data for Starting and Relief Pitchers, 1990–2007

Dependent Variable	R-Squared	P-Value of Data	Sign of the Effect (If there is one)
Innings pitched (SP)	.003	.31	N/A
Innings pitched (RP)	.003	.19	N/A
Games (RP)	.0016	.30	N/A

Dependent Variable	P-Value of Chi-Square Test	Sign of the Effect (If there is one)
Seasons qualified for ERA title	.98	N/A
Seasons of 45 or more game appearances (with other stipulations)	.45	N/A

Altbaum of Westport, Connecticut, categorized injuries that led to being placed on the disabled list. The eight categories that he employed were non-baseball injuries, injuries that are unlikely to be related to a pitcher's height, nagging pitching injuries, serious injuries to body parts other than the arm, precursors to arm injuries, serious arm injuries, minor injuries, and injuries that are unable to be determined. Injuries that are unlikely to be related to height are injuries like blisters and infections. "Nagging injuries" are relatively minor injuries to parts of the body other than the arm; examples would include groin strains and knee tendinitis. Precursors to serious arm injuries are arm injuries—such as elbow strains and rotator cuff tendinitis—that, while not serious in themselves, can lead to serious arm injuries. Serious arm injuries are injuries— such as torn ulnar collateral ligaments or torn rotator cuffs—that prevent the pitcher from continuing to pitch for some time, may require surgery, and may threaten the pitcher's career. These are the three types of injuries to which shorter pitchers are supposedly more susceptible.

None of the p-values for any variable with respect to disabled-list stints is below .05, the maximum level for statistical significance. This means that there was no evidence of a statistically significant correlation between height and the number of disabled-list stints,

the number of days spent on the disabled list or disabled-list stints due to nagging injuries, to serious arm injuries, or to precursors to serious injuries.

These data demonstrate that there is no statistical evidence that shorter pitchers are more or less durable than taller pitchers. The statistics suggest that they are just as prone to each type of injury, they recover at the same rate and they get injured as often. Given that durability is the most often cited concern for baseball executives when drafting shorter pitchers, the evidence in this study that durability does not correlate to a pitcher's height is highly significant. Brad Steil explained the prevailing theory as "You know, a large, strong body is more durable in general."[4] However, the data contradict that claim.

THROWING ARM

There is one final piece to the puzzle. Baseball has overlooked the "height rules" for left-handed pitchers because of their dearth. The data for the left-handed pitchers could have affected the numbers for all pitchers as a whole. If height has an effect on success or durability for right-handed pitchers, then baseball teams should still draft taller right-handed pitchers over shorter ones.

The data found in tables 6 through 10 and in graphs 2 and 3 show that conclusions previously set forth are

Table 5. Disabled List, 1994–2007

Dependent Variable		P-Value of Chi-Square Test		Sign of the Effect (If there is one)
Number of disabled list (DL) stints		.63	N/A	
Number of DL stints due to nagging injuries		.27	N/A	
Number of DL stints due to precursor to a serious arm injury		.36	N/A	
Number of DL stints due to a serious arm injury		.82	N/A	

Dependent Variable	R-Squared	P-Value of Data		Sign of the Effect (If there is one)
Games	.006	.0018	Negative*	
Games started	.002	.096	N/A	
Innings pitched	.00001	.88	N/A	

* The taller the fewer games appear in

Graph 1. Games by Height for Players Who Appeared on the Disabled List

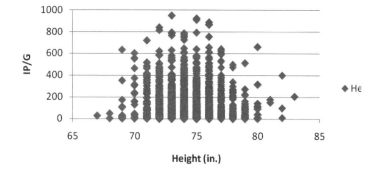

unaffected when separated by throwing arm. The highest r-square for right-handed pitchers was .009, meaning that only .9 percent of the data was explained by the graph. The highest for a left-handed pitcher was .033, so that 3.3 percent of the data was explained by the graph. The only variables for which the p-value was lower than .05 was the earned-run average of left-handed relief pitchers, the number of games appeared in by right-handed pitchers who had spent at least one stint on the disabled list, and innings pitched (per season) by left-handed starting pitchers. There is no apparent explanation for these correlations, especially absent any correlation for the other variables. Indeed, the correlation for the earned-run average of left-handed relief pitchers—the taller the pitcher the higher his earned-run average—is the reverse of commonly accepted wisdom. Again, the taller the player, the fewer games he appeared in. While the number of innings pitched per season by left-handed starting pitchers is in the hypothesized direction, it is questionable what is the cause and what is the effect. Since there is no difference in this statistic for right-handed starting pitchers, the reason shorter pitchers throw fewer innings may be that they're less durable or it may be that managers and baseball executives believe that shorter pitchers are less durable. Even if starting left-handed pitchers who are shorter are in fact less durable, the difference, while statistically significant, is still not that great.

The data speak for themselves. Baseball organizations have been scouting, signing, and developing players based on a fallacious assumption. Shorter pitchers are just as effective and durable as taller pitchers. If a player has the ability to get drafted, then he should be drafted in the round that fits his talent.

The opportunity for major-league clubs is currently at its greatest potential. Clubs that value short pitchers with talent have an opportunity similar to those of clubs that, a decade or more ago, valued on-base percentage at a time when many of their competitors did not. ∎

Table 6. Right-Handed versus Left-Handed Pitchers, Established Major-League Starting Pitchers, 1990–2007

Dependent Variable	R-Squared		P-Value of Data		Sign of the Effect (If there is one)	
	Right	Left	Right	Left	Right	Left
Walks / 9 innings pitched	.002	.007	.47	.38	N/A	N/A
Earned run average	.001	.013	.56	.22	N/A	N/A
Home runs / 9 innings pitched	.002	.006	.44	.43	N/A	N/A
Strikeouts / 9 innings pitched	.0001	.007	.27	.39	N/A	N/A
Strikeouts / walk	.0002	.004	.82	.52	N/A	N/A
WHIP	.0001	.01	.84	.28	N/A	N/A

Table 7. Right-Handed versus Left-Handed Pitchers, Established Major-League Relief Pitchers, 1990–2007

Dependent Variable	R-Squared		P-Value of Data		Sign of the Effect (If there is one)	
	Right	Left	Right	Left	Right	Left
Walks / 9 innings pitched	.001	.0111	.49	.15	N/A	N/A
Earned run average	.0016	.0195	.38	.05	N/A	Positive*
Home runs / 9 innings pitched	2.64e-6	.0069	.97	.25	N/A	N/A
Strikeouts / 9 innings pitched	.0012	.0144	.45	.10	N/A	N/A
Strikeouts / walk	.0003	.00005	.68	.92	N/A	N/A
WHIP	.0019	.0074	.34	.24	N/A	N/A

*The taller the higher the ERA)

Graph 2. Left-Handed Pitchers, Earned-Run Average by Height

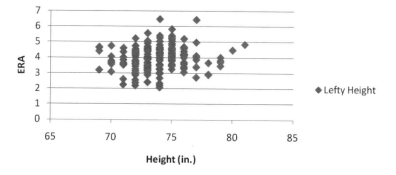

Table 8. Right-Handed versus Left-Handed Pitchers, Rule 4 Amateur Draft, 1985–2002

Dependent Variable	P-Value of Chi-Square Test		Sign of the Effect (If there is one)	
	Right	Left	Right	Left
Round drafted	1.48e-12	4.07e-7	Positive *	Positive*
Highest level got to in professional baseball (Majors, AAA, etc.)	.22	not enough data	N/A	not enough data
Becoming established major league pitcher	.43	.81	N/A	N/A
Becoming established major league starting pitcher	.006	.45	Positive**	N/A
Becoming established major league relief pitcher	.80	.45	N/A	N/A

* The taller the higher the round drafted
** The taller the more likely to become an established MLB SP

Table 9. Right-Handed versus Left-Handed Pitchers, Disabled List, 1994–2007

Dependent Variable	P-Value of Chi-Square Test		Sign of the Effect (If there is one)	
	Right	Left	Right	Left
Number of disabled-list (DL) stints	.11	not enough data	N/A	not enough data
Number of DL stints due to nagging injuries	.14	not enough data	N/A	not enough data
Number of DL stints due to precursor to a serious arm injury	.29	not enough data	N/A	not enough data
Number of DL stints due to serious arm injury	.78	not enough data	N/A	not enough data
Days spent on the DL	.71	.43	N/A	N/A

Dependent Variable	R-Squared		P-Value of Data		Sign of the Effect (If there is one)	
	Right	Left	Right	Left	Right	Left
Games	.009	.003	.0013	.24	Negative*	N/A
Games started	.0004	.005	.49	.12	N/A	N/A
Innings pitched	.0009	.003	.31	.27	N/A	N/A
Walks / 9 innings pitched	.001	.0111	.49	.15	N/A	N/A

* The taller the fewer games appeared

Table 10. Right-Handed versus Left-Handed Pitchers Starting and Relief Pitchers, Durability Data, 1990–2007

Dependent Variable	R-Squared		P-Value of Data		Sign of the Effect (If there is one)	
	Right	Left	Right	Left	Right	Left
Innings pitched (SP)	.0002	.033	.81	.05	N/A	Positive*
Innings pitched (RP)	.0006	.0044	.60	.36	N/A	N/A
Games (RP)	.0019	.0018	.33	.56	N/A	N/A

Dependent Variable	P-Value of Chi-Square Test		Sign of the Effect (If there is one)	
	Right	Left	Right	Left
Seasons qualified for ERA title	not enough data	not enough data	not enough data	not enough data
Seasons of 45 or more game appearances (with other stipulations)	not enough data	not enough data	not enough data	not enough data

* The taller the more IP

Graph 3. Right-Handed Pitcher with DL Time, Game Appearances by Height

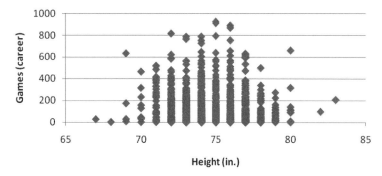

Graph 4. Left-Handed Starting Pitchers – Innings Pitched (Season) by Height

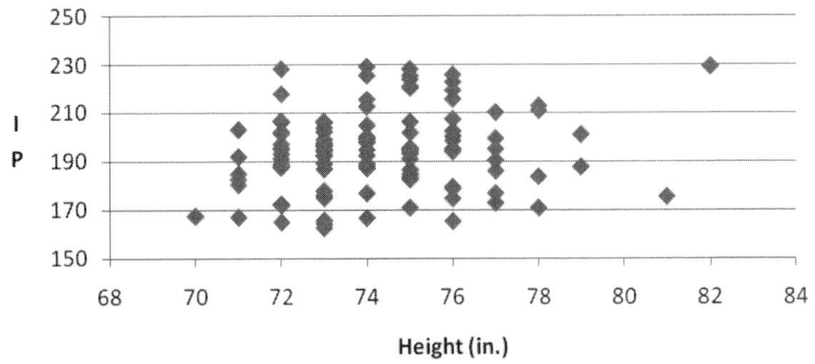

Appendix

Everyone with an interest in baseball bandies about baseball statistics. Even the most casual fan can spot trends and correlations, such as the tendency of players' performance to decline after a certain age. Statisticians, however, examine trends not through casual inference but rather through applied mathematics.

One thing a statistician does is look for mathematical correlations between two variables. Statisticians find correlation, or lack of correlation, between two variables in a number of ways. One is by making scatter-plot graphs and seeing how "closely" different types of lines fit (accurately represent) the data. The lines are linear regressions, and the statistic that shows how closely the lines fit is called the "R-square value." R-squares range from a "no fit" of 0 percent, or 0.00, to a "perfect fit" of 100 percent, or 1.00.

When the line does not perfectly fit, there are residuals, which are the differences between the line and the actual data. A graph of residuals should demonstrate no pattern; the graph should look random. If the residuals do not look random, then the data need to be altered to see correlations by creating "transformations." Transformations include things like squaring data. The same rules for the r-squares of a linear regression apply for transformations.

Another way statisticians look at correlations is through p-values. "P-value" is the common term used to express probability. Things either happen by chance or they are not random and are deemed "statistically significant."

When an event or correlation between two variables occurs, the statistical question is, "What is the likelihood that this is due to chance?" For example, if two events are linked and the probability that this occurred by chance is only 1 in 1,000, we would say the p-value

is .001. Since the likelihood that it occurred by chance is so low, we assume the linkage is not random and therefore is statistically significant. The lower the p-value, the lower the possibility the correlation is by chance and the greater the likelihood it is significant. By convention, statisticians say a p-value ≤ 0.05 (the probability of an association by chance is less than or equal to 1 in 20) is called statistically significant.

There is another way to find correlations, and that is size of the effect. Size of the effect is a measure of the strength of a relationship between two variables. While this way of testing is popular among some statisticians, using p-values and r-squares are far more common in publications. Also, finding the size of the effect would most likely have yielded no difference in the results, and so size of the effect is not included in the data.

Notes

Anthony Van Daalen and Graham Schneider provided help with the statistical analysis. President Robert Oden and Athletic Director Leon Lunder of Carleton College provided generous financial support. Professor Charles Pavitt (University of Delaware) provided help with general information on this subject. Baseball coach Aaron Rushing (Carleton College) and Brad Steil (director of baseball operations for the Minnesota Twins) contributed important insights. Robert Altbaum, M.D., of Westport, Connecticut, provided assistance with the medical issues involved. However, the conclusions are solely those of the author.

1. Wayne Coffey with Peter Botte, "Short-Sighted: Smaller Pitchers Don't Measure Up to Scouts, Teams," *New York Daily News*, 10 June 2001.
2. Brad Steil, e-mail interview, 8 May 2009.
3. David Cameron, "Prospecting: Short Pitchers," Baseball Prospectus, 3 July 2003, http://www.baseballprospectus.com/article.php?articleid=2064.
4. Brad Steil, telephone interview, 8 May 2009.

Great Streaks

Jim Albert

I N AN ARTICLE IN THE 2008 ISSUE of *The Baseball Research Journal*, Trent McCotter argued that hitting streaks are achieved more frequently than if there were no "hot hand" effect.[1] Here, the author acknowledges that finding, but argues that the effect is so small that it can be ignored for practical purposes. In addition, he uses the original researcher's technique to identify the most seemingly-unlikely (although not necessarily longest) streaks of the past several baseball seasons.

INTRODUCTION

Recently for the *Journal of Quantitative Analysis in Sports* I wrote an article where I looked carefully at the streaky patterns of hitters during the 2005 season.[2] After I wrote this, I vowed never again to write about streakiness. But after reading the recent article by Trent McCotter in *The Baseball Research Journal*, I had to break my vow. McCotter's interesting look at streaky hitting and the statements made in the article deserve some explanation and comments. Also, he describes an attractive method for assessing streakiness and it is straightforward to apply his statistical approach to identify extreme hitting streaks in recent seasons. Using this methodology, I find some "great streaks" during the 2004 through 2008 baseball seasons.

COMMENTS ON *BRJ* ARTICLE BY McCOTTER

In the *BRJ* article, McCotter wishes to construct a test of the common hypothesis that the individual batting outcomes of a particular player during a season represent independent, identically distributed trials. (We'll call this the "IID assumption" or the "IID model.") Essentially this hypothesis says that the batting outcomes are similar to flips of a coin where the chance of a hit on a single at-bat is equal to the batter's "true" batting average.

To test this hypothesis, the author looks at the pattern of game hitting streaks of all players for the seasons 1957 through 2006. Suppose we collect the game-to-game hitting records of Mickey Mantle during the 1961 season. We record all his hitting streaks for this season—maybe he started with a hitting streak of one game, a second hitting streak of three games, a

third hitting streak of four games, and so on. If the IID assumption is true, then the pattern of hitting streaks for Mantle is simply a by-product of chance variation. If we randomly rearranged his game-to-game hitting statistics, then that wouldn't change the pattern of streaks. The general question is whether Mickey Mantle's observed pattern of hitting streaks (and the streak patterns for other players) is consistent with the random patterns from a model with the IID assumption.

The author performs a computationally-intensive simulation of the patterns of hitting streaks for all players and seasons for the period 1957–2006. For each player's game log for a season (for all 50 seasons), he randomly arranges the batting lines. Then he computes the lengths of all hitting streaks for all players for all seasons. Then he repeats this simulation process for a total of 10,000 iterations. When he is done, one has an empirical distribution of the lengths of hitting streaks under the IID assumption, and one can see if the actual lengths of streaks are consistent with this distribution.

The conclusions of the paper can be summarized by two tables that show that the actual number of long hitting streaks (of length 5 and greater) are consistently larger than the mean number of long streaks predicted from the IID model. Moreover, the differences are highly statistically significant. The author concludes by saying:

> This study seems to provide some strong evidence that players' games are not independent, identically distributed trials, as statisticians have assumed all these years, and it may even provide evidence that things like hot hands are a part of baseball streaks. . . .

> From the overwhelming evidence of the permutations, it appears that, when the same math formulas used for coin tosses are used for hitting streaks, the probabilities they yield are incorrect.

Much of the article is devoted to a discussion of this conclusion, giving some possible explanations for the presence of long streaks.

Generally I'm fine with the statistical methodology used in the paper. As I'll illustrate later, the permutation test procedure is an attractive method for testing the IID assumption and the results described in the article are interesting. But I am concerned about some of the author's statements and conclusions about this analysis.

First, the author seems to make the implicit assumption that all statisticians believe in the IID assumption. The IID assumption is an example of a statistical model that we may use to fit baseball data. Any model we apply is actually wrong—that is, the real process behaves in a much more sophisticated manner than the model suggests. For example, take the standard IID assumption that individual at-bats are coin-tossing outcomes with a constant probability of hitting success p. Do I believe this is true? Of course not. I believe that the hitting talent of a player goes through many changes during the season and it depends on many other variables such as the quality of the pitcher, the game situation, whether the game is at home, etc. So if the IID model is wrong, why do we use it? Well, the IID model has been shown to be useful in understanding the variation of baseball data. One thing that I have found remarkable in my baseball research is that good simple models (like the IID model) are really helpful in predicting future baseball outcomes.

Second, the author gives the impression that this statistical analysis gives evidence for the hot hand effect in baseball. Suppose you reject the IID assumption—what does this mean? It could mean that there is a dependence structure in the batting sequence. That is, one's performance in one at-bat is helpful in predicting the performance in successive at-bats. But there is a second possible explanation. Maybe the outcomes are independent, but the chance of getting a hit changes across the season. Either explanation, a dependence pattern or a change in hitting probability, would explain the presence of long streaks. Also these two characteristics are confounded and it is difficult statistically to isolate their effects. So it is wrong to say that long streaks imply a dependence pattern in the hitting sequences. People love to believe in the hot hand and I'm concerned that this paper adds fuel to their hot-hand belief.

Last, what is the practical significance of the results? To find these streaky effects, the author had to consider all hitting sequences in 50 seasons of baseball data. This is a ton of data—the author was likely considering streaks present in over 30,000 player seasons! But we live in the context of a single season and these results really don't say that the IID assumption is inappropriate for understanding the lengths of hitting streaks for a single season. I suspect that in the context of a single season, these streaky effects are relatively small and can safely be ignored. The author is concerned about the difficulty of devising a more accurate modeling method since he has shown that the IID assumption is incorrect. But that's okay, since statisticians don't need "exact" models. If the streak effect is "real" but small in size, then I'll continue to use the IID model since I believe it is an attractive approximate model that works.

IS THERE EVIDENCE OF LONG STREAKS FOR THE PAST FIVE SEASONS?

After reading this paper, it seemed natural to explore the presence of long streaks in the context of a single season. McCotter demonstrated that there was a streakiness effect, but didn't measure the size of this effect. If the streakiness effect was substantial, then I would think it should manifest itself in a single season.

So I replicated the author's analysis for each of the five recent baseball seasons from 2004 through 2008. I'll carefully outline what I did for the 2004 season which may help explain the author's method in the *BRJ* article.

→ Using play-by-play files from Retrosheet, I collected the game-to-game hitting data (number of hits and number of at-bats) for all 959 players who had at least one official at-bat in the 2004 season.

→ For each player's game log, I collected the lengths of all hitting streaks. For example, for the 2004 John McDonald, I record if he got a hit (Y) or not (N) for each of the 40 games he had an official at-bat in the season. (See table 1.)

Table 1.

Game	0	0	0	0	0	0	0	0	0	1	1	1	1	1	1	1	1	1	1	2	2	2	2	2	2	2	2	2	2	3	3	3	3	3	3	3	3	3	3	4
Number	1	2	3	4	5	6	7	8	9	0	1	2	3	4	5	6	7	8	9	0	1	2	3	4	5	6	7	8	9	0	1	2	3	4	5	6	7	8	9	0
Hit?	N	N	N	N	Y	N	N	N	Y	N	N	N	N	N	Y	N	Y	Y	N	N	N	N	N	N	N	N	N	Y	Y	Y	Y	Y	Y	Y	N	N	N	N	N	N
Streak					1				1						1		1	2										1	2	3	4	5	6	7						

I collect the hitting streak lengths 1, 1, 1, 2, 7. Likewise, I collect the streak lengths for all other 958 players.

→ Next, I wish to simulate batting logs for all players under the assumption that the game order in each player's batting log is recorded is not important. For each player's batting log, I randomly permute the Y's and N's. For the simulated batting log, I again collect all of the streak lengths for all players. When I am done, I collect the number of streaks of length 1, the number of streaks of length 2, and so on.

→ I repeat this simulation method in part 3 one thousand times, obtaining 1,000 sets of streak lengths.

→ Last, I compare the distribution of simulated streak lengths with the actual streak lengths observed in the 2004 season. A sample of results is displayed in the following table. Suppose we are interested in the number of "long" streaks that are five or longer. Under the "Actual" column, we see that we observed 1707 streaks of length 5 or higher in the 2004 season. In the simulation, the mean number of streaks that were 5 or higher was 1690 and the standard deviation of the number of 5+ streaks was 24.2—these numbers are placed in the "Mean" and "Stand Dev" columns. We notice that we observed more streaks than one would expect under the IID model. Is this significant? To answer this question, we compute the p-value which is the probability that the simulated number of 5+ streaks is at least as large as the observed number of 5+ streaks. If the p-value is small (say, under 0.05), then we reject the IID model. Here we compute that the p-value is 0.25—the conclusion is that we have insufficient evidence to say that the data rejects the IID hypothesis. (By the way, the *BRJ* article didn't contain p-values and I think the inclusion of those numbers would help the exposition.)

The above procedure was repeated for each of the five seasons and the results are displayed in the following five tables. In each table, we look at the number of streaks of length 5 or more, the number of streaks of length 10 or more, the number of length 15 or more, and the number of length 20 or more. The p-values indicate the consistency of the strength lengths with the IID model—small p-values indicate that the observed strength lengths are longer than one would expect under the IID model.

2004 Season

Streak Length	Actual	Mean	Stand Dev	P-value
5 or more	1,707	1,690	24.2	0.25
10 or more	235	227.4	12	0.28
15 or more	35	35.8	5.6	0.58
20 or more	7	6.2	2.4	0.42

2005 Season

Streak Length	Actual	Mean	Stand Dev	P-value
5 or more	1,707	1,665.3	23.7	0.04
10 or more	228	214.5	11.6	0.14
15 or more	29	32.7	5.2	0.79
20 or more	9	5.8	2.3	0.13

2006 Season

Streak Length	Actual	Mean	Stand Dev	P-value
5 or more	1,729	1,689.8	24.4	0.07
10 or more	231	227.6	11.9	0.40
15 or more	34	35.6	5.4	0.65
20 or more	9	6.2	2.3	0.16

2007 Season

Streak Length	Actual	Mean	Stand Dev	P-value
5 or more	1,712	1,691.6	23.9	0.20
10 or more	238	226.3	11.8	0.16
15 or more	46	35.4	5.5	0.04
20 or more	11	6.2	2.4	0.04

2008 Season

Streak Length	Actual	Mean	Stand Dev	P-value
5 or more	1,663	1,688	24	0.87
10 or more	236	227.1	12	0.24
15 or more	38	35.5	5.4	0.35
20 or more	4	6.2	2.3	0.87

What do we learn from this analysis? The p-values for the 2004 and 2008 seasons are large, indicating that for these seasons the streaks were consistent with the IID model. In contrast, the 2006 and 2007 p-values are small, suggesting that the streakiness is significant for these seasons, and the 2005 p-values are less conclusive. From this brief analysis, the IID model appears useful in explaining the variation in strength lengths for some seasons. The size of the streakiness effect is small enough that it is not detectable statistically for particular seasons. McCotter did find significant streakiness in his study of 50 seasons of data, but the practical significance of his result is questionable by this analysis.

Using a permutation test to identify great streaks In baseball, we simply define a long streak by the consecutive number of official games in which a player gets at least one base hit. On the web page www.baseball-reference.com/bullpen/Longest_Hitting_Streaks are listed all of the hitting streaks in baseball history of length 30 or greater. In my *JQAS* article, I explain that the length of a hitting strength is confounded with two variables. Better hitting players are more likely to have long streaks since they are more likely to get a hit in a game. Also, regular players who play all the games in a season are more likely to have long streaks than utility players who have fewer opportunities to hit. It is desirable to get a measure of streakiness that is not related to hitting success or number of games played.

The permutation test described in the *BRJ* article provides a simple method of assessing the size of a particular hitting streak that adjusts for player ability and number of games played. We illustrate the calculation using John McDonald's data for the 2004 season.

We show again his game data. We see that his longest hitting streak was 7 games. Was this a noteworthy streak? (On the surface, you probably would say no, since 7 doesn't sound very large.) (See table 2.)

As in the previous analysis, we simulate hitting sequences assuming the IID model. For each of the ten lines below, we randomly arrange the sequence of 12 Y's (games with a hit) and 28 N's (games with no hit), and then compute the length of the longest hitting sequence in each of the random permutations. (See table 3.)

If we repeat this exercise for 10,000 simulations, we obtain the empirical distribution of the longest hitting streak for McDonald if the game results were truly a random sequence. To see if McDonald's streak of 7 is extreme, we compute the p-value, the probability that the longest streak length in the random sequence is

John McDonald's longest hitting streak in 2004, when he was with the Indians, was 7 games, which may not sound remarkable but is, according to Jim Albert, so statistically improbable as to be actually "impressive."

Table 2.

Game Number	Hit?
01	N
02	N
03	N
04	N
05	Y
06	N
07	N
08	N
09	Y
10	N
11	N
12	N
13	N
14	N
15	Y
16	N
17	Y
18	Y
19	Y
20	N
21	N
22	N
23	N
24	N
25	N
26	N
27	Y
28	Y
29	Y
30	Y
31	Y
32	Y
33	Y
34	N
35	N
36	N
37	N
38	N
39	N
40	N

Longest hitting streak = 7 games

Table 3.

Simulation Number	Sequence hitting	Length of longest streak
1	N N N N N N N Y N N N Y N N Y Y N N N N Y N N N Y Y Y N Y N N Y N N N N N Y Y	3
2	N Y N Y N N Y N N N Y N N N Y N N N N Y N Y N N Y Y Y N Y N N N N N N N N N Y	3
3	N N N N Y Y N N N N N N N N Y Y N Y N N Y N Y Y N N Y N N N N N N Y Y N Y N N	2
4	N Y Y N N N Y N N N N Y N N N N Y Y N Y N N N N N N N Y N Y N N N Y Y N N N Y	2
5	N N N N Y N N N N Y Y N N Y Y Y N N N N N N N N N N Y Y N Y Y N Y Y N N N N N	3
6	N N N N N N Y Y N N Y N Y N N N N N Y N Y N Y N N N N N Y N N N Y Y N N N N Y Y N	2
7	N Y Y Y N N Y N N N Y N N N Y N N Y N Y N N N N Y N N N Y N N N Y Y N N N N N	3
8	N N N Y Y Y N Y N Y N N N N Y Y N N Y N Y N Y N N N N Y N Y N N N N Y N N N N	3
9	N N Y Y Y Y N N Y N N N N N Y N N N N Y N Y N N N N N Y Y N N N N N N Y Y N	4
10	Y N N N N Y N N Y N N N N N N Y N Y Y N N N N N N N Y N N N N Y Y N Y Y N	3

Table 4.

Streak Length	1	2	3	4	5	6	7	8	9
Count	78	4,344	4,010	1,197	291	63	15	1	1

p-value = P(Random Streak Length >= Observed Length) = P(Random Streak Length >= 7) = (15+1+1)/10000 = 0.0017 -log10(p-value) = 2.77

7 or higher. We see from the output below that the p-value is 0.0017, a pretty small number. We conclude that McDonald's hitting streak of 7 is pretty impressive since the chance of getting a streak this large by chance is so small. (See table 4.)

Table 5. Hitting Streaks, 2004–2008, Where –Log10(p-values) > 2.5

Season	Player	–Log10(p-value)	Length of streak
2004	Robb Quinlin	3.1	21
	John McDonald	3.05	7
	Ross Gload	2.72	16
	Carlos Lee	2.72	28
2005	Jimmy Rollins	> 4.0	36
	Maicer Izturis	2.64	13
2006	Chase Utley	4	35
	Willy Taveras	3.4	30
	Chris Gomez	3.1	18
	Manny Ramirez	2.89	27
2007	Javier Valentin	2.82	14
	Mike Napoli	2.66	14
	So Taguchi	2.54	18

I used this procedure to assess the greatness of the longest streak of hits for every player in the five seasons 2005 through 2008. To pick out a relatively small number of streaks, I arbitrarily decide that a streak is "great" if the p-value is smaller than 0.0032 (that is, if –log10(p-value) exceeds 2.5).

Table 1 displays 13 great streaks in this five-season period that satisfy this criterion. There are some obvious great streaks listed such as Jimmy Rollins's streak of 36 games in 2005, Chase Utley's streak of 35 in 2006, and Willy Taveras' streak of 30 in 2006. But there are several surprising names on this list including John McDonald, Mike Napoli and So Taguchi. But remember that this streaky measure automatically adjusts for the hitting ability and number of games of the player. This measure essentially lists the most surprising hitting sequences as identified by the permutation test.

CLOSING COMMENTS

Have we learned anything new about streakiness in baseball? McCotter proposes an interesting method of detecting streakiness using a large dataset (50 years of baseball) and he did show that "true" streakiness existed. But I believe his conclusions are similar in spirit to the conclusions in my *JQAS* paper. We see much streaky behavior in baseball data, but most of the variability in this behavior of it can be explained using simple probability models such as the IID model here. Although simple models explain most of the behavior, I concluded in my article that some players exhibited more streakiness than the models would predict. Moreover, it seems hard to find statistical evidence for players who are consistently streaky across seasons.

One interesting by-product of this work was the use of the permutation test to identify unusually long hitting streaks. By looking all at players instead of the regulars, one can identify players such as John McDonald, who exhibit strong streaky performances despite hitting for a poor average. ■

Notes

A version of this article appeared in *By the Numbers* 18, no. 4 (November 2008): 9–13.

1. Trent McCotter, "Hitting Streaks Don't Obey Your Rules," *The Baseball Research Journal* 37 (2008): 62–70.
2. Jim Albert, "Streaky Hitting in Baseball," *Journal of Quantitative Analysis in Sports* 5, issue 3 (2008).

Hitting Streaks

A Reply to Jim Albert

Trent McCotter

In a previous article in *By the Numbers*, Jim Albert found that there was no significant difference in the expected and actual number of hitting streaks over individual seasons. Here the author argues that, when you aggregate all the single-season data, the result is statistically significant and constitutes valid evidence that hitting streaks are indeed more frequent than expected.

IN THE 2008 EDITION of *The Baseball Research Journal*, I published an article showing evidence that hitting streaks in baseball occur significantly more frequently than they would occur if hitting was random from game to game. I used the random permutation method to determine whether the number of hitting streaks (of lengths 5 +, 10 +, 15 +, and 20 + games) matched what an IID (independent and identically-distributed) model would look like. It turned out that it did not. Later, in the November, 2008 issue of *By the Numbers*, Jim Albert analyzed the seasons from 2004 to 2008 using the same method that I used, but taking the seasons individually. Jim found high p-values for most numbers; that is, the number of streaks in real life wasn't significantly higher than a random permutation would produce.

I have two issues with Jim's analysis and results. First, his results still show a tendency for there to be more hitting streaks in real-life than we'd "expect" using a random- permutation method—even at the single-season level. Out of the 20 matched-pairs that Jim generated (five years of data, with four different lengths of hitting streak for each year), 15 of those pairs had a higher value for the "real-life" streak total than for the average over the permutations. And the other 5 (where the real-life total was less than the average over the permutations) were pretty close to being even. So I'd say that—even at the single-season level—there is evidence that hitting streaks of pretty much every length are more likely to occur in real life than if the games were randomly permuted.

Second, even if Albert's results didn't show a tendency for there to be more streaks in real life than over a random permutation, I'd still have a major qualm with his method of trying to show that there is little difference between streak totals in real life versus the permutations. The qualm is that Albert split the 50 years of data that I used into single seasons and then said that there wasn't much significance at a single-season level. But that would be the case with almost every study. The entire purpose of conglomerating 50 seasons' worth of data is to find trends that might not be as obvious at a single-season level (although, per point 1 above, I think there actually is evidence that shows some significance at the single-season level).

If we look at each season individually and say that maybe there's a slight trend toward more hitting streaks, that wouldn't mean much; but if almost *every* season showed the exact same trend, then it would be very meaningful. In other words, the entire purpose of larger sample sizes is to smoke out trends that might not be apparent on an individual sample-by-sample basis; but if almost every sample tends to show the same pattern, then we probably have something significant going on. Of course it makes sense that—in any given season—there might not be that much evidence of a trend; the trend only becomes obvious when viewed from afar, when all the seasons are added together and their similar patterns become magnified. ■

Note

A version of this article appeared in *By the Numbers* 19, no. 3 (August 2009): 1.

JIM ALBERT RESPONDS

Sabermetrics research consists of posing a good question, collecting the relevant data, and exploring the data to answer the question. In the study of streakiness, there are different questions one can pose. McCotter asks the question: Can batting results (Hit or Out) be represented by a model where individual outcomes are independent and identically distributed (the IID model)? Another question would be: Is there evidence of significant streaky hitting ability among baseball players? A third question would be: Can we classify hitters into the two types "streaky" and "non-streaky"?

Most baseball fans and statisticians know the answer to McCotter's question. Batting results for a single player are not independent and identically distributed. So what is the point of McCotter's analysis that shows, on the basis of 50 years of data, that batting outcomes don't follow the IID model? Actually, his analysis says little since we already knew that the IID assumption is false.

I think it makes much more sense to ask a more interesting question where the answer is uncertain. If batters possess an ability to be streaky, what is the size of this streaky effect, and can we describe the characteristics of hitters who are "truly streaky"? To begin to answer this question, I believe that one has to check if there is an unusual streaky pattern of performance for individual seasons. If a pattern of unusual streakiness of hitters is not obvious for individual seasons, then it would seem that the size of the streaky effect is small. In my analysis of the seasons 2004 through 2008, I found that the streaky patterns were consistent with the IID model for two of the five seasons. This tells me that the size of the true streaky effects is generally small, and that conclusion is consistent with my earlier research on streakiness. It is difficult to find players who are consistently streaky from season to season, and so it is hard to separate players into the "streaky" and "non-streaky" groups.

Statisticians are not concerned about "exact" models. Instead they wish to find approximate models that are useful in understanding the main features of a dataset. The IID model is wrong as McCotter finds, but that's okay. Since the true streaky effects appear to be small in magnitude, one can make excellent predictions about observed streaky behavior from the IID model. For example, I believe the IID model would provide good predictions of the number of hitting streaks that exceed 10 games during the 2010 season. As I have said before, I think it is remarkable how good simple models like the IID models can be in predicting patterns of baseball hitting performance. ∎

TRENT McCOTTER RESPONDS

I'll briefly respond to Jim Albert's rebuttal. First, nobody "knew that the IID assumption was false" until my article was published in *The Baseball Research Journal*. Perhaps some of us suspected it, but it was not something "known" or assumed. In fact, it was the exact opposite: every single article that has tried to calculate probabilities of streaks in baseball relied on the IID assumption to be *TRUE*. If we all knew that it was false, then there sure were a lot of people who decided to write papers based on an assumption they already knew was wrong. Confirming that games are not randomly distributed is a big deal: after reading my paper, Steve Strogatz (a well-known lecturer and 'stats guru' at Cornell) canceled a huge simulation project he was running on 56-game hitting streaks. Why? If we can't use standard probability assumptions, then we just can't calculate probabilities. At least not meaningful ones.

Second, I agree that the effect of this "false assumption" seems small at a single-season level. But when we look at a 50-year stretch, we see that there have been many more hitting streaks than there should have been. We have seen 43 percent more twenty-game hitting streaks—and 171 percent more thirty-game hitting streaks—than we should have. Surely these differences are not "small in magnitude" and can be ignored, as Albert proposes. That the effect is small on a single-season level doesn't mean that the effect is trivial; it just means it's not monumental. Long hitting streaks are rare. We can't measure them on a season-by-season basis. We must measure them over decades.

Baseball is a game of inches: Small changes can make a big difference. And the shift caused by this false assumption about how games are distributed is not something we can ignore when we calculate probabilities of streaks in baseball. ∎

Is There Racial Bias Among Umpires?

Phil Birnbaum

IS THERE WIDESPREAD RACIAL BIAS among umpires? In August 2007, a widely publicized academic study said the answer is yes. After taking a close look at the study, I'm not so sure.

"Strike Three: Umpires' Demand for Discrimination" is by Christopher A. Parsons, Johan Sulaeman, Michael C. Yates, and Daniel S. Hamermesh. Hamermesh is the most famous of the four authors and the one quoted most often in the press reports, so I'll refer to the paper as "the Hamermesh Study." It's available for free online.[1]

Based on the results of the study, the authors (and the journalists who reported on the study) make various claims about the effects of umpire bias:

> "Specifically, an umpire will . . . call a pitch a strike about 1 percent more often if he and the pitcher are of the same race."[2]

> "A reasonable estimate is that a team enjoying 162 straight games of [umpire bias] advantage would win maybe one or two extra games."[3]

> "The data revealed that the bias benefits mostly white pitchers."[4]

I don't believe these claims are justified. A closer look at the study does show some evidence for the existence of same-race bias among umpires but does *not* show how much bias there is or where the bias lies. I believe that the quantitative conclusions quoted above are based solely on the implicit assumptions in the study, assumptions the authors may not even realize they made.

THE HAMERMESH STUDY

The authors collected pitch-by-pitch data for every regular-season game in MLB from 2004 through 2006. They classified every pitcher and every umpire into one of four groups: white, Hispanic, black, or Asian. Then, for every umpire-decided pitch (a called strike or a ball) in the sample, they noted the race of both the pitcher and the umpire. (The authors correctly write "race/ethnicity" on the grounds that Hispanic is not a "race," but I'll just say "race" to keep things simple.)

Here's the data from their table that summarizes the results. (I'm leaving out Asian pitchers because there were no corresponding Asian umpires.)

Table 1. Percentage of Pitches Called Strikes, 2004–2006

	White pitcher	Hispanic pitcher	Black pitcher	Average
White umpire	741,729	236,937	25,108	
	32.06	**31.47**	**30.61**	**31.88**
Hispanic umpire	24,592	7,323	845	
	31.91	**31.80**	**30.77**	**31.86**
Black umpire	46,825	13,882	1,765	
	31.93	**30.87**	**30.76**	**31.66**
Average	**32.05**	**31.45**	**30.62**	

The top number is the number of pitches in the sample; the bottom number is the percentage of called pitches that were strikes. It's the bottom number that's the important one here, which is why it's in bold.

If you examine the table, you'll see that there is indeed a tendency for umpires to call more strikes for pitchers of their own race. For white pitchers, they got the most strike calls when the umpire also was white. For Hispanic pitchers, they got the most strike calls when the umpire also was Hispanic. And, for black pitchers, they came within a hair of getting the most strike calls when the umpire was also black.

You'll also see from the table that white pitchers throw more strikes than Hispanic pitchers do, who in turn throw more strikes than black pitchers. Also, white umpires call more strikes than Hispanic umps do, and black umpires call the fewest strikes of all. That's not necessarily any indication of racial bias—the groups are naturally composed of different human beings, with different characteristics, and it could be just coincidence that, for instance, black umpires have smaller strike zones than white umpires. It's probably also just coincidence that the race order for pitchers just happens to be the same as the race order for umpires.

What matters is that the cells on the diagonal—the ones where the pitcher and umpire are of the same race—seem higher than they should be. For instance, white umpires called more strikes, by 0.59 percentage points, for white pitchers than for Hispanic pitchers.

But Hispanic umpires called only 0.11 percent more strikes for white pitchers than for Hispanic pitchers.

The authors ran a regression (which we'll discuss in more detail later), where they tried to predict the level of same-race bias that would best fit the nine cells of the table. They found a result of about 0.27 percentage points. That is, when facing a same race-umpire, a pitcher would be credited about one extra strike for every 400 called pitches.

However, it turned out that the result was not statistically significant. So, even though the data show more called strikes than expected when the pitcher's race matches the umpire's, the difference is so small that it could easily have happened just by chance.

MONITORING

If that were all there was, the authors of the paper would have concluded that there's no evidence of bias, and that would have been it. But they noted that there are times when umpires will find it easier to "get away" with biased calls and times when that will be harder.

For instance, in some parks, the QuesTec system electronically second-guesses umpires' ball-strike calls. For games in those parks, umpires are graded by MLB on the accuracy of their calls. In that case, you'd expect the umps' racial bias to be diminished. After all, people respond to incentives; when the umpires are punished for making the wrong call, you'd expect them to make fewer wrong calls.

Also, the authors argue, umpires can get away with more discrimination when attendance is low, because there are fewer people scrutinizing them. This I'm not sure I believe, but, as we'll see, the results do support it, so I'll go along with it.

If umpires are making the wrong calls due to racial bias, it effectively "costs more" for them to do so when they are being more heavily scrutinized. And so you'd expect them to respond to the "higher price" of discrimination by doing less of it. That's what the title of the paper is all about: umpires' "demand for discrimination" means they indulge in less discrimination when it becomes expensive to do so.

The authors found that was indeed what happened. In QuesTec parks, and games with higher attendance (when, presumably, more fans would notice), the bias disappeared—in fact, there was a bias in the *opposite* direction, as if the umpires were overcompensating. But in parks where there was no QuesTec, and where attendance was low, the apparent racial bias was much higher: statistically significant to a large degree.

Specifically, the breakdown by QuesTec status was:

+0.63	without QuesTec
-0.35	with QuesTec
+0.27	overall

That is, when QuesTec was not in effect and the umpire was of the same race as the pitcher, same-race bias resulted in a bump of 0.63 percentage points, which is one extra strike every 159 called pitches.

The breakdown by attendance was

+0.68	low attendance
-0.21	low attendance
+0.27	overall

That's one extra strike every 147 called pitches, when attendance is low and the umpire's race matches the pitcher's.

Both of the high positive results were statistically significant, which led the authors to conclude that there is indeed racial bias among major-league umpires.

REPRODUCING THE STUDY

As I said earlier, I'm unconvinced that what the authors found is really significant evidence of widespread umpire bias. Let me start by trying to reproduce the authors' results, for the low-attendance case, which showed the most evidence for bias.

For the same years the authors used (2004–6), I used Retrosheet pitch-by-pitch data to produce the low-attendance equivalent of the table 1. My results are just an approximation to what they did, but the logic that follows shouldn't be affected by the numbers being slightly different.[5]

So here's what I got for games with low attendance:

Table 2. Percentage of Pitches Called Strikes, 2004–2006 Low-Attendance Games

	White pitcher	Hispanic pitcher	Black pitcher	Average
White umpire	376,954 31.88	107,434 31.27	10,471 31.27	31.73
Hispanic umpire	10,334 31.41	2,864 32.47	258 28.29	31.58
Black umpire	23,603 31.22	6,585 31.21	695 32.52	31.25
Average	31.83	31.31	31.28	31.70

Note the similarities between this table (from my data) and table 1 (from the original study). In both cases, white umpires call the most strikes, followed by Hispanic umpires and then black umpires; in both cases, white pitchers throw the most strikes, again followed by Hispanic and black pitchers. Also note that the numbers of pitches are in pretty much the same ratios. These factors suggest that I was able to reproduce their numbers reasonably well. (They didn't provide this particular table, which is why I had to create it.)

Also, this confirms the authors' finding that the apparent bias is higher in these low-attendance games. In table 1, white pitchers were only 0.01 above their overall average with white umpires; here, they are 0.05 above average. In table 1, Hispanic pitchers were only 0.35 above their average with Hispanic umpires; here, they are 1.16 above average. In table 1, black pitchers were 0.14 above their average with black umpires; here, they are 1.26 above average. Furthermore, in table 1, black pitchers actually got slightly fewer strike calls with black umpires than with Hispanic ones; here, however, they do significantly better with the black umps.

To make things easier to read, I'm going to redraw table 2 but without including the averages and numbers of pitches.

Table 3. Percentage of Pitches Called Strikes, 2004–2006
Low-Attendance Games (Like table 2, but with less stuff in it)

	White pitcher	Hispanic pitcher	Black pitcher
White umpire	31.88	31.27	31.27
Hispanic umpire	31.41	32.47	28.29
Black umpire	31.22	31.21	32.52

Now, clearly, and as we saw above, this table shows evidence of same-race bias. How much bias?

To answer that question, what we want is a reasonable estimate of what the table "should" look like in the absence of bias. How can we come up with that estimate?

What the authors did is to make some assumptions about how the cells get their values. Specifically, their model assumes that

Percentage of strikes in a given cell =

Overall percentage of strikes +

Adjustment factor for the race of the pitcher +

Adjustment factor for the race of the umpire +

An extra factor for when the umpire's race matches the pitcher's race (what they call "UPM").

If you assume that the cells should all get their values that way, then you can run a linear regression to try to come up with the best estimates for all those factors, given those assumptions. It's the same technique you use to fit a straight line to a set of points—you're just trying to fit a "new table" to the "old table."

If I use the authors' technique, here's the "best fit" table I get:

Table 4. Best Fit for Table 2 Using Hamermesh Model

	White pitcher	Hispanic pitcher	Black pitcher
White umpire	31.88	31.27	31.22
Hispanic umpire	31.88	32.29	31.48
Black umpire	31.20	31.34	32.05

It's actually a pretty good fit . . . in the cells with the most pitches, the numbers hardly vary at all. The biggest differences are in the situations that didn't occur often, like black pitcher with Hispanic umpire (only 258 pitches).

The fitted matrix has roughly the same evidence of racial bias as in the original. You can see that the three diagonals still look a lot higher than they should—they're the highest numbers in their row and column, by a fair bit.

It turns out that the extra "race matching" UPM factor came out to 0.76 percentage points. (Remember that this is for my attempt to reproduce the original. It compares well to what the authors found, which was 0.68 points, again suggesting that I was reasonably able to reproduce the authors' work.) The 0.76 coefficient works out to be significant at the 5 percent level ($p = 0.0443$), which is generally the threshold for taking it seriously.

If we subtract 0.76 points from each of the diagonals (the cells where the pitcher is of the same race as the umpire), we get:

Table 5. Best Fit for Table 2 after Eliminating the Racial-Bias Estimate under the Hamermesh Model

	White pitcher	Hispanic pitcher	Black pitcher
White umpire	~~31.88~~ 31.12	31.27	31.22
Hispanic umpire	31.88	~~32.29~~ 31.53	31.48
Black umpire	31.20	31.34	~~32.05~~ 31.29

That, according to the authors' model, is the best estimate for what the results would look like if there were no racial bias among umpires. And, indeed, this updated table looks pretty unbiased. No matter who the pitcher is, Hispanic umpires call about 0.3 percent more strikes than white umpires do. No matter who the umpire is, black pitchers throw about 0.1 percent more strikes than white pitchers do. And so on.

How many pitches are affected? Well, we can multiply the 0.76 difference by the number of pitches in each of the diagonal cells. Here's what we get:

Table 6. Estimate of Number of Pitches Miscalled Due to Racial Bias under the Hamermesh Model

	White pitcher	Hispanic pitcher	Black pitcher
White umpire	+2,864		
Hispanic umpire		+22	
Black umpire			+5

By this logic, same-race umpires called 2,891 more strikes than they should have for same-race pitchers, out of 539,198 total called pitches. That suggests that about 1 pitch in 187 is affected in total. Of course, if you consider only pitches where the pitcher and umpire are of the same race, the percentage is 0.76, which is 1 in 132.

One called pitch in 132 is a bit less than one per game, I think (gotta check). Turning a single ball into a strike is worth somewhere between 0.1 and 0.14 runs. So, if we believe this analysis, having your pitcher match the umpire is worth about one tenth of a run off your ERA. That's a lot.

And you'll also notice that the advantage appears to go disproportionately to white pitchers. Even though our assumption was that all umpires are equally biased, the fact that there are so many white umpires (87) and so few minority umpires (6) means that white pitchers see an umpire who likes them almost 14 times as often as they see an umpire who doesn't like them. The study's authors conclude, therefore, that minority pitchers are disproportionately harmed by umpires' discrimination and therefore are better pitchers than their statistics suggest.

HIDDEN ASSUMPTIONS

But, as I wrote, I don't believe this is necessarily correct. There's nothing wrong with the study's math—it's the hidden assumptions that I have a problem with.

Specifically, the authors of the study insist on using the same "race bias" adjustment for each cell on the diagonal. That is, they insist on assuming that every race of umpire has exactly the same level of bias in favor of pitchers of his own race and against pitchers of other races.

Does that sound right? Not to me. I would imagine that people of different races will have different kinds and levels of bias. In almost every aspect of life affected by real, proven bigotry, it almost always goes one way. Whites used to lynch blacks; did blacks ever lynch whites? Are there gangs of gay men who roam public parks looking for handholding heterosexuals to beat up?

Even where it's obvious that two groups mutually dislike each other, does it really follow that one group will be *exactly* as biased as the other? Is a Republican boss exactly as unlikely to hire a Democrat as a Democrat boss is to hire a Republican? Even if they're equal today, what about tomorrow? When Barack Obama does something controversial overnight, don't you think that Republicans will get a lot more upset than Democrats and that the relative bias will wind up a little bit more against Democrats than it was yesterday?

If you agree that it's reasonable that the races would have different levels of bias toward each other—and even if you don't—you have to qualify the results of the study. Instead of saying

> The best estimate of racial bias is 0.76 percentage of pitches.

what you need to say is

> *If* racial bias is the same across all races, *then* the best estimate of racial bias is 0.76 percent of pitches.

Since we don't know that bias is the same across the races (and I think we have reason to believe that it's not), we can't just assume that the 0.76 percent is the right number.

And, indeed, if you relax that assumption, your conclusions can change—a *lot,* and in many different directions. There are many other ways to make the original table unbiased than by changing the three diagonals equally. Suppose we adjust it like this:

Table 7. One Way to Adjust the Results to Produce Unbiasedness

	White pitcher	Hispanic pitcher	Black pitcher
White umpire	31.88	31.27	31.27
Hispanic umpire	31.41	~~32.47~~ 30.80	~~28.29~~ 30.80
Black umpire	31.22	~~31.21~~ 30.61	~~32.52~~ 30.61

This matrix is perfectly unbiased: Pitchers get the same treatment relative to their other-race colleagues regardless of who's calling the balls and strikes. But, under this assumption, a lot fewer pitches are affected.

Table 8. Number of Pitches Affected by Bias, Based on the Adjustment in Table 7

	White pitcher	Hispanic pitcher	Black pitcher
White umpire			
Hispanic umpire		+48	-4
Black umpire		+40	+15

Here, only 106 pitches are affected—not 2,891, as in the other hypothesis. Also, instead of minority pitchers being advantaged, the exact opposite is true: Under this hypothesis, minority pitchers are the *beneficiaries* of umpire bias, not the victims!

Is there reason to believe one of these hypotheses is more plausible than the other? Maybe, but by argument, not by mathematics.

This particular hypothesis suggests that all the racial bias is shown by Hispanic and black umpires against Hispanic and black pitchers and that white umpires have no bias at all. Does that sound more likely or less likely than the Hamermesh study's hypothesis that all the races are biased equally? I don't know. But—and this is the important point—*both hypotheses are absolutely consistent with the data.*

There is literally an infinity of ways you can rejig the table to remove any evidence of bias. They all lead to different assumptions. The Hamermesh study arbitrarily chose one. There is no reason, in my opinion, to favor that one over all the others. And so, I'd argue, you can't read anything into the results.

With one exception: I believe the study does constitute evidence that there is *some* bias going on. The logic goes something like this:

Suppose that there was absolutely no bias. Then, their hypothesis, that all groups have equal bias, would be correct—all the groups would be equally biased at zero! But the study showed that, if all groups are indeed equally biased, it's unlikely to be at zero. So we have to reject the hypothesis that there's no bias going on.

But, as for the rest of the Hamermesh results . . . those are true only if bias is equal among the races. And, now that we've rejected the idea that bias is equally zero, there's no good reason to believe that bias is equal at any other level. And so there's no reason to believe that the rest of the results are consistent with what's happening in the real world.

The study has found evidence of bias but is unable to pinpoint either *how much* bias there is or *where* the bias is. Any conclusions on either of those issues are completely a result of the assumptions that went into the model.

INDIVIDUAL UMPIRES

Just as there's no justification for the assumption that all races are equally biased, there's also no justification for the assumption that all *umpires* are equally biased. That almost goes without saying. Think about the people you know in your everyday life. We all know people who are more biased than others. We know people who are a little bit biased. We all know people who believe in equal treatment. And we all know people who are so concerned about bias against race X that they argue for policies such as affirmative action. (And, depending on what kind of people you hang out with, you may even know some virulent racists.)

Umpires probably vary in their view of other races just as much as anyone else does. The idea that *all* umpires are biased in favor of their own race, and to exactly the same extent, doesn't seem plausible to me at all.

In that light: Is it possible that the entire effect we're seeing could be caused by only a few umpires, or even just one?

Tables 7 and 8 showed a way that the entire effect could be created by 116 miscalled pitches. Is it possible that a small number of umpires could be responsible for enough of those 116 pitches that they can push the result from statistically insignificant to statistically significant?

To check, I took every umpire in the study and compared his strike percentage with black pitchers to the strike percentage with white pitchers. If there was lots of bias, you'd expect the four black umpires to be very different from the rest—they would favor black pitchers, while the other umpires would disfavor them. If you put the umpires in order of how much they favor black pitchers, you might expect the five black umpires to be clustered at the top of the list.

They weren't *all* at the top, but they leaned toward it. Here's a graph representing where the black umpires rank in how they evaluated black pitchers:

X I I I I I I I I X I I I I I I I I I I X I I I I I I I I I I I I I I I I I I I I I X I I I I I I I

Each vertical line represents two white umpires; each *X* represents a black umpire and a white one. As you can see, the black umpires are indeed leaning to favoring black pitchers, as there are more of them at the top (left) of the "favors black pitchers" list than the bottom. But the tendency is not huge.

Here are how the umpires rank in how much they favor Hispanic pitchers:

I I I X I I I I I I I I X I I I I I I I I I I I I I I I I I I I I I I I I I I I I I I I I I I I I I I I I

Again, they're closer to the top of the list than the bottom.

(Keep in mind that this doesn't necessarily mean that black and Hispanic umpires alone are biased—if white umpires are biased the other way, that would move the vertical lines toward the right side of the line, which would be enough to cause the *X*s to move left. All we can say here is that the black umpires call more strikes on black players *relative* to the other umpires—but we can't tell whether the source of the bias is the minority umps, the white umps, or a combination of both.)

Basically, these two graphs represent what the study is all about—all those numbers, charts and regressions are just a formal mathematical way of representing what you see on these two lines. Actually, the formal method is slightly more accurate, because it takes into account the magnitude of the results, not just the rank. But, still, these Xs and vertical lines are 90 percent of the issue.

And so, you can see that it *is* possible that one umpire could be responsible for the finding of bias. Because, as it turns out, if you remove the leftmost Hispanic umpire from the study, the leftmost X in the Hispanic umpire graph disappears, and the results no longer end up so significant. And if you remove the leftmost black umpire from the study, the leftmost X disappears from the black umpire graph, and again the results are no longer significant.

And, as you can tell just by eyeing those two graphs, if you were to remove the three leftmost minority umpires, not only would the results not be significant but the bias would be almost completely gone! The three remaining Xs would be pretty evenly spread along the graphs.

So it's very possible that one umpire is responsible for the finding of significance and that three umpires are responsible for the entire effect.

But isn't it also possible that most, or all, umpires are still biased? Yes, of course, it's possible. It just seems unlikely that in a world where (it seems to me) there are more staunch antiracists than there are racists, a large group of umpires would all fall on the "racial bias" side. I may be wrong about this, and it's a matter of opinion . . . but, if you asked me to bet, I'd say it's much more likely to be a minority of umpires.

And, it should be said, there's a reasonable chance that there's no racial bias at all. A significance level of 0.04 isn't that extreme—it means that, one time in 25, it would happen by chance. Racial bias is a big topic in the literature, and studies that find evidence of bias are more likely to be published than studies that don't. Isn't it plausible that 25 researchers set out to find bias in baseball, and these are the only ones who did, just by chance? I think it's reasonable to argue that the jury should still be out.

CONCLUSIONS

But, anyway, there are ways to get a real answer to the question, instead of just speculating:

Run the same study for other seasons and see if you get the same results. If you were to find the same level of bias for (say) 2000–3 that you did for 2004–6, that would be strong evidence that what the authors found is real.

Look closely at the actual calls from the umpires on the left side of the line—the ones who wound up calling the most strikes for pitchers of their race. Get independent judgments about their borderline calls. If their calls look less accurate than other umpires' calls, see if that's enough to have driven the results the authors found.

Until someone actually does this further research, we can only conclude that

There is indeed some evidence of umpire bias in favor of same-race pitchers.

The bias appears at about an 0.04 level of significance.

The bias appears in low-attendance and non-QuesTec situations.

When attendance is higher or QuesTec is in use, the bias actually goes the other way.

We can't tell which umpires are biased, how many umpires are biased, or even what races of umpires are biased.

We can't tell how many pitches are affected by the bias. It could be as few as 116, or it could number in the thousands.

We can't tell which races of pitchers are beneficiaries of the bias and which races are harmed by it.

So: there's statistically significant evidence for bias, but we don't know which races are affected, how many umpires have it, or how strong the bias is. Quite unsatisfying for fans, reporters, and researchers alike—but I think that's all this study gives us. ■

Notes

1. Christopher A. Parsons, Johan Sulaeman, Michael C. Yates, and Daniel S. Hamermesh, "Strike Three: Umpires' Demand for Discrimination," at Social Science Research Network, http://papers.ssrn.com/sol3/papers.cfm?abstract_id=1318858.
2. Alan Schwarz, "Keeping Score; A Finding of Umpire Bias Is Small but Still Striking," *New York Times*, 19 August 2007.
3. Ibid.
4. Katie Rooney, "Are Baseball Umpires Racist?" *Time*, 13 August 2007.
5. Technical note: To save time, I only approximated what the Hamermesh authors did. I didn't correct for count, score, home/road pitcher, batter, or umpire, which they did. I selected games by actual attendance (less than 30,000) instead of the study's 70 percent of capacity. For umpires, I considered only Angel Hernandez and Alfonso Marquez as Hispanic, and C. B. Bucknor, Laz Diaz, Chuck Meriwether, and Kerwin Danley as black. The original study included one additional Hispanic umpire and one additional black umpire, but I don't know which ones those are. Also, for Hispanic pitchers, I used only those born in one of the countries listed in the study; and, for black pitchers, I used only those in the list "African-Americans in MLB, 2007" at Black Voices (www.blackvoices.com). But I got similar results both the in relative number of pitches seen, and in the effect of those pitches. So I figure it's close enough.

"No, I'm a Spectator Like You"

Umpiring in the Negro American League

Bob Motley as told to Byron Motley

Bob Motley umpired in the Negro American League from 1947 through 1958. The only surviving umpire from the Negro Leagues, he tells of his experience in *Ruling Over Monarchs, Giants and Stars: Umpiring in the Negro Leagues and Beyond* (Champaign, Ill.: Sports Publishing, 2007), which he coauthored with his son Byron Motley, and from which the following article is excerpted. The authors would like to thank Tony Yoseloff and the Yoseloff Foundation for the Yoseloff/SABR Baseball Research Grant that helped make the book and this article possible.

PEOPLE DIDN'T LIKE the umpire back in the days of the Negro Leagues, and they still don't really like umpires today. Some things never change!

It was pretty common in the Negro Leagues, that if the catcher didn't like the way an umpire was calling balls and strikes, he would purposely let a pitch go by and let it smack the umpire right in the facemask. That happened to me at least a half a dozen times.

Of course the catcher would apologize profusely, trying to act as if he had just misjudged the ball, but it was always obvious he had done it deliberately. Of course after he'd pull this stunt, I'd eject him. One time after throwing out Memphis Red Sox catcher Casey Jones for doing this, Buster Haywood had the nerve to come out to question why I was tossing his catcher. So just to get his ire up for asking such an insane question, I tossed out his pitcher too!

When you get hit in the throat, chin, forehead or face (even wearing a mask) by a 90- or 95-mile-an-hour fastball, believe me, you know you've been hit. It stings much worse than a foul-tipped ball because it's a direct hit. Sometimes the ball would be thrown so hard it would actually get stuck in the mask. Once a ball came through my mask, just nipping on my cheekbone. Thank God the front part of the mask bore the brunt of the impact before it slipped inside.

Back in those days, players would do anything to try to upset the umpire. A good number of the times they would get away with it. Sometimes when a baserunner was sliding into the bag, if he knew he was going to be thrown out he would slide wide and barrel right into the umpire and spike him, just out of spite. Oh, the players did horrible things to us umpires. But we were troupers and brushed it off and kept right on going.

If you think the players in the Negro Leagues were a handful to deal with, they were a cakewalk compared to the fans. Fans were relentless and showed no mercy on umpires.

The fans loved razzing the umpires, even on routine plays. One minute they'd applaud you for making a good call (especially if you put a little extra zip in your hip), but they would turn on you in a second if you made a call they didn't like.

In a few of the cities, like Birmingham, Indianapolis, and Cincinnati, the fans had a little song they chanted that was a crowd favorite, "*Kill the umpire, Kill the umpire!*" It was so common and popular among the fans that I expected to someday turn on the radio and hear Count Basie's band or somebody else make a real version of the song. The chant got crowds so worked up into a frenzy that it was almost hard to hear yourself think. The organist always added to the madness by pounding out a weird-sounding dirge that got the entire stadium chanting, growling, and tomahawking in unison. It was weird! It was unnerving at first, but I quickly realized that it was just all in the fun of the game experience for most fans. Others, however, took it to be a literal declaration!

Once in Birmingham, our umpire crew came out of the stadium after a game only to find that the car we were riding in had been turned upside down by disgruntled fans. Blaming us for the loss of their Black Barons, the fans decided to take their angst out on us umpires.

In all honesty, I was never really fearful of fans, but I always knew to keep my wits about myself in dealing with them just in case. For instance, when exiting a stadium after a home team had lost, if someone approached me and asked, "Hey, weren't you one of the umpires?" I'd calmly answer back, "No, I'm a spectator like you." A couple of times I even added, "If you see that bastard, let me know, 'cause I'm looking for him too!" I learned quickly how to adapt to every situation.

As umpires in the Negro Leagues we also learned

COURTESY OF BYRON MOTLEY

Fans, Bob Motley observed, "never blamed their team for a loss, it was always the umpire. A player could have bobbled a ball or made an errant throw and the fans would blame the umpire. . . . The fans would always find something that had happened in the game, no matter how badly their team may have got beaten, and find fault with the umpire. As sickening as it sometimes was, I was always impressed by their dedication."

to *never* hold a long conversation with a fan. When I did affirm that "yes, I am an umpire," I always kept walking (with facemask in hand) and never slowed down to engage someone in a lengthy conversation, even if their team had won, just in case they'd flash back to a previous game or call and decided to turn on you. As umpires we had to be thinking and aware all the time.

One thing about Negro League fans, they never blamed their team for a loss, it was *always* the umpire. A player could have bobbled a ball or made an errant throw and the fans would blame the umpire. A pitcher might give up hit after hit or a batter might strike out time after time, swinging nonetheless, but guess who'd get the blame? The fans would always find something that had happened in the game, no matter how badly their team may have got beaten, and find fault with the umpire. As sickening as it sometimes was, I was always impressed by their dedication.

Several times when crowds were really pissed off about a loss, the umpire crew would have to wait for the entire stadium and parking lot to clear before we'd exit. We didn't want to take any chances.

In one particular game at my beloved Blues Stadium, in front of my now adopted hometown folks of Kansas City, I found out just how intense the wrath of Negro League fans could get.

I think I've blocked out the exact scenario that led up to the particular incident, but it's the only time I was actually afraid of the fans. All I remember is that, on the last out of the game, fifteen thousand Monarchs fans decided to blame Bob Motley for the team's loss. All of a sudden a sea of Coca-Cola bottles started sailing past my head like bazookas being fired from Uzis. Bottles came out of the stands like it was raining. A

couple actually hit me and some of the other players who didn't have a chance to run off to the safety of their dugouts, thankfully without breaking and injuring any of us. As we stood around the field stunned at what was happening, Buck O'Neil and Oscar Charleston ran from their respective dugouts and told me to start walking toward second base, where it was harder for the bottles to reach. The bottles kept coming by the dozens from all directions, and within minutes the field was littered with them! Fearing an out-and-out riot, Buck and Charleston escorted me all the way to the center-field wall and we made an escape. How the three of us scaled that wall and they got me to safety is still a mystery to me, but we did.

True to the spirit of Negro League competition, the next week all was forgiven and everybody acted as if nothing had ever happened.

To me, the Negro League fans were the greatest fans in the world. They were devoted, passionate, fanatical, crazed, and raucous. In short, they *loved* their baseball. They enjoyed every aspect of the game—from getting dressed up in their finest attire, to the tailgating-like picnics, to the carnival-like atmosphere of pregame activities such as concerts, beauty contests, and other activities that different teams provided as entertainment, to the games themselves. People came out to enjoy a full day of fun at the ballpark.

The concessions at a Negro League game usually consisted of the standard popcorn, peanuts, Cracker Jacks, hot dogs, candy, and soft drinks, which were served in bottles. At Martin Stadium in Memphis they even went a step further, serving chitterlings in a cup, which I always enjoyed, arriving early to make sure I got filled up before a game.

No alcohol was served at Negro League games to

my knowledge. Those who wanted to indulge in spirits during a game had to sneak in their favorite booze. You would see people all over the ballpark with different styles of flasks—disguised as transistor radios, cameras, and binoculars—and sipping away and indulging in their favorite adult beverage.

To demonstrate just how serious the fans took their baseball: On Sundays, all over the country where there was a Negro League game scheduled, preachers cut their sermons short because they knew that, come 11, 11:30 at the latest, the entire congregation was going to start filtering out, making their mass exodus to the ballfield for the noon game. This tradition had gone on for years and continued in the Negro American League well into the mid-1950s.

To underscore the importance of black baseball during this time: You must realize that, before the height of the Negro Leagues, black Americans had very few heroes we could identify with. As far as sports figures were concerned, there were only a handful— Joe Louis, Jack Johnson, and Jesse Owens. There were also few political leaders, fewer successful black businessmen or -women, and even fewer professionals such as lawyers, doctors, or dentists. So, ballplayers and musicians, along with clergymen and schoolteachers, were the role models for most black Americans. That is why, even today, sports and entertainment are a big part of black culture and will probably always be. They are entrenched in our culture.

Unlike today in the sports community, it was rare that you heard a fan badmouth a Negro League player, especially one of their hometown guys. Fans were loyal to the bitter end, no matter who was on the roster. Even if a player jumped ship and moved over to another team, fans for the most part held each player in high regard, even the opposing team.

Interestingly enough, women were more fanatical about the game than men. They came in droves and were always dressed to kill in their sundresses, flowery hats, and high-heeled shoes. In the days preceding a big Sunday game, beauty shops would give discounts to women so they could get their hair done and ready for the big day. During the week you might see a woman's hair looking pretty nappy, but come Saturday before the game, you'd walk down 18th and Vine in Kansas City, or Main and McCall in Memphis, and you could practically smell the hair burning from the hot combs and curling irons that beauticians were using getting those "'do's" done!

Yes, the women were dedicated supporters. I've been called "you no-good so-and-so umpire" or "you blind bat" by more women from the stands than a male spectator would ever have thought about doing. Women loved their hometown teams. A buddy of mine told me once about catching the fury of a group of women in the old Blue Room tavern in Kansas City, for badmouthing the Monarchs after a game. They jumped and beat him, not brutally, but enough that he never said another negative word about the Monarchs in public again. ■

The Law Firm and the League

Morgan, Lewis and Bockius LLP, Major League Baseball, and MLB.com

Ross E. Davies

THIS IS (ROUGHLY) THE TENTH ANNIVERSARY of the transfer of a unique and valuable baseball property. On September 6, 2000, Major League Baseball and Morgan, Lewis and Bockius LLP (a very big and very prominent Philadelphia-based international law firm)[1] issued a joint press release announcing "that the law firm has transferred its domain name—**mlb.com**—to Major League Baseball."[2]

From today's perspective in the current age of the Internet, as we look back at a time when the rise of that age (or at least its angle of ascent) was not at all clear, it seems like a bizarrely fortuitous set of coincidences:

- In 1994, the initials of big-time baseball (Major League Baseball = MLB) and the initials of one of big-time baseball's longtime, big-time outside law firms (Morgan, Lewis and Bockius = MLB) were the same (and still are);

- In 1994, it was the law firm that had the foresight, or luck, to move relatively early to register the Internet domain name "mlb.com."

And then . . .

- Several years later, in 2000, when Major League Baseball started to aggressively market itself on the Internet, Morgan Lewis and Bockius was, for a variety of reasons described below, willing to part with mlb.com for a song, or perhaps even less.

At the time of its consummation, the mlb.com transaction got a lot of attention in the news media, as well it might.[3] Because by 2000, it was obvious that the Internet was big business, and transactions in Internet domain names were sufficiently common and significant to inspire government regulation of that market.[4]

But even in the new and booming and volatile domain-name market, the mlb.com deal qualified as unusual in at least two respects. The deal also illustrates the difficulty of placing a value on a favor, at least between lawyer and client, in the context of the business of baseball.

THE PRICE

First, the price. Morgan, Lewis and Bockius ("Morgan Lewis" for short) reportedly gave, not sold, "mlb.com" to Major League Baseball ("MLB" for short). According to *The American Lawyer*, a leading magazine covering the legal profession, "After the league announced that it wanted to make a brand out of its initials, a la the National Basketball Association, Morgan, Lewis turned over its registered domain name, MLB.com, to the league—free of charge, of course."[5]

It is possible, but unlikely, that *The American Lawyer* got the story wrong. The magazine did not cite a source for its report, and the exact terms of the deal are beyond our reach because it was a "confidential transfer agreement."[6] As the *Philadelphia Inquirer* explained at the time, "While domain transfers typically are cash transactions, the parties in this case would not reveal terms—or even give a ballpark figure, if cash was involved."[7] Nevertheless, a few media outlets (none of which cited a source or gave a dollar figure) did report that Morgan Lewis was asked by MLB to "sell" mlb.com,[8] and commentators willing to assert in print (again without a source or dollar figure) that Morgan Lewis did in fact extract compensation from MLB were in even shorter supply.[9] Most news stories, however, implied it was a gift, or at least not a sale. They reported—without mentioning a sale or a price—that Morgan Lewis "surrendered mlb.com to Major League Baseball,"[10] or that "Morgan Lewis would transfer the mlb.com domain name to Major League Baseball,"[11] or that MLB "secured" it courtesy of Morgan Lewis, or that Morgan Lewis "relinquish[ed]" it to MLB,[12] or something of the sort.[13]

In any event, based on the available news stories—and they are just about all we have to go on—it appears that MLB probably got something quite valuable for nothing, or at least for a price it has gone to the trouble to keep secret for a decade. How valuable? By the late 1990s, a short and commercially identifiable Internet domain name could be, and often was, worth a small fortune.[14] Indeed, in a domain-name lawsuit involving the National Football League and a couple of its teams, the presiding federal judge described the situation in 2000 as follows:

[I]t cannot seriously be disputed that domain names have become a valuable commodity in today's economy. In the battle to obtain as many website "hits" as possible, companies have paid hundreds of thousands, and sometimes millions, of dollars for domain names that consumers will remember and use when browsing the Internet.[15]

Law firms, including Morgan Lewis, are for-profit enterprises. Why might such an enterprise give away such a valuable asset?

THE CONNECTIONS

The answer springs pretty obviously from the second unusual feature of the mlb.com-to-MLB deal: the fortuitous connections between the original owner (Morgan Lewis) of the valuable domain name and the entity (MLB) seeking to acquire that name. Those connections—which added up to a long and fruitful if sometimes rocky relationship, described in some detail below—probably made the sweetheart mlb.com deal possible. In other words, giving up mlb.com might well have been a small price for Morgan Lewis to pay if it meant preserving and perpetuating a valuable relationship between the firm and MLB.

But the story of the connections leads to one last question: In September 2000, was all the history between MLB and Morgan Lewis, combined with the prospect of more collaboration in the future, really enough to justify Morgan Lewis's decision to turn over mlb.com to MLB?

Connections, 1978–1994

In September 2000, when the mlb.com deal was consummated, Morgan Lewis could boast of connections to baseball dating back at least to 1978, when Michael Fremuth, a young lawyer working at the firm, moonlighted as a pitcher for the Alexandria Dukes of the Carolina League.[16] The firm's legal work involving baseball began no later than 1981, when it was defense counsel in *Dudley Sports Co. v. Berry*, a case in Florida state court in which a boy and his parents sued the manufacturer and distributor of a pitching machine after the boy was injured in an accident involving the machine.[17]

By the mid-1980s, Morgan Lewis's baseball involvement went directly and deeply to MLB itself. The firm, which had then and has today a reputation as one of the strongest management-side law firms specializing in labor-management relations, was receiving some publicity for its work representing teams at salary arbitration hearings.[18] But it was in October 1987 that the first of the two most important moments in the firm's relationship with MLB occurred. Murray Chass wrote about it at length in the *New York Times*:

> In what could be a significant change on the labor front, baseball management has made a change in its legal lineup.
>
> For more years than Tommy John has pitched in the major leagues, Willkie Farr and Gallagher [a very big and very prominent New York–based international law firm[19]] has been the law firm that handled the owners' labor matters, sometimes to the detriment of the owners. The most noted legal-labor blunder occurred in 1975 when the owners were advised not to negotiate a settlement of the Messersmith–McNally grievance, but to let the arbitrator rule and then have his decision overthrown in court if the ruling went against them. However, the decision of Peter Seitz was upheld in court, and the free agency that followed became far more costly to the owners than it might have been.
>
> Willkie Farr does not specialize in labor law, and some owners think that has hurt them in their dealings with the union. Now, after many years, the Player Relations Committee, of which Rona [MLB spokesman Barry] is executive director, has hired a Washington firm, Morgan, Lewis and Bockius, which represents management in labor relations.
>
> "There are a number of labor lawyers there with great labor law expertise," Rona said. "Willkie Farr will continue to operate in corporate and general law and tax areas, where their strength and expertise lie."[20]

For most of the next decade, Morgan Lewis lawyers were important figures in a range of matters involving labor–management relations in the major leagues,[21] including especially the negotiation of collective bargaining agreements with the players' union, the Major League Baseball Players Association (MLBPA), during the early and mid-1990s.[22]

Mlb.com, 1994. And then, in 1994, in an exercise of real and remarkable techno-marketing savvy (generally speaking, no one thinks of lawyers as savvy techno-marketers, not even lawyers themselves),[23] Morgan Lewis registered the domain name "mlb.com." This display of Web-based foresightedness happened a decade after the firm had begun working closely with the major leagues and seven years after it had been hired as what amounted to MLB's chief outside labor-relations counsel. Which makes one thing clear: MLB did not hire Morgan Lewis just in order to acquire mlb.com from the firm. A conventional client–lawyer relationship long predated the Internet connection.

Moreover, neither side seemed to have a strong desire to move mlb.com from the law firm to its client at the time. Indeed, in an interview in 2000, an MLB spokesman recalled, "I think we knew they had [the domain name] early on, but we didn't think much about it because the Internet was not a big thing back then." Conversely, a Morgan Lewis official recalled that, "[f]rom the beginning, Major League Baseball had an interest in using the mlb.com name. . . . And in the early years we weren't interested in considering that because we had just started the Web site."[24]

Connections, 1994–2000

In baseball, 1994 was something of a high-water mark for Morgan Lewis. Firm partner Charles O'Connor, who had represented MLB during the 1990 spring-training lockout, was again serving as counsel to MLB's labor-relations arm, the MLB Player Relations Committee, as it negotiated with the MLBPA for a new collective bargaining agreement to replace the one that had expired at the end of 1993.[25] It was those negotiations that eventually triggered the 1994–95 baseball strike. O'Connor and several of his colleagues at the firm played prominent roles not only in the contract negotiations but also in the related litigation in 1995, including the famous *Silverman v. Major League Baseball Player Relations Committee* case before then Judge (now Supreme Court Justice) Sonia Sotomayor in New York federal court.[26]

Silverman was the second (and far less beneficial) of the two most important moments in the firm's relationship with MLB. Unfortunately for O'Connor and Morgan Lewis, management lost in *Silverman*.[27] The firm was portrayed in the media as one of the goats—or perhaps scapegoats (often in the company of MLB labor-relations executive Richard Ravitch)—of the debacle.[28] The reportage in the *Philadelphia Inquirer* was impressively thorough and well written, but the basic angle taken on the role of MLB's lawyers was not atypical of newspaper coverage in general at the time:

> Bill Buckner let a ground ball roll between his legs.
>
> Jim Fregosi let Mitch Williams pitch to Joe Carter.

Oh, those agonizing, enduring errors of baseball lore.

And now another has been added. Only this time, the guys in pinstripes who blundered were not ballplayers but lawyers—the ones representing the owners in their dealings with the union.

Faulty strategy is what the judges in the Second U.S. Circuit Court of Appeals called it. The lawyer at last week's hearing in New York, Frank Casey [of Morgan Lewis], got the umpire treatment from the judges, who interrupted his presentation with sarcastic retorts and accused him of "going around in circles" and trying to confuse the court with double-talk.[29]

In the aftermath of *Silverman*, it probably came as a surprise to no one that MLB hired a new lawyer—Randy Levine, who had been serving as commissioner of labor relations for New York City—to take the lead when negotiations with the MLBPA resumed in earnest in late 1995 and early 1996.[30] (Levine is now president of the New York Yankees.[31]) And in another unsurprising move a few years later, both the American League and the National League retained Levine's old employer, Proskauer Rose Goetz and Mendelsohn (another very big and very prominent New York–based international law firm).[32] Proskauer Rose partner Howard Ganz[33] served as lead outside counsel in labor disputes that were by 1999 beginning to boil over between the leagues and the umpires' union, the Major League Umpires Association.[34]

These moves might have suggested that MLB's confidence in Morgan Lewis had been shaken,[35] but other moves indicated that faith in the firm had not been utterly destroyed. For the balance of the 1990s, Morgan Lewis continued to do some labor-law work for the big leagues,[36] including work on the post-*Silverman* 1995–96 collective bargaining with the MLBPA.[37] In addition, in 1998 MLB commissioner Bud Selig hired two Morgan Lewis partners, Frank Coonelly and Robert Manfred, to serve as in-house labor-relations counsel at MLB,[38] creating between the firm and the big leagues a long-term connection that remains in place today.[39]

Mlb.com, 2000. And so, by 2000, MLB and Morgan Lewis had been through the wars together. The client had done its part: MLB had been a steady and valuable Morgan Lewis client for more than a decade and had continued to send business to Morgan Lewis even after the uncomfortable period in 1994 and 1995 when the firm spectacularly failed to carry the day for the team owners at the bargaining table or in court. And the lawyers had done their part: Morgan Lewis lawyers had stood up in court, and then in the media spotlight, to take the heat for the team owners' (and the firm's) commitment to what turned out to be an unpopular and unsuccessful bargaining position in the 1994–95 round of contract negotiations with the MLBPA.[40] And the firm had seemingly performed satisfactorily in other capacities as labor counsel to MLB both before and since that difficult time.

It was against this mixed background of deep disappointment and continuing collaboration that MLB began pressing Morgan Lewis to relinquish the mlb.com domain name. In the past, Morgan Lewis's control of mlb.com had not been much of an issue. As recently as early 1999, an official at MLB had "indicated that the organization was satisfied with the current arrangement" under which Morgan Lewis used mlb.com and included on the firm's website a link to MLB's website at www.majorleaguebaseball.com.[41] By December 1999, however, MLB wanted very much to control mlb.com, and it was negotiating with Morgan Lewis for a transfer.

What was Morgan Lewis to do? Ironically, this was the very firm whose "great labor law expertise," including its experience in negotiations with organized labor,[42] had made it such a good choice for MLB back in 1987 when the firm was hired to replace Willkie Farr and Gallagher as counsel to the MLB Player Relations Committee.[43] But negotiating with its client in 2000 over the transfer of mlb.com as it had negotiated with the MLBPA on behalf of that client over a new collective bargaining agreement in 1994-1995 might not be a good idea.

Holding out for a good price from MLB might well alienate the client. And it was a client that was building a substantial in-house legal operation (including two former Morgan Lewis lawyers) and showing a willingness, perhaps even a preference, for competitively high-powered outside counsel from another firm (Proskauer Rose and its star sports labor law partner, Howard Ganz). In other words, MLB might be willing to pay Morgan Lewis well for "mlb.com" if pressed to do so. But if the firm actually did demand payment, MLB not only probably would, but also easily could, promptly walk away from its long relationship with the firm.

Of course, if MLB was already well on its way to walking away from Morgan Lewis and likely to continue on its way, what did Morgan Lewis have to lose?

First, the firm would almost certainly lose any chance of holding on to any MLB work, let alone winning back any of what it had lost to other firms or the in-house operation. Second, trying to extract top dollar from a client for an asset that had been acquired by the firm for little money but had fortuitously turned to be of great value to that client was not likely to inspire warm feelings of confidence toward Morgan Lewis among its other clients and prospective clients.

Finally, as the abbreviations used in this article for "Major League Baseball" (MLB) and "Morgan, Lewis and Bockius LLP" (Morgan Lewis) suggest, the transfer of "mlb.com" to MLB and the switch to using "morganlewis.com" by Morgan Lewis fit well with the brand-marketing strategies of both organizations.[44] Thus, because Morgan Lewis was not going to be using mlb.com itself, the firm had little or nothing to gain from the domain name other than whatever money it could extract from MLB for it.

In the end, as *The American Lawyer* put it, "Morgan, Lewis and Bockius made the best of a tricky situation with one of its sexiest clients, Major League Baseball."[45] The deal was done on September 6, 2000.

Connections Since 2000

Without knowing what price MLB would have paid for mlb.com, and without access to the confidential MLB-Morgan Lewis agreement, it is impossible to say with any confidence whether Morgan Lewis did the right thing by (apparently) giving away that valuable domain name. But a look at what has happened to the MLB-Morgan Lewis relationship since then (or at least at the parts in the public record) might provide some basis for ruminating about what kind of value Morgan Lewis ended up getting for mlb.com.

To Morgan Lewis, the mlb.com deal must have seemed at first to be an excellent investment, and then perhaps a fruitless one, and then, for the time being at least, a pretty good one.

The months following the September 2000 transfer of mlb.com were a good time for Morgan Lewis's baseball practice. The firm began to play a prominent part on behalf of MLB in the important and well-publicized labor relations conflicts between the big leagues and the umpires.[46] And there was other work as well,[47] including an amicus brief for the Office of the Commissioner of Baseball filed in the Supreme Court of the United States in the case of *Major League Baseball Players Association v. Garvey*.[48]

In 2002, however, when the time came for MLB and the MLBPA to negotiate a collective bargaining agreement to succeed the one agreed to after the 1994-

1995 strike, Morgan Lewis was not invited. Howard Ganz of Proskauer Rose was.[49] *The American Lawyer* interpreted this development as an indicator of just how much value the mlb.com deal could have for Morgan Lewis:

> The gift [of mlb.com] won Morgan, Lewis some goodwill. But it didn't permanently win over Major League Baseball (or, should we say, MLB). That became clear recently, when the commissioner's office bypassed Morgan, Lewis and tapped New York's Proskauer Rose to handle the most important piece of work to come along in a half-decade, this winter's labor negotiations with the Major League Baseball Players Association. The stakes are big. A failure to hammer out a new collective bargaining agreement could lead to a strike or lockout at the beginning of the 2002 season.[50]

While the loss of its prestigious seat at the MLB-MLBPA bargaining table was surely hard to take, that did not mark the end or even the beginning of the end of Morgan Lewis's work for MLB. For much of the past decade, the firm has represented MLB in litigation relating to its conflicts with the umpires.[51] In recent years MLB has also enlisted Morgan Lewis to represent the Major League Baseball Players Benefit Plan in federal court in Ohio[52] and to lobby the administration of President George W. Bush to permit Cuba to participate in the World Baseball Classic.[53] Given the confidential nature of much legal work, there is no telling (from the outside) what other sorts of work Morgan Lewis may have done or might be doing for MLB.[54]

So, in the fifteen-plus years since Morgan Lewis originally registered the mlb.com Internet domain name (and since the 1994–95 MLB–MLBPA meltdown that cost baseball and its fans one World Series and parts of two seasons), the law firm and its big-league client have continued to work together. For the last ten-plus of those years, MLB has had (1) the probably free benefit of Morgan Lewis's mlb.com as well as (2) the certainly-not-free benefit of the good work of the firm's labor lawyers. In return, Morgan Lewis has enjoyed the income and prestige of having MLB as a client. Would this particular lawyer–client relationship have persisted for so long, and in the face of such intense ups and downs and competitive pressures, if MLB had not received both kinds of benefits? You make the call.

A POSTSCRIPT IN DEFENSE OF MLB

It would be difficult to read about the process by which Major League Baseball established its Internet home at mlb.com without getting the impression that, if a journalist or commentator had been in charge of the big leagues back in the early 1990s, mlb.com would have been registered by MLB long before Morgan Lewis got to it. If MLB's failure to register its natural domain name early really was a result of its "comparatively late [entry] in the game," or the "minor-league . . . quality" of its "tradition"-bound approach to the Web,[55] then it had some pretty diverse and fancy company, including such marketing/self-promotion slugs as Nissan Motor Co.,[56] Planned Parenthood,[57] Madonna (as in the music and media celebrity),[58] and the White House (meaning both the operation of which the president of the United States is the boss and the National Fruit Product Company, makers of White House Apple Sauce and other delectables),[59] to name just a few of the more famous Internet latecomers.

And according to *Sports Illustrated*, when MLB and Morgan Lewis closed the mlb.com deal in September 2000, quite a few other pillars of the sports world were still locked out of their natural homes on the Internet. The list at the time included the International Olympic Committee, the NHL's Colorado Avalanche, and the Bears, Bills, Cowboys, and Saints of the National Football League as well as the Arizona Diamondbacks and Montreal Expos.[60]

As always, wisdom after the event is easy to come by. ■

Acknowledgments

The author thanks Paul Haas (SABR member since 1983), Robert A. James, and Mike Kelly.

Notes

1. See www.morganlewis.com.
2. Bonnie P. Ciaramella (Morgan, Lewis and Bockius LLP) and Richard Levin (for Major League Baseball), "Morgan Lewis Pitches Web Address to Major League Baseball," press release, 6 September 2000 (bold type in original), copy on file with the author.
3. See, e.g., Jim Oliphant, "Morgan, Lewis Takes One for the Team," *New York Law Journal*, 10 October 2000, 6; "Big Leagues' Net Bet," *Newsweek*, 2 October 2000; Michael Klein, "Major League Baseball Gains Right to 'MLB' Internet Address," *Philadelphia Inquirer*, 9 September 2000, C1.
4. See, e.g., The Anticybersquatting Consumer Protection Act, S. Rep. 106–140, 106th Cong., 1st Sess., 5 August 1999; Anticybersquatting Consumer Protection Act, Pub. L. No. 106–113 (1999), codified at 15 U.S.C. § 1125(d).
5. Ashby Jones, "Tuck in the Bullpen," *American Lawyer*, January 2002, 18.
6. Jeff Blumenthal, "Morgan Lewis Decides to Play Ball with Client," (*San Francisco*) *Recorder*, 12 September 2000, 3.
7. Michael Klein, "Major League Baseball Gains Right to 'MLB' Internet Address," *Philadelphia Inquirer*, 9 September 2000, C1.

8. See, e.g., Matt Fleischer, Karen Donovan, and Victoria Slind-Flor, "The Talk of the Profession," *National Law Journal*, 1 May 2000, A8; Greg Auman, "Online Reports Not Necessarily On Line," *St. Petersburg Times*, 11 August 2000, 2C.

9. See, e.g., Clinton Wilder, "A New Game Plan," *TechwebNews*, 9 April 2001; Mark Conrad, "MLB Gets Web Rights in MLB.com," Mark's Sportslaw News, www.sportslawnews.com, 5 September 2000 (accessed 7 September 2010).

10. Henry Gottlieb, Charles Toutant, Sandy Lovell, and Tim O'Brien, "Who's On First?" *New Jersey Law Journal*, 25 September 2000.

11. Jeff Blumenthal, "Morgan Lewis Decides to Play Ball with Client, [*San Francisco*] *Recorder*, 12 September 2000, 3.

12. "Big Leagues' Net Bet," *Newsweek*, 2 October 2000.

13. "On MLB's Hit List: Web Plays, All-Star Ambushers", *Brandweek*, 17 July 2000, 18; Tom Hoffarth, "It's No Iceberg, It's P'urgh," [*Los Angeles*] *Daily News*, 31 July 2000; Tommy Cummings, "Underachievers Already Voted Off Packer Island," *San Francisco Chronicle*, 23 August 2000, E8.

14. See, e.g., Winn L. Rosch, "Domains: Today's Name Game," (*Cleveland*) *Plain Dealer*, 20 July 2000, 2C: "The value of easy-to-remember and -recognize names comes as no surprise. The big hits this year: Business.com sold for $7.5 million, loans.com for $3 million and autos.com for $2.2 million."

15. *Weber v. National Football League*, 112 F.Supp.2d 667, 672 (N.D. Ohio 2000).

16. "A Winner," *Legal Times*, 11 September 1978, 3; "Michael Fremuth Minor League Statistics and History," Baseball-Reference.com (accessed 15 October 2010).

17. *Dudley Sports Co. v. Berry*, 407 So.2d 335 (D. Ct. of Appeal of Fla., 3d Dist. 1981); see also *United States v. Athlone Industries, Inc.*, 746 F.2d 977 (3d Cir. 1984).

18. See, e.g., Phil Hersh and Fred Mitchell, "Durham Is No Poor Loser: Cubs Win Arbitration, 'Bull' Gets $800,000," *Chicago Tribune*, 21 February 1985, 1; see also, e.g., Christine Brandt, Karen Dillon, Robert Safian, and Sara Seigle, "Major League Baseball Arbitration," *American Lawyer*, November 1987, 30.

19. See www.willkie.com.

20. Murray Chass, "Free Agency Still Key to Future Peace, *New York Times*, 15 October 1987, B17. As Professor Larry Garvin of Ohio State University recently pointed out, "Bowie Kuhn was a partner at Willkie Farr handling baseball matters before he became baseball commissioner. It was with his departure as commissioner in 1984 that other law firms started getting larger pieces of the action. I don't know whether there was a causal link here, but it would hardly be surprising." Correspondence to the author, 10 November 2010.

21. See, e.g., Robert Safian, "Tom Roberts Breaks Into the Majors," *American Lawyer*, May 1988, 121; "Owners Gird for Costly Collusion Settlement," *Chicago Tribune*, 18 January, 1990, 3; *Cusack v. Detroit Tigers Baseball Club, Inc.*, 956 F.2d 27 (United States Court of Appeals, Second Circuit 1992).

22. See, e.g., Ross Newhan, "A New Man on the Point for Owners: Charles O'Connor took over at the last minute as lead negotiator for baseball management. Will his outlook affect the outcome of the talks?" *Los Angeles Times*, 9 December 1989, 1; Margaret Cronin Fisk, "Names Behind the News: Batter Up: Lawyers Score In Baseball Talks," *National Law Journal*, 2 April 1990, 10; Ronald Blum, "Finally, There's a Little Light at the End of the Tunnel," *Akron Beacon Journal*, 21 December 1994, C6.

23. Cf. Henry Gottlieb, Charles Toutant, Sandy Lovell, and Tim O'Brien, "Who's On First?" *New Jersey Law Journal*, 25 September 2000.

24. Jeff Blumenthal, "Morgan Lewis Decides to Play Ball with Client," (*San Francisco*) *Recorder*, 12 September 2000, 3 (quoting MLB spokesperson Richard Levin and Morgan Lewis chairman Fran Milone).

25. Julie Stoiber, "Lawyer Goes to Bat for Owners: He Represents the Major-League Clubs; As a Baseball Fan, He's Eager to See the Strike Settled," *Philadelphia Inquirer*, 18 January 1995, C1.

26. See *Silverman v. Major League Baseball Player Relations Committee*, 880 F.Supp. 246 (S.D.N.Y. 1995); "Baseball Talks May Resume," *New York Times*, 9 July 1995, 7.

27. See *Silverman v. Major League Baseball Player Relations Committee*, 67 F.3d 1054 (United States Court of Appeals, Second Circuit 1995); see also "New Lawyer for Owners in Appeal of Injunction," *Philadelphia Inquirer*, 26 April 1995, D4; Roger I. Abrams, *Legal Bases: Baseball and the Law* (Philadelphia: Temple University Press, 1998), ch. 9 (reviewing the *Silverman* litigation and the entire course and consequences of the negotiations and related disputes from 1993 to 1996).

28. See, e.g., "Baseball Owners to Replace Labor Lawyer," *Philadelphia Inquirer*, 16 April 1995, C10; "Rangers, Tettleton Agree on 1-Year Deal," *Houston Chronicle*, 13 April 1995, 6. See also, e.g., Jacques Steinberg, "Ravitch, Mayor's Choice to Run Schools, Has Extensive Public Record," *New York Times*, 17 September 1995: "Mr. [Richard] Ravitch served from 1991 until last December as the [MLB] owners' chief labor executive and was credited with bringing the teams together on a revenue-sharing plan, in which richer teams like the Yankees would help poorer teams like the Pittsburgh Pirates. But by basing that plan on a salary cap, he earned the enmity of the players and was never able to forge a new collective bargaining agreement with them. While the [MLBPA] union blames Mr. Ravitch, in part, for bringing on the strike in summer 1994, David W. Sussman, the executive vice president and general counsel of the Yankees, believes he was cast unfairly as a scapegoat. Nevertheless, soon after the strike began, the owners eased Mr. Ravitch out of his lead role at the bargaining table. He resigned in December."

29. Julie Stoiber, "Phila. Law Firm May Have Dropped the Ball for the Owners: Judges Blasted the Strategy of the Baseball Owners' Lawyers; Will the Firm Be Benched?" *Philadelphia Inquirer*, 9 April 1995, C1.

30. See David Firestone, "Labor Chief for Giuliani to Leave for Baseball Job," *New York Times*, 19 September 1995.

31. Yankees Front Office, mlb.mlb.com/team/front_office.jsp?c_id=nyy (accessed 16 October 2010). Levine is also of counsel at Akin, Gump, Strauss, Hauer and Feld LLP, yet another very big and very prominent international law firm. See www.akingump.com/rlevine/ (accessed 16 October 2010).

32. See www.proskauer.com (accessed 16 October 2010).

33. See www.proskauer.com/professionals/howard-ganz/ (accessed 16 October 2010).

34. See, e.g., Susan Hansen, "Proskauer on Deck for Baseball Owners?" *American Lawyer*, November 1995, 17; Ashby Jones, "Tuck in the Bullpen," *American Lawyer*, January 2002, 18.

35. See, e.g., "Season Opens with Replacement Umps," *Rocky Mountain News*, 26 April 1995, 8B: "The decision to replace Casey, made by the ruling executive council, signals what probably will be the phase-out of Morgan, Lewis. Several owners were angered over losing at the injunction hearing, and some want to drop Morgan, Lewis. Oral arguments on the appeal are scheduled for May 11."

36. See, e.g., Susan Hansen, "Proskauer on Deck for Baseball Owners? *American Lawyer*, November 1995, 17; *Bowen v. Workers' Compensation Appeals Board*, 73 Cal.App.4th 15 (California Court of Appeal, Second District 1999).

37. See, e.g., "Smiley an All-Star as a Replacement," *Miami Herald*, 9 July 1995, 7D.

38. See Appellants' Brief and Appendix, *Phillips v. Selig*, 2007 WL 5289093 (Superior Court of Pennsylvania, 5 November 2007).

39. See MLB Official Info, MLB Executives, mlb.mlb.com/mlb/official_info/about_mlb/executives.jsp?bio=manfred_rob (accessed 7 September 2010), identifying Robert D. Manfred, Jr. as "Executive Vice President, Labor Relations and Human Resources," and as a former "partner in the Labor and Employment Law Section of Morgan, Lewis and Bockius, LLP"). Coonelly left his position under Selig in 2007 to become president of the Pittsburgh Pirates. See Rob Biertempfel, "Bucs Hire Coonelly, President with a Plan, *Pittsburgh Tribune Review*, 14 September 2007; Front Office biographies, Frank Coonelly, President, pittsburgh.pirates.mlb.com/pit/team/exec_bios/coonelly_frank.jsp (accessed 16 October 2010): "Frank Coonelly was named President of the Pittsburgh Pirates on September 13, 2007. . . . Prior to joining the Pirates, Frank served as Senior Vice President and General Counsel of Labor in the Office of the Commissioner of Baseball

. . . Coonelly practiced labor and employment law as a Partner in the Washington, D.C. office of Morgan, Lewis and Bockius before joining the Commissioner's Office. A large part of Frank's practice consisted of the representation of Major League Baseball as outside labor counsel. In that role, Frank assisted the Commissioner of Baseball in collective bargaining and litigation matters. He also represented several individual Clubs, including the Minnesota Twins, Chicago Cubs, Montreal Expos and Atlanta Braves, in salary arbitration matters."

40. See Leonard Koppett, *Koppett's Concise History of Major League Baseball* (New York: Carroll and Graf, 2004), 456–70.

41. Ruth Singleton, "Morgan to Lewis to Bockius: Firm's Web Site Plays Major League Ball," *National Law Journal*, 19 April 1999, A23.

42. *See* Jennifer Fried, "Walking the Line: Morgan, Lewis Knows How to Bargain at the Table and Battle in the Courthouse," *American Lawyer*, January 2004, 99.

43. Murray Chass, "Free Agency Still Key to Future Peace," *New York Times*, 15 October 1987, B17.

44. Jim Oliphant, "Morgan, Lewis Takes One for the Team," *New York Law Journal*, 10 October 2000, 6. Correspondence to the author from Robert A. James, partner and board member of Pillsbury Winthrop Shaw Pittman LLP, 19 October 2010: "The marketing strategies of many large law firms have been gravitating for some time to use of the first name or names on the letterhead. Bingham, Orrick, and Paul Hastings are now promoted with shorthands rather than full names or acronyms. With their 2001 merger the Winthrop, Stimson, Putnam & Roberts and Pillsbury Madison & Sutro firms adopted pillsburywinthrop.com and discontinued use of their 'WSPR' and 'PMS' shorthands—the latter acronym having a most unfortunate connotation in the late twentieth century. The Pillsbury firm today uses the single-word Pillsbury brand, but retains the 'pillsburylaw.com' domain name to distinguish itself from the Pillsbury food brands." If Morgan Lewis had similar plans in 2000 for moving from mlb.com to morganlewis.com, the firm may have been quitclaiming the sleeves off of its vest.

45. Ashby Jones, "Tuck in the Bullpen," *American Lawyer*, January 2002, 18; see also Michael Klein, "Major League Baseball Gains Right to 'MLB' Internet Address," *Philadelphia Inquirer*, 9 September 2000, C1 ("The deal . . . was complicated by the fact that the two sides had long been business partners and enjoyed attorney–client privilege: Morgan Lewis has handled much of Major League Baseball's labor-negotiations work for a decade"); Monica Bay, "Yankee Stadium, Ringstrasse, Disney World, Dallas," *Law Technology News*, November 2000, 16.

46. See, e.g., *Bonin v. World Umpires Association*, 204 F.R.D. 67 (E.D. Pa. 2001); Defendant Office of the Commissioner of Major League Baseball's Memorandum of Law in Support of its Motion to Dismiss, *Bonin v. World Umpires Association*, 2001 WL 34898519 (E.D. Pa. 2001); *Gregg v. National League of Professional Baseball Clubs*, 57 Fed. Appx. 123 (3d Cir. 2003); Brief of Defendants/Appellees National League of Professional Baseball Clubs, *Gregg v. National League of Professional Baseball Clubs*, 57 Fed. Appx. 123, 2002 WL 32818411 (3d Cir. 2002); *Major League Umpires Association v. American League of Professional Baseball Clubs*, 2001 WL 34894718 (E.D. Pa. 2001); *Major League Umpires Association v. American League of Professional Baseball Clubs*, 357 F.3d 272 (3d Cir. 2004); Reply Brief of Appellees/Cross-Appellants, *Major League Umpires Association v. American League of Professional Baseball Clubs*, 357 F.3d 272, 2002 WL 32819168 (3d Cir. 2002); Memorandum of Law in Support of Motion of Defendants to Dismiss the Complaint, *Major League Umpires Association v. American League of Professional Baseball Clubs*, 2003 WL 23906078 (E.D. Pa. 2003); Memorandum of Law in Opposition to the Major League Umpires Association's Motion for Contempt of Court, *Major League Umpires Association v. American League of Professional Baseball Clubs*, 2005 WL 3724109 (E.D. Pa. 2005); *Phillips v. Selig*, 157 F.Supp.2d 419 (E.D. Pa. 2001); Brief and Appendix for Appellees, *Phillips v. Selig*, 959

A.2d 420, 2008 WL 2623632 (Superior Ct. Pa. 2008); Memorandum of Law in Support of the Motion of Defendants to Disqualify Patrick Campbell, Esquire and Phillips and Campbell, P.C., *Major League Umpires Association v. American League of Professional Baseball Clubs*, 2003 WL 23906093 (E.D. Pa. 2003); Memorandum of Law in Support of Motion for Summary Judgment of Defendants, *Phillips v. Selig*, 2006 WL 6048310 (Ct. Common Pleas of Pa., Phila. Cty. 2006); Complaint, *Office of the Commissioner of Baseball v. Major League Umpires Association*, 2002 WL 34447591 (E.D. Pa. 2002); see also Shannon P. Duffy, "Arbitrator's Call on Most Umpires Stands: Three See Their Cases Returned for Reassessment," *Legal Intelligencer*, 14 December 2001, 1.

47. Ashby Jones, "Tuck in the Bullpen," *American Lawyer*, January 2002, 18: "For the time being, the firm is handling the league's garden-variety ERISA and employment work. 'We're just happy that Rob and Frank are keeping us busy with other matters,' says Steven Wall, the deputy manager of the firm's labor and employment practice group."

48. Motion for Leave to File Brief Amicus Curiae and Brief Amicus Curiae of the Office of the Commissioner of Baseball in Support of the Petition, *Major League Baseball Players Association v. Garvey*, 532 U.S. 504 (2001) (Harry A. Rissetto, Counsel of Record, Morgan, Lewis and Bockius LLP).

49. Liane Jackson, *Play Ball: MLB Lawyers Strike a Deal, Corporate Legal Times*, 1 November 2002, 70.

50. Ashby Jones, "Tuck in the Bullpen," *American Lawyer*, January 2002, 18.

51. See note 46 above.

52. See Answer, *United States v. Rogers*, 558 F.Supp.2d 774, 2004 WL 3124417 (N.D. Ohio 2004); see also *United States v. Rogers*, 558 F.Supp.2d 774 (N.D. Ohio 2008).

53. See "Looper Back with Cards for $13.5 Million, 3 Years," *Chicago Tribune*, 16 December 2005, 6.

54. Cf., e.g., Rebecca A. Falk Attorney Biography, www.morganlewis.com (accessed 17 October 2010): "Recent matters include . . . Represented individuals employed by a Major League Baseball franchise in connection with the San Francisco U.S. Attorney's Office's investigation into steroid use and the related internal investigation conducted by the Commissioner of Baseball."

55. Michael Klein, "Major League Baseball Gains Right to 'MLB' Internet Address," *Philadelphia Inquirer*, 9 September 2000, C1; Clinton Wilder, "A New Game Plan," *TechwebNews*, 9 April 2001.

56. See *Nissan Motor Co. v. Nissan Computer Corp.*, 378 F.3d 1002, 1006 (9th Cir. 2004): "This appeal raises a number of trademark issues arising out of the use by Uzi Nissan of his last name for several business enterprises since 1980, his use beginning in 1991 of 'Nissan' as part of the name of a North Carolina computer store he owned—Nissan Computer Corp.—and his registration in 1994 of 'nissan.com' as a domain name. . . ."

57. See *Planned Parenthood Federation of America, Inc. v. Bucci*, 42 U.S.P.Q. 2d 1430, 1997 WL 133313 (S.D.N.Y. 1997): "On August 28, 1996, Bucci registered the domain name 'plannedparenthood.com.'"

58. See *Madonna Ciccone v. Dan Parisi*, WIPO Case No. D2000-0060, www.wipo.int/amc/en/domains/decisions/html/2000/d2000-0847.html (Oct. 12, 2000) (vis. Oct. 17, 2010): "On or about May 29, 1998, Respondent . . . purchased the registration for the disputed domain name".

59. See Charles F.C. Ruff, counsel to President Clinton, letter, to Dan Parisi, president, Infolook, Inc., news.com.com/2009-1023-207800.html? legacy=cnet (8 December 1997) (accessed 17 October 2010) "It will come as no surprise to you that the White House Counsel's Office is aware of your Internet Web site, 'www.whitehouse.com,' and that we object to your use of the names and images of the White House, the President, and the First Lady on that Web site to sell memberships in an adult video club"; discussed in "Wasting Time in Cyberspace," by Chad D. Emerson, 34 *U. Balt.* L. Rev. 161, 186–87 and n.223 (2004).

60. See "Misdirection Plays," *Sports Illustrated*, 18 September 2000.

The Macmillian *Baseball Encyclopedia,* the West System, and Sweat Equity

Robert C. Berring

THERE IS BEAUTY IN FINDING that beneath a complex system, one so large and entrenched that it seems to operate under its own power, there is a history that is quite human. The work of a person, perhaps a small band of people, fueled by energy and sweat equity, and perhaps a dollop of obsessiveness, can create a mighty enterprise. Simon Winchester wrote a bestseller about how one man, James Murray, stood at the center of *The Oxford English Dictionary.* On an abstract level, one might claim that William Blackstone created the conceptual framework of the common law that still guides us. But those two are famous figures. The real fun lies in identifying those who, by sheer perseverance and drive, create mighty dreadnoughts that sail on under their own power, growing and changing, and yet remain anonymous. Two delightful examples, related on many levels, are the individuals behind the West System[1] and the *Macmillan Baseball Encyclopedia* (MBE).

Baseball and lawyers are intricately intertwined. This is no news to the reader of this article. The magic that pulls them together may not admit to easy characterization, but there is no denying that Stevens's "The Common Law Origins of the Infield Fly Rule" created an enthusiastic body of commentary all on its own, or that the intricacy of the Baseball Rule Book maps easily onto the technical pyrotechnics of the Internal Revenue Code for specificity and opaqueness. Lawyers love the intricacies of the game of baseball and the collection of statistics. More congruence is found in the fact that the guiding light of modern baseball statistics and the conceptual blueprint for legal analysis share similar origins. There are human stories behind these grand enterprises.

BUILDING THE WEST SYSTEM

The West Publishing Company was founded by two brothers: John and Horatio. John was a salesman who noticed that some of his customers, who were lawyers, were having trouble getting their hands on recent judicial decisions. West lived in Minnesota in the late nineteenth century. Courts there were required to make written copies of judicial opinions available, and the state had an official printer of decisions, but getting

Lee Allen, the longtime historian at the Baseball Hall of Fame and himself a walking encyclopedia of baseball knowledge, had spent three decades compiling biographical data on players. David S. Neft and his team of twenty-one researchers took Allen's accumulated research as the basis of their massive reference work that was published as the Macmillan *Baseball Encyclopedia* in 1969.

access to these opinions was not easy.[2] The official printer was slow and not always reliable. This gave John West an idea.

The classic Supreme Court opinion in *Wheaton v. Peters* had established in 1834 that judicial opinions were in the public domain. These opinions could be published by anyone who wanted to do so. Many jurisdictions had official printers for their courts' decisions, but the office of official printer was often a sinecure. The resulting publications were incomplete and slow. John realized that one might make money by doing the sheer donkey work of going from court to court, making copies of the opinions, printing them, and distributing them.[3] Remember, the West brothers had no photocopy machines, let alone digital information. What they did have was an idea and the market incentive to perform the simple, hard work. It had to be done carefully and quickly. John was not a lawyer; he was an entrepreneur.

Armed with his idea and the raw materials to carry it out, he and his brother Horatio went into business. They produced the *Syllabus*, a collection of Minnesota decisions. It was a huge success. It was such a winner that the brothers began the *Northwestern Reporter*, which included decisions from courts in surrounding states. That quickly led to the full National Reporter System. This tale has been told in detail elsewhere, but what matters here is that the root from which it all grew was simple effort and obsessive attention to detail. The West Company produced and produces a more thorough and timely product than anything seen before.

The maraschino cherry on the chocolate sundae of the West story is the Key Number System. The West brothers realized that they should offer some organizational system for finding the judicial opinions in their *Reporters*. They bought a system developed by John Mallory and morphed it into the Key Number System. The Key Number System categorized opinions by classifying legal ideas. It was new and it allowed lawyers to find judicial opinions via an entirely new rubric. Several of us have contended that the Key Number System categories came to have an impact on the way lawyers think and judges write.

As the paper-based universe of information sinks slowly in the west, and the new dawn belongs to the texting, social networking, and Boolean-searching generation of multitaskers who sit in the classes that I teach, it is fitting to note that the mighty West system was the product of the obsessive work and simple plan of human beings.

THE MACMILLAN *BASEBALL ENCYCLOPEDIA*: THE BEGINNING OF A MAGNIFICENT OBSESSION

Growing up as a baseball fanatic,[4] I treasured the Macmillan *Baseball Encyclopedia*. As a boy contemplating it, I was filled with wonder. The MBE listed every player who ever had a cup of coffee in the majors. It was detailed and it was authoritative. For me it was an unquestioned source of information. Like the West System (of which I was ignorant in my elementary-school years), it seemed an enterprise bigger than any human, but in fact it was the product of the work of a small band of zealots—humans who were willing to invest the sweat equity in its creation.

David Neft was a statistician who loved baseball. Growing up in the 1950s, he saw *The Official Encyclopedia of Baseball* as his lodestone of authority. But it was incomplete in coverage, and printed only batting averages for hitters and won–lost records for pitchers. He nurtured the dream of something better. When he went to work for Information Concepts Incorporated in

1965, he proposed the idea of a computerized baseball encyclopedia that would be complete and reliable. How Neft sold his concept to ICI and then to Macmillan is a great tale.[5] The statistics were out there, but before 1920 they were not in one place, and after 1920 they were unverified. Doing the job right would mean starting over. First, the new effort would need to be certain who the players were. For that there was another compulsive information maven, Lee Allen.

Lee Allen was the longtime historian of the Baseball Hall of Fame in Cooperstown, New York. Known as a walking encyclopedia of baseball knowledge, Allen had spent three decades collecting information on players. Allen did not care about statistics; he wanted biographical data. Though official records had been kept since 1903, there had been little quality control. Allen had supplemented these records through his own research, his own drive to be accurate and complete. He visited graveyards and pursued leads on players like a Sam Spade in search of information on the black bird. He compiled a massive library of books and materials that he took with him to Cooperstown when he assumed his position as librarian there.[6] Basing their encyclopedic work on the biographies compiled by Allen, Neft, and his team went to work gathering up data. Neft hired a team of twenty-one researchers and set them to work, checking old newspapers and gathering up data. As Alan Schwarz put it:

> The staff of 21 then began its Kerouakian odyssey all over the United States, from library microfilm rooms to long lost graveyards, mortar and spades always in tow, to build the greatest book of statistics sports had ever seen.[7]

The hard work of slogging was supplemented by the effort of programming a computer to sort and check each item. It was the middle of the 1960s. Computers were primitive creatures and the task was not simple. It fell to Neil Armann. Armann was not a baseball fan, much like John West was not a legal scholar, but he took on the challenge of creating a computer program that would pull together and cross-check all statistics. Given that these were early days for computing, there is another great story here, but we shall tip our cap to Mr. Armann and move on.

The first edition of the Macmillan *Baseball Encyclopedia*, which was published in 1969, sold an amazing 100,000 copies at $25 ($150 in the dollars of 2009). The *New York Times* reviewed it three times. It carried the day. Just as the West Key Number System set the accepted categories for legal thought, *The Base-*

ball Encyclopedia established the standard for statistical categories. If you look through the volume you will find seventeen categories for hitters, and nineteen for pitchers. They became the standard way of evaluating performance. In my family's basement back in Ohio, these were the numbers that meant something to me. The *Baseball Encyclopedia* was authoritative and it created an authoritative classification system. I knew that if Kelly Heath had one at-bat in the major leagues, it would be in the MBE. As with the world of the West brothers, the information was there for the taking. It never occurred to me that actual people struggled to pull these sources together, they just existed.

Once the MBE was in place, a new world was opened. Having a source of reliable information available, others began to build. In its wake, those who were devoted to baseball statistics founded the Society for American Baseball Research (SABR), which applies the tools of modern statistics and the power of computers to generate, refine, and parse new categories of information. Indeed, new statistical categories are now in vogue, but the rock upon which it was all built was the Macmillan *Baseball Encyclopedia*.

COMMON FATE

These two great enterprises share another characteristic. They are intellectual booster rockets carrying their missions forward. And now, having served their purposes, they are falling back to earth. Each has taken us to a new level where others have built upon them. Boolean searching has largely replaced the Key Number System at the center of the search function of legal research. New digital tools, web pages, blogs and a deluge of specialty software applications have replaced *The Baseball Encyclopedia*. The tenth edition, published in 1996, was its last hurrah. Just as law libraries are shipping the old *West Digest* and *National Reporter* volumes to storage, or perhaps to a nearby dumpster, no one wants to buy a ten-pound reference book on baseball statistics when a website can tell you everything you need to know and more.

Since you have read to this point, you must be a person of the old school. One who values the feel of pages and admires the heft of a ten-pound reference book. Let us take a moment, and raise a glass of fine single malt scotch to these two very human efforts to bring order out of chaos, and to the resulting books that represent the giants upon whose shoulders we now stand. Each was a masterpiece built on sweat, and each was a financial success in its day. As with so many other great authoritative tools of the twentieth century, their days are gone, but they should not be forgotten. ■

Notes

1. This article was published originally in *The 2010 Green Bag and Almanac and Reader*, 318–21. The West System will stand for both the National Reporter System and the American Digest System. Though it is the former that is primarily of interest here, like Ruth and Gehrig they are forever conjoined.

2. For a short and charming description of the history of the distribution of legal information in the United States, see the text of the 2009 Opperman Lecture at Drake Law School, "Remarks of the Honorable John G. Roberts, Jr. Chief Justice of the United States," in the fall 2008 issue of the *Drake Law Review* at page 1. I am an admirer of any Chief Justice who can use the term "pneumatic tube" in a lecture.

3. Marvin, *History of the West Publishing Company*, provides a full account of this story. This book is very hard to find. For a more easily located version of the story try "Collapse of the Structure of the Legal Research Universe: The Imperative of Digital Information," 69 Wash. L. Rev. 9 (1994). It is my youthful attempt at telling the story, complete with edifying footnotes.

4. Growing up in northeastern Ohio, I was a Cleveland Indians fan. Since my team never won, focusing on statistics was a fine outlet for my enthusiasm. Did you know that Rocky Colavito once hit four home runs in one game? I thought not.

5. The story is well told by Alan Schwarz in *The Numbers Game: Baseball's Lifelong Fascination with Numbers* (New York: St. Martin's Griffin, 2005). Chapter 5 covers this territory but, if one loves baseball and statistics, the whole book is worth a read. It is in print in paperback.

6. Credit should also be given to John Tattersall, a shipping executive who spent his life collecting information on players from the nineteenth century. His work formed the basis of the reports on the earliest players of the game.

7. Schwarz, *The Numbers Game*, 95. Kerouakian is my word of the month.

The Fightingest Pennant Race

Brockton versus Lawrence in the Eastern New England League, 1885

Justin Murphy

IT HAS BEEN NOTED time and time again that the search for the good old days of baseball is bound to come up dry. In every period of the national pastime, there has been greed, poor sportsmanship, lying, and cheating, to name a few of the lesser offenses. The subject of this article is further evidence of the same— a hotly disputed pennant race that was contested in the newspapers, the league offices, and, reluctantly, on the diamond.

For twenty-eight days after the end of the regular season, and fourteen days after the last playoff game, Brockton and Lawrence bickered publicly about a confusing welter of complaints: whether and when postponed games should be made up, who should schedule them, and which of three teams Lawrence's star pitcher was actually under contract with. These disputes, and the heat generated by each team's loyal newspaper, required neat diplomacy and legal tact on the part of the league's board of directors.

In 1885 the Eastern New England League was in its inaugural season and comprised five teams: Lawrence, Brockton, Haverhill, and Newburyport, all in Massachusetts, and Portland, in Maine. The league schedule consisted of 80 games, with each team playing 20 games against each of the other four. Newburyport and Portland both played their way out of contention early in the season, and Haverhill ultimately faltered as well, leaving the way clear for the two powerhouses and bitter rivals, Brockton and Lawrence.

Brockton ended its regular season with a record of 48–31. Lawrence, with a record of 45–31, had three games remaining at the end of September: one against Portland and two against Newburyport. They needed to win all three to match Brockton.

On September 29, Lawrence defeated Portland, 9–1, on the strength of a four-hitter by John A. Flynn. After the game, Portland manager Chick Fulmer filed a protest. He claimed that the game should not count because the teams had already played each other the allotted 20 times. In response, Lawrence pointed out that one of the games, in Portland, had been agreed on as an exhibition, since it would have been the eleventh match between them in that city. For the first time, but certainly not the last, the *Lawrence Daily*

American entered the fray:

> This [protest] was undoubtedly due to the fact that Portland accidentally defeated Brockton Monday [September 28], and McGunnigle, who is a much better wire puller than ball player, laid a plan with Portland to win another game to make him safe. This seems to be the whole thing in a nutshell, the Brockton management being as brazen receivers of stolen goods as McGunnigle is a purloiner of the same. They evidently expect no difficulty in getting whatever they want in the board of directors. In this way only has Brockton gained a sight of the pennant, by fraud and downright theft, which no honest man would uphold.[1]

The primary object of the paper's scorn was Bill "Gunner" McGunnigle, the 30-year-old right-hander in his first season as Brockton manager. Born and raised near Boston, he'd made his playing debut with a junior team in Brockton and had several years of experience in and around New England, as well as 54 games, 19 of which he pitched, with Buffalo of the National League in 1879–80. The "stolen goods" referred to were the championship laurels that both clubs hoped to wear.

With this issue looming in the background, Lawrence still had two games left against Newburyport. These were played the next two days, and Lawrence came away with two clutch victories. In the first game, on September 30, they beat the hosts 11–6. They then returned to Lawrence on October 1 and beat them there, 8–3. Flynn started the second match on one day of rest but struck out seven, allowed only four singles, and hit a pair of doubles himself.

The two front-runners, Lawrence and Brockton, were tied atop the leaderboard. As luck would have it, though, a pair of games between them had been called off earlier in the season.

The first disputed game was played on August 14, when the two teams met in Manchester, New Hampshire.[2] The umpire did not show up, so Brockton catcher George Bignell arbitrated from behind the plate. Predictably enough, Bignell was accused of favoritism, but Lawrence managed to rack up a 6–0 lead through seven and a half innings. Brockton rallied for four runs in both the eighth and ninth innings, but three more runs for Lawrence in the top of the ninth decided the game in its favor, 9–8. The exact cause of the protest is not recorded. Presumably, Brockton claimed that the game shouldn't have counted without the umpire. After all, they'd been deprived of their starting catcher.

The second contested outcome came on August 26, in Brockton. The *Boston Globe* captured what must have been the prevailing sentiment, noting that "nearly every time the Brockton and the Lawrence teams meet upon the ball field there is more or less 'kicking' about the decisions of the umpires." The paper continued:

> The newly appointed umpire, Mr. A. W. Stewart of Ayer, was assigned to duty here today and administered the worst "roasting" ever accorded the home team. It was evident from the beginning of the game that Mr. Stewart was not a good judge of balls and strikes and his fatal misjudgments were principally bestowed upon the home team.[3]

Facing a three-run deficit in the bottom of the sixth inning, Brockton's George Tanner stepped to the plate and "knocked a ball clear over the right-field fence for a home run, but the umpire decided it was only for two bases."[4] Then, instead of returning the ball to the pitcher, Lawrence second baseman Timothy Brosnan tagged Tanner, who was not standing on the bag. Stewart promptly declared him out. "The audience protested against such a decision, and the umpire, thinking himself insulted, left the field and would not return until 35 minutes had passed. The game was then continued under protest."[5] Lawrence ended up winning, 9–3.

The validity of these two games was debated at a league meeting in September. Apparently, they were both stricken from the record and ordered to be replayed. The way the standings stood, their outcome would determine the championship.

The actions of the two clubs after the end of the officially scheduled season are, as reported by their respective mouthpiece newspapers, muddled. First, even before Lawrence's second game with Newburyport, the *Brockton Gazette* reported:

> No longer ago than this week, Secretary [H. S.] Bicknell of this city wrote to Manager [Walter] Burnham of Lawrence, inquiring if the games could not be arranged, but up to the present time no reply whatever has been received, a fact which Manager Burnham cannot deny. . . . To sum up, Lawrence cannot tie us, and knows it well, but apparently would rather resort to chicanery than to lose the pennant. We would not.[6]

In response, the *Lawrence Daily American* claimed the exact opposite, that Burnham had contacted Bicknell and received no reply. "They [Brockton] refuse to play, knowing defeat to be inevitable. They crowed over the pennant too soon and now dread having to eat their words."[7]

Despite the posturing, a directive came that same day, October 1, from league secretary Charles J. Wiggin, mandating the teams to play off the two remaining games, on October 3 in Lawrence and the following day in Brockton. The *Brockton Gazette* protested this arrangement:

> All fair-minded people are convinced that Brockton has won the championship, and nothing can shake this conviction. Brockton has a postponed game with Newburyport, why doesn't Wiggin order that to be played? Because he has nothing to say but what is in Lawrence's favor. Brockton will not play these games which have been ordered by the secretary.[8]

It is not clear why baseball men in Brockton believed they'd already won the pennant, unless it was in hopes of having the Portland protest upheld. Also, a report in the *Newburyport Germ* on October 4 indicated that the Brockton team had indeed agreed to play the games, contrary to the indication in the *Brockton Gazette* that they would defy Wiggin's order.[9] Sure enough, though, when Lawrence arrived at its field on October 3, no Brockton players were there.

Once the home team stepped onto the field, the umpire waited a specified amount of time and then declared Lawrence the winner by forfeit, 9–0. "The greatest indignation was felt by the audience," wrote the *Lawrence Daily American*, "at the shabby treatment [by] the Brockton management . . . [who know] full well that if Lawrence had been given her just dues she would now hold the pennant, which Brockton is attempting by the most bare-faced methods to steal."[10]

Several minutes after the forfeit was declared, however, a telegram arrived. It read: "Manager W. W. Burnham—I cannot play, as several players refuse to go [to Lawrence], as their contracts expired yesterday. W. H. McGunnigle." The crowd soon dispersed, "thoroughly disgusted."[11]

In the following day's *Gazette*, McGunningle elaborated, saying that "no one more than he desired to play the three postponed games [including the one against Newburyport]" but that league secretary Wiggin had overstepped his bounds in ordering the games played on October 3 and 4.[12] First, McGunnigle argued, the two teams must be given the chance to arrange the dates themselves, according to the league constitution. For his part, the Brockton manager submitted that they play on October 8 and 9. That would give him time to reassemble his team.

That same day, however, a report in the *Boston Journal* said that "Capt. McGunnigle of the Brocktons has definitely decided to play no more games during the present season." This apparent contradiction was seized on immediately by the Lawrence paper. "The two despatches given above," it dutifully reported, "settle the whole question. There is now no doubt that McGunnigle does, and does not, want to play off the three games yet to be played."[13]

The *Boston Journal* article contained another piece of news potentially much more damaging for Lawrence. On October 4, Brockton's Bicknell received a telegram from American Association commissioner Wheeler C. Wickoff. In it, Wheeler claimed that Flynn, Lawrence's star pitcher, had signed a contract with the AA's New York Metropolitans on September 15.[14] If true, this would invalidate the six games he had played for Lawrence since then, all of them victories.

With this nineteenth-century media circus in full procession, Lawrence traveled to Brockton the following day, October 5, for the second scheduled game. The Brockton players were indeed present, but the field was soaked through. The next day's *Brockton Gazette* wrote, "[Umpire] Bond looked the ground ov'r, poked the earth with his umbrella, and finally announced that he could not call [i.e., officiate] the game, as the grounds were not in fit condition."[15] What followed was bizarre.

First, both towns' papers reported that McGunnigle refused to pay Lawrence's travel expenses on being presented with a bill, as was common practice at the time. Instead, "the men left the grounds in little groups, the Lawrence club taking a barge which was in waiting, and driving . . . to the depot, where they took the 3:20 train for Boston."[16]

Neither paper revealed why McGunnigle refused to pay. He may have been miffed, however, by a nifty piece of detective work, related in the *Lawrence Daily*

A Lawrence baseball team, probably from the nineteenth century. The first recorded game in Lawrence was shortly after the Civil War. After a complicated, protracted dispute, Lawrence was ultimately declared champion of the short-lived Eastern New England League in 1885. The town went on to field teams in minor leagues, primarily the New England League, for many years through the 1940s.

American: "Some of the Lawrences went under the grand stand [after the game was called] and found a hose covered with mud and water and having every appearance of being used to flood the grounds to prevent a game."[17] The Lawrence paper, loathe to miss out on a comedic opening, deadpanned that "the Brocktons probably intend to use their ball grounds this winter for a skating rink, flooding them with water and letting it freeze over. Saturday was a little early in the season to begin flooding [it], however."[18]

The Lawrence team officially disbanded after this debacle, presumably because their contracts had expired as well. Manager Burnham wrote a terse letter to league secretary Wiggin, requesting "an early opportunity to prove these facts [i.e., McGunnigle's refusal to pay] to the board of directors and [argue] that the Brockton Base Ball club may be expelled from the Association."[19]

At the same time, Brockton leveled accusations against both Newburyport, of throwing their last two games against Lawrence, and Haverhill, "of a desire to cheat her [Brockton] out of a pennant."[20] Haverhill representatives had been present at the forfeit in Lawrence and had "denounced the trickery and meanness of McGunnigle in the loudest and most emphatic terms," according to the *Lawrence Daily American*.[21] Haverhill's William H. Moody also served as league president. A multitalented man, Moody soon abandoned baseball to dedicate himself to the law and politics. In 1906, after having served as secretary of the navy and U.S. attorney general, he was named to the Supreme Court by Theodore Roosevelt.

If ever a league meeting was needed, it was on October 8, when the team presidents finally got together at the Essex House in Lawrence. The *Biddeford Journal*, playing the role of impartial observer, had nothing but scorn for both teams involved:

> The Eastern New England League is preparing for a monkey and parrot sort of a time at its next meeting. The leading clubs, more intent upon gaining legal advantages than to meet on the ball field, have exhausted the constitutional provisions in attempts to avoid a meeting. Brockton refuses to play games when not ordered by the secretary; failed to appear at the field after agreeing to play; Lawrence went to Brockton to play when the ground was flooded, and Brockton refused to pay them for so doing; and now Lawrence asks for the expulsion of Brockton, and follows this by disbandment of the club. It seems to be a clear case of one's afraid and the other "darsn't"—and still the championship remains unsettled.[22]

Several important issues were on the docket for the meeting. First, Portland's protested game against Lawrence on September 29, which it claimed was the twenty-first match between the two teams. Second, the contractual status of Flynn, who had been claimed not only by the Metropolitans of the AA but also by McGunnigle himself on behalf of Brockton. Third, whether or not Secretary Wiggin had overexercised his power in ordering the postponed games between Brockton and Lawrence to be played. How these disputes were resolved would go a long way toward determining the champion.

The next day, the *Lawrence Daily American* pronounced all problems "amicably arranged." Concerning Flynn, there proved to have been a miscommunication among Brockton management:

> Mr. Mills stated that he had protested the game because McGunnigle telegraphed him that Flynn and [Lawrence catcher George] Moolic were under contract with him [McGunnigle]. The matter of whether this was so or not was discussed and [Brockton secretary Bicknell] said they based their information on the statement of Manager [Jim] Mutrie,[23] of the Metropolitans,

and did not claim that Brockton had any hold on Flynn. McGunnigle corrected Bicknell, saying that it was under a belief that they could hold Flynn that they telegraphed Mr. Mills as before stated.[24]

In light of this confusing development, Mills dropped his protest, and the men moved on to the question of whether Flynn had signed with the Metropolitans. To answer this, they summoned Flynn himself, who averred that "he had signed with no club but Lawrence, and that he had never told any person that he had."[25]

In the end, and at Mills's suggestion, all of the problems were bundled into one elegant solution. Lawrence and Brockton agreed to play a three-game series for the championship—on October 10 in Brockton, October 13 in Lawrence, and October 15 in Boston, if necessary. The clubs further agreed to "waive all protests and matters at present except the eligibility of Flynn. In case Flynn was found to have played while ineligible, the Brocktons [were] to take the pennant."[26] Lawrence re-signed its players, and the recalcitrant foes were finally ready to play ball.

On the field as in the newspapers, Lawrence and Brockton were very well matched. The former team was carried by the 21-year-old Flynn, who had joined the club for the stretch run after playing for Meriden earlier in the year (more on that later). He was the unquestioned ace of the staff and also the best hitter, with a .432 average in 44 at-bats. His batterymate was fellow Lawrence native George H. Moolic, a competent defensive catcher who went by the nickname Prunes. Other standouts included second baseman (and captain) Timothy Brosnan, first baseman Pat O'Connell, and center fielder John Kiley. The team did not hit for much power but was far above average defensively and outscored its opponents by 46 runs over the course of the season. The roster included John Tener, a young Irishman from County Tyrone, who didn't make much of an impression during his time in Lawrence but did go on to serve as National League president from 1913 to 1918 and as governor of Pennsylvania from 1911 to 1915.

For Brockton, third baseman James "Jumbo" Davis was the centerpiece of a fearsome offense. He later went on to a fairly lengthy career with various teams in the American Association, and led that league with 19 triples in 1887. Ed Crane was another reliable hitter, and Jim Cudworth patrolled center field with grace. The main starting pitcher for Brockton was John Moriarty, and he faced Flynn in the first game of the series.

Brockton drew blood in the first inning of the

opener, as first baseman Bill Hawes reached first on a muffed third strike by catcher Moolic, advanced to second on a wild throw by the same, and scored on a passed ball. In the second inning, however, Lawrence put up three runs of their own on hits by O'Connell, Brosnan, and Flynn. Also in that inning, Brockton's Davis got into a heated argument with the umpire and stormed off the field.

The Lawrence nine continued to add runs incrementally throughout the game. They scored two in the third, one in the fifth on "Flynn's terrific hit to extreme left field for three bases,"[27] two in the sixth, and one in the seventh. Brockton scraped together three more runs, but it was not enough to prevent a 9–4 loss. Flynn allowed five hits, walked five, and struck out nine; Moriarty allowed ten hits, walked three, and struck out seven.

The second game of the series, in Lawrence, was scheduled for October 13, but rain pushed it back two days. Brockton's loss had evidently not diminished its healthy swagger; in their Lawrence hotel guestbook, the players signed themselves in as "Champions of New England." The *Lawrence Daily American*, noting this, dryly compared them to "lads of tender years, who delight to scribble their names on the walls of every conceivable place they enter."[28]

When play finally began, Lawrence jumped out to an early lead, scoring two runs in the first on "an opportune hit by O'Connell."[29] In the fourth inning, Brockton answered with three runs of its own on a double by Ed Crane and a balk by Lawrence's Flynn. In the next two innings, though, Lawrence reclaimed the lead and extended it considerably, scoring five unanswered runs, then four more in the eighth and ninth innings. O'Connell, Bill Conway, and John Burns each recorded multiple hits, Moolic had an RBI double, and Flynn allowed only five hits. Lawrence took the game by the final score of 11–4, winning the three-game series and the pennant.

Afterward, a hastily arranged parade carried the players through the town and dropped them off at the Brunswick Hotel, where they were the object of much speechifying by local bigwigs. "There was a feeling of great gratification at the result of the game expressed in the countenance of each one present, and after the repast cigars were circulated among the guests."[30] Pitcher Dick Conway was presented with a winter overcoat, "with the hope that he would accept it and continue to cherish as kindly feelings toward Lawrence people as they did towards him." The night wore on, "songs were rendered by several present, and at a seasonable hour the party broke up with Auld Lang

Syne, much pleased with the celebration in honor of securing the pennant."[31]

As the revelers dined, the scribes at the *Lawrence Daily American* must have been fairly cackling at their desks. In a swipe at Brockton's self-styled "Champions of New England," the next day's delirious headline read, "HELLO, BROCKTON! What Are You Going to Sign Yourself Now?"[32] Along with the recap was a lengthy column of vindictive gloating, aimed primarily at the *Brockton Gazette*:

> Well, Gazette, take it all back and tell your readers you don't know a little bit about base ball anyway. It is a bitter pill, but you must take it. . . . It is dreadfully hard, but you were, as usual, just a trifle previous, to say the least, and indiscreet beyond a doubt. We pity you, indeed we do. Ta-ta.[33]

In fact, many different New England newspapers chimed in regularly through the dispute. After the final game, the *Boston Globe* opined that "the Brocktons won the championship and the Lawrences got the pennant,"[34] while the *Boston Post* wrote:

> The managers of the Brockton team may well feel heartily ashamed of themselves. . . . That they lost the pennant is entirely their own fault. Brockton, with the chances greatly in her favor, took just the one course that should have been avoided, disbanded the team and attempted to win the championship by bluff.[35]

A third Boston paper, the *Herald*, believed that "in the opinion of a large majority of the base ball public in New England . . . the Brockton club fairly and squarely won the championship on the ball field."[36] To which the *Lawrence Daily American*, ever judicious, replied: "In the opinion of a large majority of the base ball public in New England, the Herald base ball man has a big head."[37]

Incredibly, though, the affair was not yet decided. In a new tactic, Brockton alleged that Flynn and his batterymate, Moolic, had been under contract not with the Metropolitans but with Meriden of the Southern New England League. Both men had indeed played for Meriden earlier that year and joined Lawrence on September 17, only after Meriden folded. According to the secretary of the SNEL, Meriden had disbanded on September 15. According to Meriden's own secretary, however, that team never actually disbanded officially. A meeting of the Eastern New England League was called on October 28 to settle the dispute.[38]

In the meantime, some further digging by the *Boston Globe* showed that on August 12 the Meriden club released all of its players—with the exception of Flynn and Moolic.[39] At the same time, however, Flynn was owed $200 by management, which the *Lawrence Daily American* believed "released him from all obligations to them long before he signed in Lawrence."[40] The SNEL secretary, however, admitted, "I don't know any rule in our League by which contracts become invalid when salaries are not paid." In the same telegram, he counted himself among the befuddled: "Lord only knows when the Meriden club disbanded."[41]

As October turned toward November, the *Brockton Gazette* commented that "base ball talk is getting rather wearisome at the present time."[42] Though Brockton had a vested interest in the conversation, many New England baseball fans likely agreed. On October 28, four weeks after the last scheduled game of the season, the league board of directors finally awarded the championship—to Lawrence. At that evening's meeting, Lawrence's representatives—Flynn among them—provided proof that not just Meriden but the entire SENL had disbanded by August 15, if not before. League secretary Moody concurred.[43] The long, hard season was over, on the field and in the boardroom.

Old habits die hard—the following day, Brockton promised an appeal. "It is ten to one," the *Boston Globe* surmised, "that they will never carry out this threat, and a hundred to one that . . . the matter [will not] come before the arbitration committee."[44] Indeed, no appeal was ever filed.

The weather worsened, and, though the principal parties (or, rather, their supporters in the press) continued to snipe at one another, public interest moved elsewhere. Flynn, who had found himself in the eye of a hurricane on and off the field, signed with Chicago of the National League. Lawrence's manager, Burnham, went to head the new Meriden franchise and was replaced by former Detroit player Frank Cox.

In 1886, the two teams would again battle in the standings, but somewhat farther down the ladder— they both finished over 20 games out of first place. This was in the newly constituted New England League. The Eastern New England League had gone out of business after one season and one of the most heated pennant races in baseball history. ■

Acknowledgments

The author would like to thank Tony Yoseloff and the Yoseloff Foundation for the Yoseloff/SABR Baseball Research Grant that helped make this article possible. Thanks also to the staff at the Lawrence History Center and Lawrence Public Library. Baseball-Reference.com was an indispensible resource for statistics.

Notes

1. *Lawrence Daily American*, 30 September 1885.
2. Sources disagree on the date of the game and on the identity of the umpires. One source gives the date as August 12. Another source gives the date as August 18 and identifies the umpire as Winslow [Sylvester?]. The *Boston Globe* of 15 August 1885 refers to the Lawrence–Brockton game of August 14.
3. *Boston Globe*, 27 August 1885.
4. Ibid.
5. Ibid.
6. *Lawrence Daily American*, 1 October 1885. Quotes from the *Brockton Gazette* and other regional newspapers, with the exception of the *Boston Globe*, come from the *Lawrence Daily American*, which published lengthy excerpts from competing newspapers throughout the season.
7. Ibid.
8. *Lawrence Daily American* 2 October 1885.
9. *Lawrence Daily American*, 5 October 1885.
10. *Lawrence Daily American*, 3 October 1885.
11. Ibid.
12. *Lawrence Daily American*, 5 October 1885.
13. Ibid.
14. Ibid.
15. *Lawrence Daily American*, 6 October 1885.
16. Ibid.
17. Ibid.
18. Ibid.
19. Ibid.
20. Ibid.
21. *Lawrence Daily American*, 3 October 1885.
22. *Lawrence Daily American*, 8 October 1885.
23. The manager of the Metropolitans in 1885 was James Gifford. Mutrie, who had managed them in 1883–84, moved to the New York Giants in 1885.
24. *Lawrence Daily American*, 9 October 1885.
25. Ibid.
26. Ibid.
27. *Lawrence Daily American*, 10 October 1885.
28. *Lawrence Daily American*, 14 October 1885.
29. *Lawrence Daily American*, 16 October 1885.
30. Ibid.
31. Ibid.
32. Ibid.
33. Ibid.
34. Ibid.
35. Ibid.
36. *Lawrence Daily American* 17 October 1885.
37. Ibid.
38. *Lawrence Daily American*, 20 October 1885.
39. *Lawrence Daily American*, 26 October 1885.
40. Ibid.
41. Ibid.
42. *Lawrence Daily American*, 21 October 1885.
43. *Lawrence Daily American*, 29 October 1885.
44. *Lawrence Daily American*, 30 October 1885.

It's Not Fiction

The Race to Host the 1954 Southern Association All-Star Game

Ken Fenster

FOR THE FIRST ELEVEN DAYS of July 1954, the Atlanta Crackers, the Birmingham Barons, and the New Orleans Pelicans fiercely battled each other on the playing field for the honor of hosting the Southern Association All-Star game. Their intense struggle culminated in a spectacular, tense game that ended in grand storybook fashion in Atlanta on July 11. The race in general and this game in particular were something right out of an epic novel. There was drama, anxiety, excitement, a hero, a villain, a damsel in distress, and catharsis. The All-Star game itself, played on July 15, was decidedly anticlimactic.[1]

The story of the great race to host the 1954 Southern Association All-Star game began in December 1953. At their annual meeting, league directors changed the rules for determining the site of the game for the upcoming season. In previous years, the team in first place after the completion of games played on July 4 hosted the midseason event on July 15. For 1954, that privilege would go to the team in first place after games played on July 11. League directors made this change to avoid the possible embarrassment of the first-place team on July 5 sliding to third or even fourth place—it had happened in the past—by the time the All-Star game arrived.[2]

OPERATION TICKTOCK BEGINS

To be sitting atop the league standings on that midseason date predetermined by league officials was tantamount to winning the first-half pennant of a split season. It gave the team and its city bragging rights.[3] Moreover, the owner and the players had financial motives for wanting to host the All-Star game. For the owner, hosting the All-Star game meant an extra payday at the gate, and it could be lucrative. Attendance at fifteen previous All-Star games had averaged slightly more than 10,100. Four All-Star games in Atlanta had averaged more than 13,450.[4] For Earl Mann, the Crackers' owner, whose only source of income was his baseball franchise, an extra gate of this magnitude would be a financial bonanza. The players on the team hosting the game received from the league a wristwatch valued at $75, a considerable sum—the average monthly salary in the Southern Association was about

$600.[5] The Atlanta players nicknamed the race for the 1954 All-Star game Operation Ticktock.[6]

Operation Ticktock began in earnest on July 2, with the Atlanta Crackers, the Birmingham Barons, and the New Orleans Pelicans all in the chase. Atlanta clung to a slight lead. The top four teams in the standings on that date:

	Won	Lost	Winning Percentage	Games Behind
Atlanta	47	31	.603	
Birmingham	48	34	.585	1
New Orleans	45	36	.555	3.5
Chattanooga	42	40	.512	7

Between July 2 and July 11, Atlanta and New Orleans played twelve games, and Birmingham eleven.[7] Their schedules were nearly identical. Atlanta had four games with New Orleans, four with Mobile, and four with Birmingham. Birmingham played four against New Orleans, three against Mobile, and four against Atlanta. New Orleans had four with Atlanta, four against Mobile, and four with Birmingham. The schedule put each team's destiny in its own hands. The Crackers, the Barons, or the Pelicans were all in the same position: The team that took care of business in their games with the other two contenders—regardless of what other teams did on the field—would win the race.

However similar the schedule for the crucial next ten days may have been for the three top teams, it slightly favored New Orleans at the expense of Atlanta and Birmingham. New Orleans and Atlanta had one more game against the weak, sixth-place Mobile Bears than did Birmingham. New Orleans played eight of its next twelve games at home; of its next twelve, Atlanta played only four at home; and the unfortunate Barons played all their next eleven games on the road. Birmingham had only one doubleheader between July 2 and July 11. New Orleans and Atlanta had excruciating back-to-back doubleheaders on July 4 and July 5, a situation that could wreak havoc with their pitching staffs. At least the Pelicans played their doubleheaders on their home field. Atlanta had the extra burden of playing its doubleheaders on the road and in two different cities, New Orleans on July 4 and Mobile on July 5.

NATIONAL BASEBALL HALL OF FAME LIBRARY, COOPERSTOWN, N.Y.

Cracker first baseman Frank Torre, whose mother, sister, and brother Joe traveled from New York to Atlanta to watch his team in a crucial game against the rival Birmingham Barons on July 8, 1954.

The three teams each played .500 ball in their first series in July. Atlanta and New Orleans split their four-game set, and the Barons split a brace of games with the Mobile Bears. The Crackers and the Pelicans caught a huge break when rain cancelled Birmingham's game with Mobile on July 4. After games played on July 4, Atlanta still led the league by a slim one-game margin over Birmingham. The standings were:

	Won	Lost	Winning Percentage	Games Behind
Atlanta	49	33	.598	
Birmingham	49	35	.583	1
New Orleans	47	38	.553	3.5
Chattanooga	46	40	.535	5

On July 5, Atlanta split a doubleheader with Mobile, losing the second game in the eleventh inning on right-fielder Chuck Tanner's costly error. Meanwhile, in New Orleans, the Pelicans and Barons were rained out, forcing them to play back-to-back doubleheaders on the July 6 and 7. Atlanta wasted a second golden opportunity to pull further ahead of its pursuers when the team lost another game it should have won, 1–0, to the lowly Bears. In the end the Crackers salvaged a split in the series, winning the final game 3–1 behind the stellar hurling of Leo Cristante, the league's leading pitcher. In New Orleans, the Pelicans beat the Barons three out of four games to move within 2.5 games of league-leading Atlanta. After games played on July 7, with each contending team having four games left to play through July 11, the standings were:

	Won	Lost	Winning Percentage	Games Behind
Atlanta	51	35	.593	
Birmingham	50	38	.568	2
New Orleans	50	39	.562	2.5
Chattanooga	48	41	.539	4.5

Although Atlanta had played mediocre ball since July 2, the team had gained a full game over Birmingham. But New Orleans had moved one game closer to first. Any of these three teams could still win the honor, and the upcoming four-game series between the Crackers and the Barons in Atlanta's Ponce de Leon Park between July 8 and July 11 now loomed crucial. This "All-Star Series" or "All-Star Showdown," or "July's own Little Dixie Series," as the Atlanta sportswriters called it, excited fans in Birmingham and Atlanta and generated hometown boosterism in both cities. The Atlanta sportswriters predicted large crowds for the series, especially for the opener on July 8, which could potentially determine the winner of the race.[8]

SHOWDOWN SERIES: BIRMINGHAM AT ATLANTA

Of the three teams vying for the All-Star game, Atlanta certainly had the best chance. To bring the game to Atlanta, the Crackers had to win only one of their four games with the Barons while the Pelicans had to lose one of their four games with the Bears. That outcome would give Atlanta first place by .002 points over Birmingham and .008 points over New Orleans. Two Atlanta wins over Birmingham would give the Crackers the All-Star game even if the Pelicans swept four games from Mobile. For Birmingham to win the honor, the Barons would have to sweep their four-game series on the road in Atlanta. For New Orleans to get the game, the Pelicans would have to sweep the Bears while the Barons took three of four from the Crackers.

Conditions were perfect for baseball when the Crackers and the Barons squared off on July 8 in Ponce de Leon Park for the opening contest of their decisive four-game series. The temperature at game time was a comfortable 77 degrees under clear skies. An excited crowd of 6,537, one of the largest of the season to date, came to cheer on the Crackers to, as they hoped, a victory that, combined with a Pelican loss in Mobile, would give Atlanta the All-Star game. The throng included the mother, sister, and fat teenage brother, Joe, of Cracker first baseman Frank Torre—they had traveled from New York to watch the slick-fielding infielder and his teammates take on the Barons.[9] The Crackers did not disappoint. They convincingly defeated the Barons 6–3 behind Bill George's stellar pitching, third baseman Paul Rambone's sensational defense, which stifled three Baron rallies, and an offense that banged out eleven hits, including eighth-inning home runs by catcher Jack Parks and shortstop Billy Porter that iced the game. Atlanta's victory dropped Birmingham to third place, eliminated the Barons from contention for the All-Star game, and brought the Crackers one step closer to getting it. All they needed now was a New Orleans loss to Mobile. But the Pelicans beat the Bears 4–1, keeping their slim hopes alive. The race for the midseason extravaganza would continue for at least one more day.

WSB-TV televised the game, and a slight rain had fallen during the day, but still an enthusiastic crowd of 6,770 fans turned out for ladies night on July 9. They watched Birmingham deny Atlanta the victory they needed to clinch. While Cracker batters squandered four opportunities to score, the Barons broke up a deadlocked pitchers' duel with solo runs in the eighth and ninth innings to defeat Atlanta 2–0. In Mobile the Pelicans won again, downing the Bears 5–1 and keeping their hopes alive. The location of the game was still undecided, with Atlanta and New Orleans each having two games left to play.

On Saturday, July 10, a crowd of 8,293, the second-largest of the season to date, watched the Crackers lose yet another game to the Barons, 6–4. Atlanta scored all its runs on pitcher Dick Donovan's two-run homer in the fifth inning and second baseman Frank DiPrima's two-run shot in the ninth. Otherwise, Cracker pitching faltered and the offense sputtered, collecting a measly five hits and striking out ten times, and the infield defense simply collapsed, committing errors and bad judgment. New Orleans pounded Mobile again, 12–7.

Going into games scheduled for the crucial day, July 11, the standings of the top four teams:

	Won	Lost	Winning Percentage	Games Behind
Atlanta	52	37	.584	
New Orleans	53	39	.576	0.5
Birmingham	52	39	.571	1
Chattanooga	50	41	.549	3

The race would go down to the wire in a photo finish between Atlanta and New Orleans. Atlanta still had

the better chance. A Pelican loss to the Bears or a Cracker victory over the Barons would ensure first place for Atlanta. Despite the Crackers' poor performance in the last two games, circumstances strongly favored them against Birmingham on July 11. Their scheduled starting pitcher was Leo Cristante, who, at 16-4, easily led the league in wins. Moreover, Cristante had rightly earned the nickname "Baron Killer," having beaten Birmingham eight straight times in the past two seasons.[10] New Orleans could still cop the All-Star game, but the path to it was more demanding. The Pelicans had to win again and had to depend on the Barons to defeat the Crackers one more time. With Cristante on the mound for Atlanta, that seemed a Herculean task.

"LOVE AND LUCK TO MY BROTHERS"

Earl Mann, the Crackers' owner, had staged for Ponce de Leon Park a one-hour concert, featuring some of the biggest names in country-western music, to take place before what was now shaping up as the most important game of the season.[11] While Hank Snow, the Smith Brothers, Boots Woodall, and other performers created a carnival atmosphere for the fans—the official attendance was 8,385—Atlanta manager Whitlow Wyatt, the former pitching star for the Brooklyn Dodgers, created a sober, solemn atmosphere in the Cracker clubhouse. He read aloud to the players an inspirational and heartwarming letter he had received from a 15-year-old girl, Billye Hinson, an only child from Lawrenceville, Georgia.[12] It was dated July 8. Greeting him as "Pop," the youngster was thrilled that Wyatt, a total stranger and a very busy and famous man, had responded to her first letter. Although she had heard before the advice Whitlow had offered her, "never did it mean so much, or was it said so beautifully as it was in your letter. I guess that's because this time it came from someone great, who has really had a chance to know." Billye was especially elated with Whitlow's permission to adopt him and the players as her brothers. She provided her new "wonderful brothers" with a religious poem, extolling the virtues of Christian labor. The young girl concluded with an appeal for patience and understanding: "I hope you don't mind hearing all my problems and troubles, and I hope you don't mind how often I write. All I can say is thanks for everything. Give my love and luck to my brothers. You have my prayers, blessings, luck and best wishes for all." Whitlow and some of the playerschoked up during the reading, struggling to hold back tears.[13]

Just before the start of the game, Whitlow again surprised his players and everybody else. This time he

Operation Ticktock is what the Atlanta players nicknamed the race to host the Southern Association All-Star game in 1954. Players on the hosting team would receive a wristwatch valued at $75. Shown here is the watch awarded to Cracker infielder William Porter.

irked Leo Cristante and shocked the sportswriters and fans on hand at the ballpark by giving the starting pitching assignment to left-hander Bill George. Whitlow believed that Birmingham had difficulty against left-handers, and George had already defeated the Barons once this series. When asked about Cristante's uncanny string of victories against Birmingham, Wyatt tersely responded, "I never beat anybody with a jinx yet. You beat or get beat on the field, not with a jinx."[14] Whitlow's strategy backfired—badly.

CRUNCH TIME

Working on only two days' rest, George yielded four hits and four runs in one-third of an inning before Wyatt replaced him with another left-hander, Dick Kelly. The park organist, Johnnie Nutting, played "Say It Isn't So."[15] But it was. The Crackers were in grave danger of losing again to the Barons and of losing the All-Star game to the Pelicans, who were leading the Bears 1–0 in the third inning.

The Crackers battled back, pushing across two runs in the second inning and two more in the third to tie the score 4–4. And with Cristante finally on the mound, victory seemed hopeful. The "Baron Killer" promptly gave up two runs, giving Birmingham back the lead, 6–4. In the fifth and again in the sixth innings, the Crackers put the tying runners on base, but the offense floundered, stranding them. The score remained 6–4 when news arrived that New Orleans was leading Mobile, 3–1, in the sixth inning.

JIM SOLT

With Birmingham still holding its 6–4 lead, the Crackers had a man on first with two out in the bottom of the seventh inning. Atlanta then caught a huge break when three Baron defenders allowed a high fly ball hit by Cracker catcher Jack Parks to fall harmlessly to the ground in foul territory near the right-field line. Parks walked, and for the third inning in a row the Crackers had two runners on base. Whitlow then called on Jim Solt, the other half of the Cracker catching platoon, to pinch-hit for Cristante, a good-hitting pitcher. Once again the Atlanta manager's strategy surprised the sportswriters in the press box and the fans in the stands.[16] With the count two balls and one strike, Solt guessed that Baron pitcher Dave Benedict would throw a curve. Solt guessed right, and he launched the ball over the left-field fence, just beyond the outstretched glove of left-fielder Dick Tettlebach, for a three-run home run that put the Crackers ahead 7–6. The crowd erupted. The Cracker players mobbed their teammate as he crossed home plate. Solt's electrifying home run thoroughly demoralized the Barons and made the Pelican victory over the Bears irrelevant.[17]

The hard-fought race to host the Southern Association All-Star game, a race that had begun ten days earlier, was now finally over. Solt's improbable blast traveled 350 feet in Atlanta and "was clearly heard 373 miles away in Mobile."[18] Among the shouts heard in the Cracker clubhouse, where the players were celebrating and congratulating each other, especially Solt, with hard slaps on the back, was "operation tick tock completed."[19] The standings after the completion of games played on July 11:

	Won	Lost	Winning Percentage	Games Behind
Atlanta	53	37	.589	
New Orleans	54	39	.581	0.5
Birmingham	52	40	.565	2
Chattanooga	50	43	.538	4.5

On July 15, one day after Atlanta experienced record-setting 98-degree heat, hail, high winds, heavy rain, and the worst electrical storm in years, a crowd of 16,808 fans, the largest to date for a Southern Association All-Star game, turned out to watch the Crackers take on the league's best at Ponce de Leon Park. They crammed every nook and cranny of the ballpark, which seated only 14,500.[20] They "rocked the joint," according to one report, "and most of 'em went away hoarse."[21] Fans began shouting and cheering in the second inning, when the Crackers took a 4-0 lead, and did not stop until the game ended. The Crackers trounced a powerful offensive All-Star lineup, 9–1. A trio of Atlanta hurlers yielded only four base hits, giving up a meaningless run in the eighth inning. Cracker left fielder Bob Montag hit two solo home runs. Catcher Jack Parks hit a three-run home run and had four RBIs. League sportswriters voted Parks the game's most valuable player.

Ironically, Jim Solt, whose home run gave Atlanta the honor of hosting the All-Star game, was not in the lineup. In fact, he was not even in uniform, and he was not at the ballpark. He was at his home in Charleston, South Carolina, tending to his young wife, who was dying of a brain tumor.[22] Mae Jeanette Solt died on November 5, 1954, about five weeks after the season ended.[23]

Jim Solt continued his baseball career for several more years, but never again would he or the Atlanta Crackers experience anything like the first eleven days of July 1954. The great race to host the Southern Association All-Star game ended when Solt, a part-time player and a most unlikely hero, hit the most dramatic home run of his then seven-year career. Furman Bisher, sports editor of the *Atlanta Constitution*, compared it to Bobby Thomson's 1951 shot heard 'round the world. "Solt," he wrote, "is only a cotton-picking Thomson, for his shot was heard just around the Southern Association, not the world. But the situation had everything it takes for a heart attack."[24] Years and even decades later, Solt, Earl Mann, Whitlow Wyatt, and Furman Bisher vividly remembered the most famous and thrilling home run in more than fifty years of Atlanta Cracker baseball history.[25] ∎

Notes

The author would like to thank Tony Yoseloff and the Yoseloff Foundation for the Yoseloff/SABR Baseball Research Grant that helped make this article possible.

1. This article is based primarily on the two Atlanta daily newspapers, the *Atlanta Journal* and the *Atlanta Constitution*, 1–16 July 1954.
2. *Atlanta Journal*, 3 December 1953; *The Sporting News*, 9 December 1953.
3. The Southern Association had used a split season in 1928, 1933, 1934, 1943, and 1944. From 1935 through 1942 and beginning again in 1945, the Southern used the Shaughnessy Playoff system. See Charles Hurth, *Baseball Records: The Southern Association, 1901–1957* (New Orleans: Southern Association, 1957), 7–8.
4. All-Star Game attendance data from Hurth, 130.
5. For reference to the watch and its value, see *Atlanta Constitution*, 13 July 1954; for Southern Association salaries in 1954, see U.S. Congress, House, *Organized Professional Team Sports: Hearings Before the Antitrust Subcommittee of the Committee on the Judiciary*. 85th Cong., 1st sess., 1957, 2483–84.
6. Cracker outfielder, team comedian, and team elder statesman Earl "Junior" Wooten came up with the slogan "Operation Ticktock," and the rest of the players adopted it as their battle cry. See *Atlanta Constitution*, 12 July 1954; *Atlanta Journal*, 13 July 1954.
7. For the 1954 Southern Association schedule, I have used *The Baseball Blue Book*, 1954, 64.
8. *Atlanta Constitution*, 7 and 8 July 1954; *Atlanta Journal*, 7 and 8 July 1954.
9. Photo of the Torres and caption in *Atlanta Constitution*, 9 July 1954.
10. *Atlanta Journal*, 11 July 1954.
11. *Atlanta Constitution*, 6 and 9 July 1954.
12. This letter is printed in full in *Atlanta Journal*, 12 July 1954.
13. *Atlanta Journal*, 12 July 1954.
14. *Atlanta Constitution*, 12 and 13 July 1954.
15. Ibid., 12 July 1954.
16. Ibid.
17. *Atlanta Journal*, 12 July 1954; *Atlanta Constitution*, 12 July 1954. In addition to the game reports and commentary, the *Journal* has a photo sequence of Solt hitting the home run, and the *Constitution* has a photo of the Crackers greeting Solt at home plate.
18. *Atlanta Constitution*, 12 July 1954.
19. Ibid.
20. For seating capacity at Ponce de Leon, I have used *The Baseball Blue Book*, 1954, 25.
21. *Atlanta Constitution*, 16 July 1954.
22. *Atlanta Journal*, 16 July 1954.
23. *Atlanta Constitution*, 17 November 1954.
24. *Atlanta Constitution*, 13 July 1954.
25. Clipping, 1956, Jim Solt file, Sporting News Archives; clipping, *Atlanta Constitution*. 19 July 1958, Charlie Roberts Collection, Atlanta History Center, MS 552, box 12, folder 7; interview with Whitlow Wyatt by Loran Smith (1976), Georgia Sports Hall of Fame Archives; interview with Furman Bisher by the author, 24 February 1999.

Departure Without Dignity

The Athletics Leave Philadelphia

Robert D. Warrington

THE OUTLOOK WASN'T BRILLIANT for the Philadelphia Athletics in 1954. In fact, it was downright bleak. The franchise was beset by problems from all sides. A bad team, sparse crowds, burdensome debt, and internal strife all were set against the backdrop of playing in an old ballpark located in a declining neighborhood with limited parking and bad transportation. Grumblings were being heard from other American League clubs that were dissatisfied with the paltry receipts they were getting from games played in Philadelphia.

It hadn't always been this way. After their founding in 1901, the Athletics had achieved unparalleled success in Philadelphia baseball. After league titles in 1902 and 1905, the club won four more pennants and three World Series championships from 1910 through 1914. A second dynasty emerged when the A's won the AL title three years in a row, 1929 through 1931, and the World Series twice (1929–30).[1] Some baseball historians consider the 1929 team to be the greatest ever to take the field.[2]

WOES ON THE FIELD . . .

Glory days became a dim memory, however, as Connie Mack dismantled his second dynasty, selling off star players, and the Philadelphia Athletics descended into the AL's second division. Last place was where the A's typically could be found in the standings. The World War II years were a particularly awful time for the club. The 1943 team was so awful, with a record of 49–105, that it finished 49 games out of first and even 20 games behind the club in next to last place.[3]

The Athletics showed some signs of resurgence in the late 1940s, finishing above .500 in 1947–49. The 1948 team even contended for the league lead before falling off the pace late in the season. Still, it ended up in fourth place, the club's only finish in the first division from 1934 through 1951.

The A's were supposed to be contenders in 1950. It was the golden jubilee of the AL and of Connie Mack's reign as manager. The club adopted the rallying cry "One more pennant for Connie!" In a blockbuster trade before the season, the Athletics sent four marginal players and $100,000 to the St. Louis Browns for star third baseman Bob Dillinger and outfielder Paul Lehner. The franchise also invested in upgrading Shibe Park. It spent $300,000 to install additional box seats and for other park improvements. In addition, the ballpark's electrical plant was overhauled for $100,000.[4] These were heady sums for an organization known for its lack of funds.

But 1950 turned out to be a bust for the Athletics. The team never was in contention, and Dillinger turned out to be a major disappointment. He was sold to the Pittsburgh Pirates in July for $35,000.[5] The Athletics ended the year at 52–102, firmly in the cellar—and a full 46 games out of first place. To add insult to injury, the Philadelphia Phillies won the National League pennant in 1950, further solidifying that club's status as the ascendant baseball team in the city.

The last four years, 1951–54, of the A's stay in Philadelphia offered little hope for salvation. After a dismal 1951 season that saw the team wind up in sixth place, a brief glimmer of hope appeared in 1952 when the A's again clawed their way up to fourth place with a record slightly above .500 (79–75). But it quickly descended into the all too familiar territory of the AL's second division. The 1953 Athletics finished in seventh place, and the 1954 club notched a woeful record of 51–103, claiming the cellar and trailing the first-place club by a horrifying 60 games.

. . . AND AT THE TURNSTILE

As a rule, fans flock in droves to watch winners and trickle in sparingly to look at losers. This obvious fact was painfully evident as the fortunes of the Philadelphia Athletics unfolded in the late 1940s through mid-1950s. The 1947 A's, playing barely above .500 ball, attracted 911,566 fans through the turnstiles at Shibe Park—a franchise attendance record. When the Athletics actually contended for the pennant in 1948, the club set another attendance record, 945,076. It was the last time the A's would ever outdraw the Phillies.[6]

The disastrously disappointing 1950 Athletics could lure only 309,805 fans to Shibe Park. While the 1952 club boosted the figure to 627,100 with its fourth-place finish, the truly awful 1953 and 1954 A's teams could achieve figures no better than 362,113 and 304,666 respectively.

Not surprisingly, fan support, or lack thereof, affected the organization's financial health. The Athletics' combined profits for the good years of 1947–49 totaled $450,000. However, the 1950 team—it was a flop from the very beginning of the season—wound up losing the franchise $315,000 that year.[7] The Athletics continued to hemorrhage money as the 1950s unfolded. Roy Mack, Connie's son and club vice president, warned early in 1954, "We can't stand another year as bad as the last one."[8]

Lean gate receipts motivated the Macks to cut costs wherever they could, even if it meant sacrificing the team's performance on the diamond. After the 1953 season, the Athletics traded Harry Byrd and Eddie Robinson, whose salaries were on the high end of the club's roster, to the New York Yankees for minor leaguers and marginal players who drew small paychecks for their services. The Yankees also kicked in $25,000 on the deal.[9] This and other belt-tightening player moves helped the A's trim their payroll from more than $400,000 in 1953 to less than $300,000 in 1954.[10]

Front-office personnel moves were also made to cut costs. General manager Arthur Ehlers, who had been with the club since 1950, was fired after the 1953 season, and his responsibilities were transferred to Earle Mack, another of Connie's sons, who already held the portfolio of chief scout. This saved the $20,000 salary that Ehlers had been earning. In addition, A's manager Jimmie Dykes was released after the 1953 season.

Shortstop Eddie Joost was named the team's player-manager at only a 25 percent increase in salary. Again, payroll was saved.[11]

The A's farm system was reduced to six clubs for 1954. With the drawdown, the organization hoped to break even on its minor-league-affiliated clubs, instead of losing money—as much as $200,000—as it had in recent years. Desperate to survive, the A's could not fund efforts to build a talented supply of ball-players for the future.[12]

The impact of the meager finances was devastating to the club. Jimmie Dykes recalled the desperate nature of the times: "The club was sinking into the quicksand of financial catastrophe. . . . Philadelphia had become indifferent to the Athletics. . . . Long years in the second division were taking their toll. . . . We had no money to plug holes, no bench strength."[13]

THE MACK–SHIBE LEADERSHIP

Connie Mack was synonymous with the Philadelphia Athletics. The team's manager since its inception in 1901, Mack was the "Tall Tactician," the "Spindly Strategist," and the "Grand Old Man of Baseball." In his fifty-year tenure (1901–50) at the helm of the A's, Mack notched 3,582 victories, a total exceeded only by his 3,814 defeats.[14] As time marched on, the losses mounted faster than the wins. When in 1943 the club experienced a 20-game losing streak, Mack expressed bewilderment and despair. "I can't understand it," he observed. "It would seem, under the very law of averages that we would get in a winning game somewhere."[15]

Fans vented their ire at the continual losing, and much of it was directed at Connie Mack. Letters to the A's made clear the fans' preferences. One declared, "Why doesn't he [Connie] step down and give a younger man a chance?" Another wrote, "He should know the parade has passed him by."[16] Patrons clearly wanted Mack to go as the Athletics' manager, and they linked the prospect of his departure to any chance the team would have to turn around its abysmal performance.

The great drawback in having Connie Mack as both president and manager of the Athletics became increasingly apparent as the years passed. Only he could fire himself as manager, and he lingered on far too long in that unfulfilled quest for one more pennant-contending team.

With Connie Mack's election as president of the Athletics in January 1937, the Mack family now controlled all of the senior leadership positions in the club's front office. From left: Earle, Connie, and Roy Mack in 1937.

Any other franchise would have let him go at some point during the seventeen years before 1950, a period during which the club finished in the first division only once. But Mack stubbornly held on, defying the wishes from within and outside the organization that he step aside as manager.[17]

As the years passed, Connie Mack's encroaching senility grew more pronounced. The deterioration in his mind was apparent by the mid-1940s, and the team suffered from his mental lapses. Poor trades, incorrect signals from the bench (the most obvious of which coaches would override), sudden acts of emotional rage,[18] and lapses into bygone days during gametime (calling out for past players to pinch-hit) all contributed to the team's woes on the field.[19]

The abysmal 1950 season was the last straw. Sons Roy and Earle pressured Connie, then 87 years old, to give up his managerial role after the season.[20] In the end he agreed, but reluctantly. "I'm not quitting because I'm getting old," he said. "I'm quitting because I think people want me to."[21]

Connie Mack still retained the club's presidency, although he was little more than a figurehead president, given his mental decline. Jimmie Dykes, who followed Mack as field manager, described in his autobiography a meeting with Connie in 1953: "One day before spring training began I went to Roy Mack's home to confer with Mr. Mack. He lay in bed. For an hour and a half I discussed the team. I say discussed the team for he was showing obvious signs of his advanced age. His mind often wandered."[22]

A plan of succession had been devised by Connie Mack. He envisioned the Mack and Shibe families perpetually controlling the Philadelphia Athletics (more on the Shibes later). Mack's intentions were explained in his 1950 autobiography *My 66 Years in the Big Leagues*:

It is my desire always to have a Mack–Shibe combination in our national game. . . . My son Earle will succeed me as manager of the Philadelphia Athletics. My sons Roy and Connie, Jr ., will be associated in the business end and the financial operations. . . . Some people may charge me with forming a dynasty in our national game. Call it what you will. I assure you that the Macks and Shibes are imbued with the spirit of American democracy and will always remain true to the best traditions of American sportsmanship.[23]

Connie Mack signs copies of his 1950 autobiography, *My 66 Years in the Big Leagues*, for young admirers. The book described Mack's intention to perpetuate Mack–Shibe leadership of the Athletics indefinitely, but it was not to be.

After a brief playing career with the Athletics, consisting of one game in 1910, one game in 1911, and two games in 1914, Earle honed his managerial skills for a decade in the minor leagues. He managed teams in the North Carolina League and the Blue Ridge League. In 1924 he was called back to Philadelphia, where he served as the A's coach and assistant manager, positions he would hold for the next twenty-six years.[24] Occasionally, Earle would manage the club in his father's absence. He was universally viewed, including by himself, as the A's heir-apparent manager.[25]

Roy Mack also served his time in the minor leagues, but his role was in the front office, not on the field. He worked as business manager for the Baltimore Orioles for five years and then moved on to become president of the Newark Indians (later Bears). In 1924 he took over as general manager of the Portland Beavers of the Pacific Coast League—an Athletics-affiliated minor-league club. In 1936, Roy was named vice president and secretary of the Philadelphia A's.[26]

Connie Mack Jr., a product of the senior Mack's second marriage, also joined the A's hierarchy. He learned the business of baseball while holding various positions—including managing the concession stands at Shibe Park—in the A's organization in the years before the Second World War. Connie Jr. was appointed assistant treasurer of the Athletics in 1938, and in 1950 he was elevated to the position of club treasurer when Connie Sr. relinquished it.[27]

Then there was the Shibe–MacFarland family. Benjamin Franklin Shibe was the original president of the Philadelphia Athletics, and his sons, Tom and John, held the positions of vice president and secretary–business manager, respectively. When Ben Shibe died in 1922, Tom was elevated to the presidency of the club, while John added the vice presidency to his portfolio of responsibilities.[28]

Tom Shibe died in February 1936. His brother John became A's president the same month, ensuring that a Shibe would remain in that position. With the positions of vice president and secretary now open, Roy Mack was brought into the front office, taking over both posts. John Shibe lasted less than one year in the job, resigning in August 1936, because of illness; he died in 1937. In January of that year, Connie Mack Sr. became A's president, a position he would hold as long as the Athletics continued to call Philadelphia home.[29]

The death of John Shibe marked a fundamental turning point in the ownership of the Philadelphia Athletics. The 50–50 Shibe–Mack ownership structure that had served the A's so well came to an end, and now the preeminent voice of the club's front office belonged solely to the Macks. After John Shibe's death, Connie Mack bought 141 shares of A's stock from his estate, thereby giving the Macks majority ownership of the franchise for the first time. The Mack family held 891 shares to the Shibe–MacFarlands' 609.[30] (The MacFarland family name was added to the list of the Athletics' owners when Ben Shibe's daughter married Frank MacFarland.)

The Shibe–McFarland family did retain some positions in the front office. Benjamin Shibe MacFarland, son of Ben Shibe's daughter, served for years as the traveling (road) secretary of the A's and was promoted to the post of secretary in 1950 when Roy Mack left the job to take on a greater role in helping his aged father run the franchise. Another son, Frank MacFarland Sr., became assistant treasurer in 1950 when Connie Mack Jr. was promoted to treasurer. Finally, grandson Frank MacFarland Jr. entered the A's front office in 1950 as the new traveling secretary, replacing Benjamin Shibe MacFarland.[31]

The diminished role of the Shibe–MacFarland faction in the club's operation after John Shibe's death was clearly reflected in the composition of the Athletics board of directors. Members of the board in 1950 were Connie Mack, Sr., Roy Mack, Earle Mack, Connie Mack Jr., and Benjamin Shibe MacFarland.[32] That year,

1950, proved far more pivotal for the Athletics off the field than on it. A family feud over control of the organization had been festering for several years and pitted the "first" Mack family against the "second" Mack family. The disagreement boiled over with ultimately disastrous consequences for the club and its fans.

THE FAMILY FEUD

There were three intersecting fissures in the Mack family—based on marriage, generation, and sex—that created conflict over the question of who would take the reins of power once Connie Mack departed the scene. Mack had two families. His first wife, Margaret, bore Connie two sons, Roy and Earle, and a daughter, Marguerite, before dying at a young age in 1892, less than three weeks after giving birth to Marguerite. Connie married again in 1910, and his second wife, Katherine, gave birth to four girls and one boy, Connie Mack Jr.[33]

Connie Mack wanted his three sons to succeed him in running the Athletics. But between Roy and Earle on one side and Connie Jr. on the other, there was a general divide that soon enough began to manifest itself in their different approaches to running the club. Harry Paxton captured the dilemma in his assessment of the franchise:

> Young Connie had come to share the dissatisfaction of many Philadelphians with the cautious, low-budget manner in which the family was operating the team. He was constantly proposing changes—which just as consistently were opposed. In the eyes of Connie Jr., Roy and Earle were old mossbacks blindly resisting progress. To Roy and Earle, young Connie was an interfering upstart with a lot of half-baked ideas.[34]

The situation was made worse by the mental incapacity of Connie Mack Sr. As club president, he was positioned to arbitrate and settle such disputes, but his lack of fortitude contributed to prolonging the friction. "Old Mr. Mack," as Paxton notes, "then well into his eighties and grown somewhat indecisive, was swayed first by one side and then the other."[35]

Intent on having his three sons eventually take over the club, Connie Mack transferred 163 of his shares each to Roy, Earle, and Connie Jr. He also gave 100 shares of A's stock to his wife, Katherine, the mother of Connie Mack Jr. Connie Sr. kept the remaining 302 shares of stock for himself.[36]

The daughters of the first and second marriages got

nothing. The decision to exclude the daughters, who never had any role in the organization, provoked considerable tension between Connie and his wife. Bruce Kuklick, in his landmark study of the Athletics' Shibe Park and its place in Philadelphia history, notes that Connie Sr. envisioned the three male heirs—Roy, Earle, and Connie Jr.—running the franchise in concert once he (Connie) gave up the reins of power.[37] Kuklick writes of the discord that resulted from the senior Mack's decision to exclude his daughters from the ranks of stockholders:

> His wife had other ideas. Mack's plan would ultimately give power to Roy and Earle, the surviving children of the first marriage. The second Mrs. Mack proposed that her husband distribute stock in equal shares to her, to each of her five children (four of whom were female), to Roy, to Earle, and to the children of Mack's deceased daughter from his first marriage. Controlling interest in the club would then go not to the men but to the family of the second marriage (and, indeed, to the women). So adamant was Katherine Mack that the couple separated, her husband leaving the house when they could not agree.[38]

This unpleasantness occurred in 1946–47. The couple reconciled after a few months, but Connie did not relent on the stock allocation. Resentment within the Mack family over the issue lingered, and, as will be seen, it also had adverse consequences for the business relationship between the Mack and Shibe–MacFarland families. The discord would surface with particular ugliness in 1950.

The generational difference that divided Connie Jr. from Roy and Earle strained their ability to cooperate, according to Paxton. The proposals of Connie Jr. to invigorate the Athletics and refurbish Shibe Park were opposed by Roy and Earle because of the sizable price tags associated with the moves. As Roy often pointed out, the last time the A's had declared a dividend for stockholders was in 1931 (the team's last trip to the World Series). He was not inclined to spend large sums on the team or its ballpark, preferring instead to keep expenses down, especially given the club's low attendance figures.[39]

In the face of this resistance and supported by his mother, young Connie broke ranks with the "first" Mack family and made an alliance with the Shibe–MacFarland clan before the 1950 season. By adding

Katherine and Connie Mack in 1946 around the time they separated temporarily in a dispute over how Athletics' stock should be divided among the children of the first and second Mack marriages.

his 163 shares to his mother's 100 shares, and combining it with the Shibe–MacFarland's 609 shares, the coalition amassed by Connie Jr. could outvote his half-brothers and father 872 to 628.[40]

With this shift in power, Paxton notes, the A's started making major moves, including the investment of those significant sums to improve Shibe Park in 1950; Bob Dillinger was acquired to increase the Athletics' offensive punch. To introduce some new blood to the coaching staff for the 1950 season, Al Simmons and Earle Brucker were fired and replaced by Mickey Cochrane and Bing Miller.[41]

The alliance between Connie Mack Jr. and the Shibe–MacFarland family also recognized that it was time for Connie Sr. to retire as manager, but for several reasons it decided not to press the issue until after the 1950 season. First, the "Golden Anniversary" of the A's founding and Mack's longevity as the team's manager was central to the club's promotional and advertising campaign for 1950. Removing him during the season would undermine whatever sentimental motivation the club hoped to generate among fans to come to the ballpark to honor the venerable team manager on this special anniversary.

In any case, Mack's role as manager was actually only marginal. Most on-field decisions and daily operations were being handled by the coaches. Yet another reason for postponing the delicate business of relieving Connie Sr. of his managerial duties was that it was soon apparent that the 1950 season was going to be another losing campaign and that replacing him wouldn't salvage the situation. He could be eased out later, during the off-season, under the guise of retirement, instead of in a potentially messy effort to try to force him out during the season. The former course would appear voluntary and dignified, while the latter could alienate fans, who might view it as unseemly and harsh treatment for such a revered figure. Roy and Earle actually agreed with Connie Jr.'s group on the need for a new manager.

Shaking up the A's hierarchy, however, began long before Connie Sr. was eased out as manager at season's end. At a meeting of the board of directors on May 26, 1950, Earle Mack was removed as assistant manager of the Athletics and replaced by Jimmie Dykes.[42] Dykes would direct day-to-day operation of the team and be positioned to take over as manager after the 1950 season. It was also at this meeting that Mickey Cochrane was named the A's general manager.[43]

Earle's role as manager in waiting, as Connie Sr.'s hand-picked successor, was ended; he was given the job of "chief scout" in the club's minor-league system. These moves were orchestrated by Connie Jr.,[44] who, according to Kuklick, voted with his allies against his father for the first time.[45] Outside the Mack family, the move was regarded as positive. Earle was not respected by Athletics players. "You wouldn't listen to him," one of them said. Another commented, "Earle, I don't think he knew too much about baseball."[46]

The split between Connie Jr. and his two older half-brothers was now out in the open. Power was slipping from the hands of Connie Sr., Roy, and Earle. But the situation had become untenable. The Athletics were losing games and bleeding money throughout the 1950 season. Leadership tensions and factional rivalries were contributing to problems on and off the field. Something had to be done to eliminate the fractured hierarchy.

ROY AND EARLE TAKE OVER

Connie Jr. made the first move. As the 1950 season unfolded disastrously, he came to the conclusion that the Athletics would never prosper under the Mack family. His solution was to sell all the stock to a new ownership group that would have the resources, unity, and drive to resuscitate the club. Young Connie was supported in this conviction by his mother and the Shibe–MacFarland family.[47]

James P. Clark, a local trucking magnate, who two years earlier had organized a syndicate to buy the Philadelphia Eagles football team, expressed interest in buying the Athletics. Baseball writer Art Morrow of the *Philadelphia Inquirer* broke the story.[48] Other groups also showed interest. On June 12, the A's announced that the club would not be sold in 1950.[49] Roy Mack declared that, if Connie Jr., his mother, and the Shibe–MacFarland family wanted to sell their A's stock, they should first give the other Macks a chance to buy it. "Eventually," Paxton notes,

> this was agreed to. On July 31, it was announced that Roy and Earle—not always in agreement on other things but united on this issue—had been given a thirty-day option to purchase the stock of young Connie's group. If they failed to do so, then the other side would have forty-five days to buy out Roy and Earle.[50]

The price set for the 872 shares of stock held by Connie Jr., his mother, and the Shibe–MacFarland family was $2,000 a share, or a total of $1,744,000. Connie Jr. did not believe Roy and Earle could raise that kind of money and never expected the option to be exercised.[51] He was wrong.

In mid-July, Roy began planning to take out a loan for the money. One of his attorneys, Frank Schilpp, pitched the proposal to Gordon Burlingame, a Philadelphia-based representative of the Connecticut General Life Insurance Company. Within three weeks, a mortgage for $1,750,000 had been approved for the American Base Ball Club of Philadelphia. Shibe Park was used as collateral for the loan.[52] Roy and Earle could now buy out Connie Jr.'s group.

The long struggle waged by the Mack family for control of the Philadelphia Athletics ended on August 28, 1950, with the signing of papers in a Philadelphia law office.[53] The stock held by Connie Jr., his mother, and the Shibe–MacFarland family was bought in the name of the club rather than by Roy and Earle as individuals. All of the 872 shares went into the club treasury. The only active A's stock remaining were the shares held by Connie Sr. (302), Roy (163), and Earle (163).[54]

Ending the family battle over control of the Athletics did not ease the club's chronic financial straits or result in success between the white lines, but it did create a burdensome debt to repay. Unlike payrolls, mortgages couldn't be cut. Paxton writes:

> The mortgage payments were set at $200,000 a year for the first five years, and $160,000 a year for the next five, at the end of which the princi-

ple will be down to $483,000. Without this extra burden, the Mack brothers would be in good shape today [1954]. As it is, they still have a tough row to hoe. They can't afford even moderate losses for very long.[55]

After Roy and Earle took control of the Philadelphia Athletics, the franchise broke even in 1951 and 1952, according to Roy, and lost $100,000 dollars in 1953, a disappointing season.[56] To help make the mortgage payments in full and on time, the Mack brothers turned over to Connecticut General the rent that the club got from the Phillies to play at Shibe Park.[57]

Temporarily short of working capital on some occasions, the Mack brothers took cash advances from Jacobs Brothers, the company that now ran the concession stands at Shibe Park, and they may also have borrowed capital from the American League treasury.[58]

But scraping by financially was hardly a formula for long-term stability or success. One observer commented in 1954 that "Roy and Earle have neither the talent nor the money to keep the A's fighting."[59] Moreover, although they were now running the show, Roy and Earle were fighting over operation of the franchise. They sniped at each other from different offices in Connie Mack Stadium. (Shibe Park was renamed Connie Mack Stadium before the 1953 season.)

The club announced that it needed at least 13,000 fans at every home game to reach its goal of an attendance of 550,000 for the 1954 season. Reaching that figure, according to the A's, would enable them to meet their financial obligations. But average attendance at home games throughout the season stayed stuck at less than half that figure, resulting in the end-of-year total of only a sliver more than three hundred thousand.[60]

In June 1954, the Mack brothers informed Philadelphia mayor Joseph Clark that they would have to sell the Athletics unless attendance at A's games leapt dramatically. Sale of the franchise, they warned, most likely would result in its relocation to another city. Roy and Earle may have hoped to rally public opinion around the A's and improve the club's finances, but it was an ill-fated gambit. Fans were not roused by threats about the team's uncertain future. Clark turned out to be an apathetic ally of the Athletics, and the "Save the A's" campaign largely fizzled.[61]

THE MACKS' PERSPECTIVE ON THE FUTURE OF THE A'S

Three options loomed large for the future of the Philadelphia Athletics once the 1954 season had ended. First, the Macks could sell the team to Philadelphia buyers who would keep it in the city. Second, the Macks could continue operating the A's in Philadelphia but share power with new investors who would have money to revitalize the club. Third, they could sell to outside buyers who would move the club elsewhere. What did the Macks want?

Connie Mack Sr., architect of the Athletics' former greatness, had spent years planning for the franchise to remain under the perpetual control of the Mack and Shibe–MacFarland families. With the buyout of the Shibe–MacFarland and "second" Mack families in 1950, that dream was over, but nonetheless he held on to his vision of the Athletics remaining a Philadelphia franchise and the permanent property of the "first" Mack family. Connie still wanted the A's to remain the permanent property of the "first" Mack family and for the club to stay in Philadelphia. But his skills and judgment eroded by increasing senility, he was long past being the dominant force in charting the club's future. A figurehead president who still owned the largest block of A's shares, Connie Sr. in 1954 could express his preferences, but no longer could he impose his will.

No longer destined to manage the club, Earle Mack was content to sell his shares and retire. Like his father, Earle preferred that the Athletics stay in Philadelphia, but he was not insistent that the club remain under sole Mack control or that he be given a position in the new leadership hierarchy. One commentator, writing in 1954, noted that Earle "would be happy to retire," and Earle himself was quoted as saying, "If the team goes to another city, I won't go with it."[62] His inclination to take the money and leave made Earle more of a passive observer of events as they unfolded than an active participant in them.

With Connie's infirmity and Earle's docility, the power to decide the Athletics' future fell, by default, to Roy Mack. As vice president, he represented the A's at AL ownership meetings, wielded power in the club's front office, and would represent the franchise in any negotiations about its future. Unlike his brother, Roy wanted to preserve the club as Mack property, with himself in charge. Roy was determined to become the A's president even if it meant bringing in outside investors to buy out Connie and Earle. Indeed, Roy went so far as to state that he wanted to run the Athletics even if it meant moving the club out of Philadelphia and to a new location.[63]

The Philadelphia Athletics board of directors would pose no problems for whatever the Macks decided. Connie Mack Jr. and Benjamin Shibe MacFarland had been removed from the board after they sold their

The long struggle over control of the A's ended on August 28, 1950, when Roy and Earle took out a loan to buy the shares held by Connie Mack Jr., Katherine Mack, and the Shibe family. The loan left the club heavily in debt. Shown at the signing of the purchase agreement are, from left, attorney Robert Walker and Connie, Earle, and Roy Mack.

stock in 1950. In 1954, the board consisted of Connie Sr., Roy, Earle, Tommy Richardson (president of the Eastern League and a longtime Mack family friend), and Gordon Burlingame, representing the Connecticut General Life Insurance Company. As a condition of the deal that Roy and Earle made with Connecticut General to secure the loan in 1950 that enabled them buy out other shareholders, it would have a representative on the board. The agreement, however, also stipulated that the representative would have no say in club policy as long as the franchise did not become delinquent in its mortgage payments. In addition, the company would make no effort to have the A's sold or moved as long as mortgage installment payments continued to be paid on time.[64] They always were.

SUITORS APLENTY

There never was any shortage of suitors seeking to buy the Philadelphia Athletics. As noted, Jim Clark exhibited strong, serious interest in 1950. Earle in 1951 was on the verge of selling his stock to a Philadelphia group that pledged that the franchise would not be relocated and that Connie Sr. would remain the club president. When they heard of the idea, however, Roy and his father pressured Earle to kill the deal, which he did.[65]

Reports surfaced that several Philadelphia-based groups were forming in 1954 to buy the A's and keep the club in the city. Two such initiatives, one organized by advertising executive Babe Alexander and the other by restaurant owner Jim Peterson, were said to be underway, but it is unclear if either of these efforts

ever got beyond the talking stage.[66] A more serious undertaking was led by Harry Sylk, president of Philadelphia's Sun Ray Drug Company, who promised to match the price offered by any other potential buyer and to not move the A's out of the city if Connie Sr., Earle, and Roy would agree to sell their stock to his investment group.[67]

No deal was struck to buy the Athletics during the 1954 season because Roy was not prepared to sell the franchise outright. He needed and sought an infusion of funds from outside investors. His goal was to buy out his father and brother, not exit with them in relinquishing ownership. Roy recognized, of course, that any investment group would want a role in running the Athletics. He was prepared to have seated on the board of directors representatives who would replace Connie and Earle—an arrangement along the lines of the one with Connecticut General. But Roy wanted to run the Philadelphia Athletics as its new president, a position he had spent many long years coveting since becoming vice president in 1936

Exactly what role and influence Roy would have under a new leadership arrangement (that is, once Connie and Earle had left) was a thorny issue for all potential suitors. Most accepted that Roy and his son Connie Mack III would have to be given front-office posts to gain Roy's acquiescence to a deal. Given Roy's dubious record in running the club, however, no investors wanted him to become the A's president or wield operational control of the franchise.[68] Besides, if a "new" Athletics club was going to emerge from the debris of the "old" Mack regime, it would make sense that the change would start at the top, with a non-Mack being put in charge. Roy's desire for the presidency and its authority remained a stumbling block in negotiations, and he would not be dissuaded from his goal until events forced him to abandon it.[69]

Not all of the potential buyers were Philadelphia-based. Hovering around the Athletics like a vulture circling a wounded animal was Arnold Johnson, a Chicago businessman, investor, and vice chairman of the Automatic Canteen Co. of America. Eager to buy the club and move it to Kansas City, Missouri, Johnson was backed in his bid by the powerful owners of the New York Yankees, with whom he had extensive personal and business dealings. Johnson owned Yankee Stadium.[70]

In August 1954, Johnson officially made his bid to purchase the Philadelphia Athletics, offering $4.5 million for the franchise with the avowed intention of moving it to Kansas City. Johnson's assessment of the A's was that there was "nothing wrong that a few million dollars won't cure."[71] According to some reports, Connie and Earle expressed interest, but the recalcitrant Roy declined the offer, still seeking funds that would enable him to buy out his father and brother so he could take control of the club.[72]

JUST SELL THE PHILADELPHIA ATHLETICS OR SELL AND RELOCATE THEM?

A fundamental question that surrounded the various offers being made to buy the A's was whether the franchise should be sold to new owners who would keep it in Philadelphia or to new owners who would move it to a different city. Precedent had been established by Major League Baseball the previous two years in dealing with cities that had two clubs one of which was beleaguered. The beleaguered clubs had been relocated.

Boston and St. Louis each had fielded two major-league clubs, and in both cases the weaker team had been transferred to a new city in an effort to improve its fortunes. The Boston Braves had moved west after the 1952 season to become the Milwaukee Braves, and after the 1953 season the St. Louis Browns had moved east to become the Baltimore Orioles. The new locations had had an initial galvanizing effect, at least as measured by attendance. The Boston Braves had drawn 281,278 in 1952, and the next year the Milwaukee Braves drew 1,826,397. Similarly, the St. Louis Browns drew 297,238 in 1953, and in 1954 the Baltimore Orioles drew 1,060,910.[73]

Fan interest in a ballclub recently relocated could not be sustained indefinitely by the initial enthusiasm over its arrival in its new city. Still, the explosion in attendance that followed the transfer of the Braves and Browns to new cities strongly suggested that moving the Philadelphia A's would produce the same result for the short term.[74] This influenced the owners in their deliberations about what to do with weaker franchises. Their goal was not just to stabilize tottering clubs but also to maximize the profitability of gate receipts for all franchises on the road.

Those who felt that selling the Athletics but not moving them was an inadequate remedy to the club's problems embraced the notion that relocation was essential to the project of rescuing floundering franchises. AL president William Harridge was convinced that the Athletics' situation in Philadelphia could not be salvaged because the club could never again attract enough fans to save it from financial collapse. His position was that the A's must be moved.[75] The extent to which Harridge's belief was shared by AL owners would become apparent as they gathered to discuss what to do about the Athletics.

THE AL OWNERS MEET

On September 28, 1954, AL owners met in New York to discuss the sale and transfer of the Athletics.[76] The meeting ended inconclusively, but league owners made it clear that they wanted the problem to be resolved and the Athletics to be returned to sound financial footing. Roy was given two weeks to obtain enough funding to buy the club from Connie and Earle. AL owners met again on October 12 in Chicago, where Roy informed them that he had been unable to raise enough money[77] and, after a fair amount of browbeating by Harridge and those owners in favor of the Johnson offer, agreed that that deal should go through.[78]

Earle didn't need much convincing. He was eager to be bought out and to retire comfortably. "We're licked," he said after the September 28 meeting. "We haven't a chance and I can't imagine why Roy insists upon trying."[79] On his way to the AL owners' meeting of October 12, Earle commented that "before I left Philadelphia last night, my stepmother [the second Mrs. Connie Mack] told me that I had to press for a sale to Johnson because, if I didn't, my father and I would be broke."[80]

Other offers to purchase the club, including those originating from Philadelphia, were rejected as inadequate at the October 12 meeting. "They talked in millions," Harridge observed about the other suitors, "but they produced no money."[81] Johnson was given the go-ahead to finalize a settlement with the Mack family. In giving his consent to sell Johnson all of the A's stock, Roy added a proviso that he and his brother be given until the following Monday, October 18, to contemplate and complete the sale.[82]

AN APPEARANCE OF SALVATION

Little noticed at the meeting was a Philadelphia sales executive, Jack Rensel, who told a story about a syndicate that was being formed to rescue the Athletics and keep them in the city. When Roy announced at the end of the meeting that he was going back to Philadelphia to discuss the club's sale with his wife, there was Rensel at his heels and whispering into his ear.[83]

On October 15, a group of wealthy Philadelphia businessmen, headed by auto dealer John P. Crisconi, announced they could pay top dollar to buy the Athletics and keep the team in Philadelphia. The prospect of a last-minute rescue of the A's, one baseball historian has written, "had overtones of an old-time melodrama."[84]

It was a dramatic turnabout. The Macks agreed to sell the Athletics to the group of Philadelphia businessmen, and, in an event that was well covered by the press, signed papers formalizing the sale on October 17, 1954.[85] This was one day before the deadline Roy had established to finalize the sale of the club to Johnson.

One of the photographs accompanying this story captures the moment: Roy Mack affixes his signature

to the documents of sale. Standing in the back row are Roy's son (Connie Mack III) and members of the syndicate who organized to buy the Athletics. The photograph's original caption begins: "Philadelphia Athletics baseball team will remain in Philadelphia."

According to the agreement, nine persons would each hold an equal share of the total stock of the Philadelphia Athletics. The syndicate would put up $4,000,000 to buy the club and get it out of debt. Connie Mack Sr. would receive $604,000 in cash for his 302 shares; Earle would get $450,000 in cash for his 163 shares; Roy would get the same amount as Earle for his shares but would take only $200,000 of it in cash and then, as a partner in the new ownership, would reinvest the remaining $250,000 for his one-ninth share of the club. Roy also would be given a senior position in the front office to help run the club.[86] The Connecticut General Life Insurance Company would get $1,200,000 to pay off what remained of its mortgage on the A's ballpark. Another $500,000 of the syndicate's investment would be used to liquidate other debts the club had accumulated.[87]

Roy emerged from the meeting apparently delighted. "I have notified William Harridge, president of the American League," he said, "that we have agreed to sell to this fine group of civic-minded Philadelphia businessmen. I have requested league approval. I am very, very happy to be able to keep the A's in Philly. That has always been my goal."[88] Harridge

Roy Mack affixes his signature to an agreement selling the Athletics to the Philadelphia syndicate on October 17, 1954—a commitment Roy would betray just a day later in a backroom deal with Arnold Johnson. Standing left to right in the back row: Paul Harron, Barney Fischer, Ted R. Hanff, Connie Mack III, Jack Rensel, Morton Liebman, Isadore S. Sley, John Crisconi, and Joseph Liebman. Sitting left to right at the table: Arthur A. Gallagher; Roy, Connie, and Earle Mack; and Arthur Rosenberg.

instructed Roy to send him a telegram containing complete details of the sale and conceded that Johnson's gambit to buy the Athletics looked dead. Harridge commented to the press that "it was a case of Roy Mack changing his mind after he told us he was willing to sell his stock to Mr. Johnson."[89]

THE FISHERS ROAD FIX

Arnold Johnson was on an airplane flying from Chicago to Philadelphia with his attorney Edward L. Vollers when sale of the A's to the Philadelphia syndicate was announced. Johnson was thunderstruck at the announcement, which he heard about after his plane had landed. "It doesn't sound too good to me," he was quoted as saying. "Roy Mack had a much better deal with me. I was going to make him a vice president at a high salary and he would have been a key factor in the Kansas City setup."[90]

Johnson didn't mention Earle, who was still eager to sell his shares and retire. After the sale to the Philadelphia syndicate was announced, Earle was asked by reporters what role, if any, he would play in the new organization. "I'll hang around the ballpark," he said, "and advise a little bit on some of the players."[91]

Roy, however, wanted to continue working in the front office after the club was sold, even if he couldn't be president, and to secure a management position in the organization for his son, Connie Mack III.[92] This provided some of the leverage Johnson needed to work on Roy and change his mind about selling the Athletics to the Philadelphia syndicate before AL owners met again on October 28, purportedly to finalize the sale of the A's to new ownership.[93]

Johnson sought an immediate meeting with Roy to talk over the situation. On the evening of October 17 he sent Roy a telegram, which read in part:

> Dear Roy: Unbelievable that you would not talk to me or let me see you before you went off the deep end [that is, agreed to sell the club to the Philadelphia syndicate]. Would appreciate courtesy of you calling me at Warwick [hotel] in the morning. Suggest you do not sign until you get all the facts. Your future and your son's future are at stake.[94]

Johnson went on in the telegram to tell Roy about certain changes that had been made to the offer that he, Johnson, was making for the A's. It was now possible for him, Johnson said, to offer Roy "a stock interest in the club in Kansas City, a substantial sum of cash, and a work contract not only for himself but for his son."[95]

The two agreed to meet on Monday morning, October 18, at Roy's house at 423 Fishers Road, Bryn Mawr, Pennsylvania. The meeting allowed Johnson to make the case that his offer was more lucrative for Roy and his son than the one made by the Philadelphia syndicate. Johnson also stressed repeatedly that his offer came with the assurance that Roy and his son would have roles in the front office of the Kansas City Athletics. Roy's wife came out on Johnson's side, describing his offer as meaning "financial assurance for all the parties concerned." During the meeting, Roy addmited that he felt he had been coerced into signing the sale agreement with the Philadelphia syndicate.[96]

If in the drawn-out and complicated process of selling the Athletics a single event could be identified as the one at which the club's fate to leave Philadelphia was sealed, it would be this meeting at Roy's house on October 18. Johnson acknowledged as much later when he said:

> After it was all over and we had the club, Roy mentioned to me that this telegram [the one, quoted above, that Johnson sent on October 17] had turned the trick. It had stated exactly what I was prepared to do. He and his wife talked over the matter and they agreed that as far as their own interests were concerned there were great advantages to my proposition as compared to the one which the Philadelphia group had made.[97]

WHAT MADE THE DIFFERENCE?

It is difficult to know precisely which features of Johnson's proposal convinced Roy to turn his back on the syndicate. Ernest Mehl, the Kansas City sports editor, in his book about the Athletics' relocation hinted at the answer when he wrote that Johnson's offer "was considerably more attractive."[98] The differences may have involved the amount of upfront cash that Roy would get for his A's stock and the circumstances under which he and his son would get positions in the front office under the new ownership. The promise of the front-office positions was common to the offers made by both Johnson and the Philadelphia syndicate. And payment for Roy's stock was the same in both cases— $450,000. The syndicate deal, however, involved Roy reinvesting more than half of that, or $250,000, to buy a one-ninth interest in the new ownership, and the front-office positions for him and his son were linked to that.

That Roy would receive the full $450,000 in cash from Johnson for his A's shares, and that positions in the front office for Roy and his son were not dependent on investing any of that money in the Kansas City

Athletics—these were probably the deciding factors for Roy as he switched his allegiance from the syndicate to Johnson. Mehl confirms that Johnson gave Roy and Earle each a check for $450,000 for their shares of Athletics' stock and that Roy and his son were given front-office positions once the club moved to Kansas City.[99]

Whether Johnson's telegram in which he offered Roy a stock interest in the Kansas City Athletics was ever acted on remains unclear. There was one report that Roy invested a portion of his proceeds from the sale of the Philadelphia A's to buy stock in the new Kansas City franchise, but the amount was unknown.[100] Johnson already had his investment group formed, however, and he did not need—and it is highly doubtful he wanted—Roy as part of that group.

SABOTAGING THE PHILADELPHIA-SYNDICATE DEAL

Roy's change of heart made an already convoluted situation even messier. He was legally bound to transfer ownership of the Athletics to the Philadelphia syndicate. That agreement, moreover, had been signed not only by Roy but also by his brother Earle and father Connie, both of whom still supported selling to the syndicate. The AL owners were scheduled to meet at the Waldorf-Astoria Hotel in New York on October 28 to review and vote on the sale of the Athletics to the Philadelphia syndicate, because that was the only deal that existed on paper. Roy had already informed league president Harridge and other AL owners of the Macks' intention to sell the club to the syndicate, not Johnson.

No formal sale agreement existed with Johnson, and, if one was to be concluded, it also would have to be signed by all three of the Macks. Johnson, however, had a powerful ally in the New York Yankees. The influence that the Yankees had on this process was, although exercised primarily beneath the surface, considerable. "In the mid-1950s," as one baseball historian observes, "what the powerful Yankees wanted was generally what happened."[101] There is no doubt what outcome the Yankees favored. "There's been no secret about our position," Yankees president Dan Topping said. "We think it would be best for the American League and best for us to move the A's to Kansas City."[102]

Initially, most AL team owners had responded with "No comment" to news of the Athletics' sale to the Philadelphia syndicate. Only Walter "Spike" Briggs, owner of the Detroit Tigers, who had consistently supported keeping the A's in the city, said he was glad the team was staying put.[103]

Before the October 28 meeting, stories began circulating that the Philadelphia syndicate had raised only $1,400,000 of its "alleged" $4,000,000 bid for the Athletics. One newspaper headline asked, "Did Syndicate Try to Buy A's on Shoestring?"[104] Some syndicate members, according to reports published in the press, were anxious to drop out of the deal because they had discovered that rebuilding the Athletics financially was going to be a far more costly project than they had been led to believe.[105] While such stories were attributed to "league sources" that were never identified, a circumstantial yet persuasive case can be made that they originated with the Yankees and other AL clubs eager to see Johnson get the Athletics.

The meeting of AL owners in New York on October 28 provided the forum for Roy, in concert with others sympathetic to Johnson's bid for the A's, to torpedo the agreement with the Philadelphia syndicate. "Roy found himself legally bound to the deal which had been made with the syndicate," Mehl wrote, "but there was one hope in this for Johnson and that concerned the American League. If it refused to grant approval to the syndicate, the contracts with the Macks were abrogated."[106]

The meeting at the hotel took six hours, and at its end an announcement was made that the sale of the Athletics to the Philadelphia syndicate had failed to receive a vote of approval.[107] A mere majority of five votes (out of eight cast) was required to approve the sale. The final vote was a tie—four in favor of the sale and four opposed. Earl Hilligan, an assistant to Harridge, told the press, "The meeting adjourned to permit the Macks to return to Philadelphia to work out their own problems."[108]

RECRIMINATIONS FOLLOW REJECTION

The rejection was a staggering blow to the Philadelphia syndicate, who, according to newspaper accounts following the meeting, fully anticipated that the deal would be approved.[109] "The decision acted like a bombshell to the members of the syndicate," Mehl wrote. "They had been confident of triumph; they sensed in the decision a reflection upon themselves. Their resentment was expressed as they glared at the retreating forms of the league directors once the decision had been announced."[110]

How the owners voted was supposed to be secret, but information on what happened at the meeting leaked out from knowledgeable sources to the press. Several major newspapers reported that Cleveland, Washington, Chicago, and Detroit voted in favor of the club's sale to the Philadelphia syndicate; New York,

Baltimore, Boston, and Philadelphia cast No votes.[111] In one account, "Other sources declared that Roy Mack, in a last-minute turn-about, walked out on the Philadelphia deal and tossed his support to Arnold Johnson, the Kansas City buyer."[112]

Roy's denial that he cast a No vote has to be viewed with considerable skepticism.[113] According to sources cited in the press after the meeting, he did vote against the deal. Not a single source said he had voted to support it. Syndicate member John Crisconi had no doubt that his group had been the victim of duplicity: "I have reason to believe," he said, "that someone handed us a double-cross. The citizenry of Philadelphia should join with me in this demand for a complete and public explanation of their [the league owners'] action."[114]

It is clear that Roy did not tell syndicate members of his behind-the-scenes deal with Johnson. There is no evidence to indicate that syndicate members were aware, or even suspected, that at the meeting Roy would abandon the agreement in favor of Johnson's bid.

Roy, other than denying he had voted against it, was assiduously vague in his statement to the press following the meeting. "I don't know what to say about anything right now," he said. "We'll have a meeting Monday or Tuesday to talk things over."[115] But in at least one newspaper article his attitude was characterized in unambiguous terms: "Roy Mack, who has been the principal figure in the negotiations, is understood to prefer the Johnson deal, which is personally more beneficial to him and his son."[116]

The owners' meeting allowed Roy to vote to repudiate without legal or financial penalty the sale agreement he had signed with the Philadelphia syndicate less than two weeks earlier. Roy's No vote, moreover, was critical in sending the Athletics on their way out of town. Had he voted Yes, there would have been a simply majority of five owners approving the sale of the Athletics to the Philadelphia syndicate (with Cleveland, Washington, Chicago, and Detroit also supporting the deal).

Roy withheld not only from the syndicate members but also from his brother and father any indication of his transformational conversation with Johnson before the owners' meeting. Connie and Earle were in favor of accepting the syndicate's offer and went into the October 28 meeting expecting that to be the outcome of the deliberations.[117] When Roy voted against it, there surfaced "a divergence of opinion" among the Macks about how their stock should be sold, according to an "insider" source at the meeting.[118] The failure of the Macks to agree among themselves on what action to

take was now an obstacle to their ever approving the sale to the syndicate.[119]

Those owners who were unaware of the backroom deal between Roy Mack and Arnold Johnson were mystified and more than a little annoyed that they had come to a meeting to consider an offer that the Macks themselves could not agree on. "I will not come to any more meetings until the Mack family has settled their own affairs among themselves," Charles Comiskey Jr., owner of the White Sox, told the press. "It seems they can't make up their minds. There are others who feel the same."[120]

That Connie Mack Sr. was blindsided by his son Roy at the meeting became apparent when before the vote the elder Mack made a personal appeal that the Athletics remain in the city under the ownership of the Philadelphia syndicate.[121] Some in the room (almost certainly the Yankees' owners, perhaps others) knew the syndicate deal was doomed, and they may have been momentarily saddened at the sight of the once powerful Connie Mack pleading for a cause that was about to be abandoned through machinations in which his own son was complicit. "Dad was in the league fifty-four years," Earle said later, expressing his own surprise and despair over the failed vote, "and only one time did he ask a favor. He asked the other owners at the meeting in New York to keep the club in Philadelphia. He didn't care who owned the club as long as it stayed in Philadelphia. They turned him down. Fifty-four years in the league and they turned him down."[122] By 1954, time had left Connie Mack behind, and now so had baseball.

THE OPEN LETTER

Connie Mack released an "open letter to Philadelphia fans" on October 29, read aloud to the assembled press by his wife Katherine, which left little doubt regarding how the "Grand Old Man of Baseball" felt about what had transpired at the owners' meeting the day before. He began by criticizing AL owners. "They simply don't want those men [the Philadelphia syndicate] to have the club," he said. "It's a runaround with an awful lot of pressure to take the A's to Kansas City. The Kansas City set-up wants the club. Everything works to that end. No matter what the Macks say or do, the answer still will be Kansas City, of course."[123]

Connie Mack saved his biggest salvos, however, for son Roy. "He's been behind everything since May, telling everybody one thing and doing something else," the statement read. "Actions speak louder than words, and Roy's been doing all the talking." It continued by noting that he, Connie Sr., had thought that at the owner's meeting "everything was going to be okay" with respect to approval of the sale of the Athletics to the Philadelphia syndicate.[124]

Earle, by contrast, was treated favorably in the open letter, if succinctly. "I don't think it's any fault of his," Connie wrote, referring to Earle. "He's been wonderful about everything."[125]

Mrs. Mack added in an ad hoc comment: "New York wants this club to go to Kansas City, and when New York's in the back and pushing it, well, there's your answer." She concluded the statement by saying that her husband "is feeling terrible about the whole thing."[126]

There can be little doubt that the open letter was composed by Katherine Mack, given Connie's debilitated condition. This "second" Mrs. Mack probably took fiendish delight in using the public forum occasioned by the controversy to join the chorus criticizing Roy for his treachery. There was no love lost between Katherine Mack and the sons from Connie's first marriage, Roy and Earle.

MAKING FINAL ARRANGEMENTS

The Philadelphia syndicate fell apart quickly. "All I know is we were looking to the Macks to gain league approval for us," member Ted Hanff commented. "They did not because they either were unwilling to do so or unable to do so. As far as I'm concerned, this is the end."[127]

Told by AL owners to go back to Philadelphia to work out their own problems, the Macks were left with the choice of resuming negotiations with Johnson or trying to operate the club for another year. Connie Mack in his open letter said that "there isn't a chance" the family would run the A's in 1955, citing insufficient funds. He also made clear his belief that selling the club to Johnson was the only agreement that would gain league approval.[128]

"There is no news to give anyone," Earle was quoted as saying on November 1. "We're just waiting— for what I don't know—but we're waiting."[129] During the period between the AL owners' meeting on October 28 and their next meeting on November 8, Roy conveniently remained unavailable for comment.[130]

Arnold Johnson was anything but dormant. With Roy now in the bag, he went to work on Earle. From the owners' meeting in New York, Johnson returned to Philadelphia to meet with Earle. In a session that "lasted all day and into the night," Johnson and his lawyer Vollers used "every possible argument" to try to persuade him. "At last, he capitulated," according to Mehl, but, ever diffident, made his agreement "subject to his father's approval."[131]

Johnson then met with Connie Mack and his wife.[132] After a brief discussion, Katherine Mack, now the primary decision-maker, agreed to the sale. She dispatched a letter to Harridge. It read in part: "This letter is being sent to you by Cornelius McGillicuddy, Earle T. McGillicuddy and Roy F. McGillicuddy to inform you that we have made an agreement with Arnold M. Johnson to sell all of the stock of the Philadelphia Athletics. This agreement contemplates the transfer of the franchise to Kansas City."[133]

Johnson paid $604,000 to Connie Mack for his 302 shares of stock, and $450,000 each to Roy and Earle for their respective blocs of 163 shares. Johnson also assumed $2,000,000 of debt that the A's had accumulated. For his money, Johnson got the Athletics and their ballpark.[134]

Of course, Johnson didn't want Connie Mack Stadium, and Robert Carpenter, president of the Phillies, reluctantly bought it, paying $1,675,000 and lamenting that he had no alternative, as the Phillies would have to continue playing there. Carpenter noted that owning the ballpark would be much more expensive for the Phillies than remaining as lessees. Since the Phillies started playing at Shibe Park/Connie Mack Stadium in mid-1938, they had paid as rent to the Athletics only ten cents on each admission.[135]

THE END COMES

The final act was played out at the meeting of AL owners on November 8, 1954. The session opened with Roy urging that the sale of the A's to Johnson be approved and that the new owner be permitted to move the club to Kansas City. Obtaining a simple majority, or five votes, to approve the sale of the Athletics to Johnson was a foregone conclusion. New York, Baltimore, Boston, and Philadelphia were sure votes, and Charles Comiskey Jr. of Chicago had signaled that he too would support the transaction now that the Mack family was united on how it wanted to proceed.[136]

But that was only a partial victory for Johnson. A three-fourths majority, or six votes, was required to approve the relocation to Kansas City. Cleveland, Washington, and Detroit still preferred that the franchise remain in Philadelphia, but Johnson had no intention of keeping it there. Following a lengthy discussion between Johnson and the owners, Tigers owner Spike Briggs switched his vote.[137] This gave Johnson the ultimate victory he had so earnestly sought for so long—not only owning the Athletics but moving them to Kansas City.[138]

In a gracious, albeit meaningless, gesture, Johnson announced after the November 8 meeting that Connie

Mack would be the "honorary president" of the Kansas City Athletics.[139] In 1955, Connie Mack attended the first Opening Day of the Kansas City Athletics. A photograph in Mehl's book shows him sitting in the third row behind Johnson, other club officials, and invited guests, including former President Harry Truman.[140] Connie Mack no longer commanded front-row seats at Athletics' games.

ASSESSING BLAME

There are plenty of fingers to point and culprits to identify in explaining why the Athletics failed to remain in Philadelphia. The fate of the A's rested primarily in the hands of three flawed men—one whose greatness advanced age had eroded and two who did not possess the ability to fill the resulting void in leadership. That is the great tragedy of this affair—it ultimately dashed any realistic hope that the club might survive to play again in Philadelphia.

CONNIE MACK

On several counts, Connie Mack bears heavy responsibility for the Athletics' demise. His stubborn refusal to relinquish his role as manager in his later years and to pass the baton to a younger, more attuned baseball man did not improve their prospects of ever climbing out of what had become for them perennial second-division finishes. Prolonged periods of losing eroded fan support, undermined the club's financial soundness, and hindered any sustained or robust effort to rebuild it into a contender.

Equally damaging was Connie Mack's refusal to give up the president's post when he could no longer carry out its responsibilities effectively. The fractious fighting between the sons of the "first" Mack family and the coalition between Connie Mack Jr. and the Shibe–MacFarland family could have been stopped only by the firm hand and wisdom of the franchise president. By the 1950s, the time for Connie Mack Sr. to exercise such authority had long since passed. He was, as noted, swayed by one side and then the other. He became a captive of others' machinations rather than their master. A cascade of events and the preferences of others dictated developments that would cripple and eventually destroy a franchise that he had helped found and spent most of his life nurturing.

In addition, Connie Mack was fixated on "the name of Mack, the house of Mack" being forever associated

Handshakes and smiles are all around as Arnold Johnson and his allies celebrate after league owners agreed to the sale and relocation of the A's to Kansas City on November 8, 1954. Shown, left to right, are Roy Mack, league president William Harridge, Arnold Johnson, and Kansas City mayor William E. Kemp.

with the Athletics.[141] The narrowness of his thinking ultimately forced the senior Mack to depend on Roy and Earle to perpetuate the empire. But, as Kuklick points out, they were "undistinguished men" not up for the task of overseeing a major-league franchise that would be successful on the field or profitable at the gate.[142] This became evident when, after the Second World War, the Athletics performed more like "a gentle comedy."[143] By 1954, they were "a truly bad ball club."[144] At his insistence, Connie Mack built "the house of Mack" to govern the Athletics, but it was a house built on sand, and it slipped away as Mack's abilities left him.

Connie Mack should have acted more quickly and decisively to expand the Athletics' ownership by bringing in partners with deep pockets, entrepreneurial drive, a willingness to restructure and invigorate the organization's operations (especially the farm system), and a determination to rejuvenate the front office with new personnel possessing baseball acumen and awareness of how the business of baseball had changed and was being conducted after the Second World War.[145] Doing that, however, would have meant sharing control of the Athletics outside the family. Mack's resistance to what he considered such an unpleasant prospect eventually resulted in the family's loss of the A's entirely.

For an example of the powerful impact that new and plentiful money could have on a club's fortunes, Connie Mack needed look no further than Bob Carpenter and the Philadelphia Phillies. The Phillies had long been a poverty-stricken franchise fielding bad teams when the wealthy Carpenter family bought the club in 1943. The renaissance that followed was unmistakable. "The Carpenters brought to the Phillies front office a substantial bankroll," Donald Honig writes in his history of the club, "a quiet dignity, and the stability that flowed therefrom."[146] Rich Westcott in his own history of the Phillies echoes the observation: "Bob Carpenter poured his energy and his family's fortune into the team. . . . Perhaps Carpenter's chief contribution to the Phillies, though, was the dignity he gave to a flimsy franchise. Bob changed the image of the club, giving it a respectability it had for so long been lacking."[147]

That the Phillies' star began ascending in the late 1940s under new and inspired ownership with deep pockets, just as the A's star was descending under old and tired ownership with empty pockets, only compounded the sense of the A's decline after the Second World War.[148] By 1954, the A's star had been eclipsed, and now they were disappearing over the horizon.

EARLE MACK

There is remarkably little to write about Earle Mack's role in the sale of the Philadelphia Athletics because it was so negligible. His passivity made Earle more a bystander than participant in the whole affair. Quotations from Earle cited earlier in this story illustrate his subservient role. In them, he refers to his stepmother's instructions to sell to Johnson, his bewilderment over what would happen next after league owners rejected the Philadelphia syndicate deal, and his willingness to sell his stock to Johnson subject to his father's approval. Newspaper accounts published between late October and early November 1954 focus very little on Earle because he was such a marginal presence in events as they transpired.

Earle had long labored in the Athletics' organization, briefly as a player and then as a coach and field lieutenant. But, it was always in the shadow of his father, and as Kuklick points out in his book, Earle acted "without motivation of his own."[149] Earle summarized his feelings after the November 8 meeting by commenting, "I'm glad it's over, but naturally I'm terribly disappointed that the Athletics had to leave Philadelphia."[150] He was not alone in being disappointed, but it is unlikely Earle could comprehend just how much he contributed to the disappointment that so many shared.[151]

Earle could have played a pivotal role in the sale of the Philadelphia Athletics, but he did not possess the fortitude—nor could he summon the determination—to do more than follow a trail that was being blazed by someone else. His father, Connie, was too infirm to lead from the front, so it fell—by default and not through ability—to Roy Mack to do so.

ROY MACK

For fans of the Philadelphia Athletics, the role of villain in this story belongs most clearly to Roy Mack. He went from supporter of retaining the Athletics in Philadelphia to conspirator in delivering the club to Kansas City. In Roy's defense, it is apparent he took the deal that held the greatest financial benefit for himself and his family, both in terms of money received for A's stock, and position held in the new ownership structure. In doing so, however, personal gain took precedence in Roy's calculations over any intention to keep the Athletics in Philadelphia. This provided the opening that Arnold Johnson was able to exploit in crafting his strategy to gain control over the A's, extract the team from Philadelphia, and relocate it to Kansas City.

Roy was the only member of the "house of Mack"

who could have thwarted Johnson's ambitions to control the Athletics. With Connie impaired by old age and the weak-willed Earle looking for someone to tell him what to do, only Roy was left to thwart Johnson (and the New York Yankees) by insisting that the club be sold to an owner who would keep it in Philadelphia. A weak man,[152] Roy was not fit for that role and actually wound up providing critical assistance to Johnson in torpedoing the Philadelphia syndicate deal and paving the way for the A's departure from the city.

Necessity, not preference, compelled Johnson to seek out and buy Roy's allegiance. It is evident that Johnson's dealings with Roy left him disenchanted with the man. Once he had purchased the A's stock of Connie, Earle, and Roy, Johnson ordered his lawyer Vollers to get the stock out of Roy's name first and to do so immediately.[153] Johnson, moreover, had told the press on October 17 following announcement of the sale of the Athletics to the Philadelphia syndicate that he had intended to make Roy "a key factor in the Kansas City set-up." After Johnson had obtained the club and approval to move it to Kansas City, he announced that Roy (and Earle) would be given three-year contracts with the new organization to work "in some capacity."[154] Roy was given the ceremonial position of vice president in the Kansas City Athletics franchise, but he had no real authority in the operation of the club.[155] Recognizing that he was nothing more than an anachronistic appendage from a by-gone era, Roy left the Kansas City Athletics after a year.[156] Earle did not accept the position offered by Johnson.[157]

Roy's descent from being "a key factor" in the new organization before the sale to working for it "in some capacity" after the sale made clear that Johnson's courtship of him was based on expediency alone and not borne of inclination or respect.

While Roy certainly does not stand alone in bearing responsibility for the departure of the Athletics from Philadelphia, he was the one who first succumbed to the siren's song of greater personal gain that Johnson sang. Avarice replaced allegiance in guiding Roy's behavior. At all of the critical AL owners' meetings, it was Roy Mack who sat at the table representing the Athletics; it was his hand that went up in the air to vote against the Philadelphia syndicate's offer, to vote for Johnson's bid, and to approve the club's relocation to Kansas City.

ARNOLD JOHNSON

If there is a hero in the sale of the Philadelphia Athletics, it's Arnold Johnson. Of course, to Kansas City he's a hero, for bringing it a major-league franchise.

To Johnson's credit, he overcame many, often seemingly insurmountable hurdles to acquire the A's. He persevered in the face of numerous delays and considerable uncertainty to get what he wanted.

But it was a pyrrhic victory for him, and the misfortunes he encountered subsequently may bring a faint smile to the most hardened of Philadelphia fans. The A's were an awful franchise during their relatively brief stay in Kansas City. While reaching as high as sixth place only once (1955), the Kansas City Athletics could most commonly be found in or near the cellar of the American League.

Johnson died in 1960 during spring training, after suffering a heart attack. He left his 52 percent share of the club to his wife and young son. Johnson's wife quickly remarried and in late 1960 sold the stock to Charlie Finley for $1,975,000. Finley then bought out the remaining 48 percent of shares held by a Kansas City investment group and became sole owner of the Athletics.[158] After a tumultuous tenure in Kansas City, where its on-field performance did not improve, Finley moved the club to Oakland following the 1967 baseball season.[159]

NEW YORK YANKEES

In assessing why the Athletics left Philadelphia, some mention must be made of the New York Yankees. It is clear that Yankees' owners meddled in the sale of the Athletics to ensure that the transaction was done to satisfy their interests. Dan Topping's statement, quoted earlier, about the transfer of the A's being "best for us," leaves no doubt about whose behalf they acted on. For the Yankees, that meant arranging for Johnson to become the A's new owner and Kansas City the club's new home. Their backing helped Johnson outdistance other suitors seeking the Athletics, and the Yankees' assistance was indispensable in sabotaging the Philadelphia syndicate's offer to buy the franchise.

Impartiality was not a criterion embraced by the Yankees in assessing the various offers made to buy the Athletics from the Mack family. As noted, the Yankees had an extensive business relationship with Johnson, and he was their favored candidate. New York had a farm team in Kansas City, the Blues, that would have to be moved elsewhere if the Athletics shifted there. Johnson, ironically, owned Blues Stadium in addition to Yankee Stadium. Fears of collusion between Johnson and the Yankees' owners were heightened when New York announced immediately after the November 8 meeting that it was waiving the indemnity payments due it for pushing its farm affiliate out of Kansas City to make room for the Athletics.[160]

In a broad sense, Johnson and the Yankees complemented each other in their effort to attain their shared goal. Johnson's job was to deliver the deal to buy the A's, while the Yankees' role was to deliver the votes of AL owners to approve the club's sale and relocation. It was an effective partnership. With president Will Harridge's connivance, the Yankees used their influence to convince AL owners to approve the club's sale and relocation. At the same time, the Yankees worked to ensure that Johnson would be welcomed into the fold of AL owners when his bid was considered.

The Yankees were rewarded handsomely for their efforts. The Kansas City Athletics became little more than a New York farm club on a major-league level.[161] Between 1955 and 1960 (the period when Johnson owned the A's), the Yankees and Athletics completed sixteen trades involving fifty-eight players. In most cases, the trades brought the Yankees prized prospects while leaving the Athletics with over-the-hill stars.[162] The Yankees won the AL title five times during that six-year period and the World Series twice.

A compelling argument can be made that the ultimate beneficiaries of the Athletics' sale and relocation were the fans not of Kansas City but of New York.

A LAST LOOK BACK AT THE DETRITUS OF DEPLORABLE DOINGS

Two of the great losers in the Athletics' sale and departure were Philadelphia and Pennsylvania. On a cold November day in 1954, both the City of Brotherly Love and the Keystone State lost representation in the American League. Teams from that league would no longer visit during the regular season—at least not until the advent of interleague play in 1997. The distinction that Philadelphia and Pennsylvania had enjoyed since 1901, having a club in both major leagues, was now gone. The loss diminished their stature in baseball and all of sports.[163]

Some in baseball recognized that the luster of the game itself was tarnished by the shabby, albeit self-induced, manner of Connie Mack's departure from the game. *Baseball Magazine* dedicated its March 1955 issue to the A's longtime skipper. John Ford, paying homage to the man, wrote:

Baseball will be a little different this year, a little sadder, for the era of one of the game's greatest figures is over. For the first time in seventy years organized ball will have to go it alone without one man, a man who, more than any other, symbolized what baseball has meant to America. That man, of course, is Cornelius McGillicuddy—Connie Mack.[164]

Ford attributed the Athletics' demise to the fair-weather and fickle fans of Philadelphia, noting that "when he [Mack] saw, finally, that the city would no longer support the team he agreed to the sale."[165] In offering that superficial explanation, Ford never addressed *why* the fans had withdrawn their support. To do so honestly would have meant criticizing Connie Mack in a way and to an extent that would have conflicted with Ford's goal of bestowing praise.

In placing the sale and relocation of the Athletics in historical perspective, one author has written, "And when the end came, it came in a tragicomedy of fits and starts, of sloppy, confusing procedures which left fans and supporters in both Philadelphia and Kansas City unhappy and disillusioned."[166]

It was an overwhelming set of unfavorable circumstances that came together in 1954 to seal the fate of the Athletics. Failed franchise leadership (the Macks), inadequate sources of revenue (vanished patrons), burdensome debt (Connecticut General and others), an aging ballpark (Connie Mack Stadium), an indifferent city administration (Mayor Clark), a suddenly invigorated rival (the Phillies), a powerful advocate for the club's relocation (the Yankees), a willingness to relocate troubled franchises (Braves and Browns), and an able suitor (Johnson) all combined in 1954 to end the A's stay in Philadelphia. It is doubtful that any lesser combination of these factors would have been sufficient to compel the team to leave. Together, they produced enough momentum to make that outcome inevitable.

The process also was punctuated by opportunities to keep the Athletics in Philadelphia. The opportunities passed by unrealized, however, because none of the men positioned to seize on them were both willing and able to do so. This fact more than any other made the Athletics' departure from Philadelphia a journey without honor. ∎

Notes

1. The Athletics' record of success dwarfs that of Philadelphia's other major-league team. In 2008, the Phillies won just their second World Series championship after 126 years of playing baseball in the city. In fifty-four years of playing in Philadelphia, the Athletics won five World Series championships. In 2009, the Phillies won their seventh National League pennant. In fifty-four years of playing in Philadelphia, the Athletics won nine American League titles.

2. Bill Kashatus, *Connie Mack's '29 Triumph* (Jefferson, N.C.: McFarland, 1999).

3. In this article, data on the Athletics' won–lost figures and place in the AL standings are taken from, David S. Neft, Richard M. Cohen, and Michael L. Neft, *The Sports Encyclopedia: Baseball*, 23d ed. (New York: St. Martin's Griffin), 2003.

4. Harry T. Paxton, "The Philadelphia A's Last Stand," *The Saturday Evening Post* 226, no. 50 (12 June 1954): 134.

5. Mark Stang, *Athletics Album: A Photo History of the Philadelphia Athletics* (Wilmington: Orange Frazer Press, 2006), 172.
6. Athletics' attendance figures are taken from the www.baseball-almanac.com.
7. Paxton, *Saturday Evening Post*, 134.
8. Ibid., 31.
9. David M. Jordan, *The Athletics of Philadelphia: Connie Mack's White Elephants, 1901–1954* (Jefferson, N.C.: McFarland, 1999), 181.
10. Paxton, *Saturday Evening Post*, 136.
11. Ibid.
12. Ibid.
13. Jimmie Dykes, *You Can't Steal First Base* (Philadelphia: J. B. Lippincott., 1967), 108–9.
14. Mack's career managerial record, 3,731–3,948, reflects three seasons (1894–96) with the Pirates, where he was 149–134.
15. Frederick G. Lieb, *Connie Mack: Grand Old Man of Baseball* (New York: G. P. Putnam's Sons, 1945), 271.
16. Bruce Kuklick, *To Every Thing a Season: Shibe Park and Urban Philadelphia, 1909–1976* (Princeton: Princeton University Press, 1991), 117–18.
17. There probably were a number of reasons Mack refused to go gently into the night. Vanity and stubbornness certainly played a part, as well as a refusal to admit that his abilities were leaving him. It is possible Mack also may have hung on in hope of tying his great friend and rival John McGraw for the number of pennants won. McGraw had captured ten National League titles during his tenure with the New York Giants. Mack was stuck at nine AL pennants with the Philadelphia Athletics.
18. One particularly notorious incident illustrating Mack's uncontrolled and spontaneous interference with the club's fortunes occurred in 1948 when the A's were contending for the pennant. In the first game of a home doubleheader on June 13, against the St. Louis Browns, Mack sent reliever Nelson Potter in during the eighth inning with the bases loaded, none out, and the Athletics holding a 5–2 lead. Potter had done a good job out of the bullpen up to that point in the season, but in this instance he couldn't hold the lead. Four Browns' runners crossed the plate before Mack yanked Potter from the game. When Potter reached the dugout, the visibly agitated Mack questioned whether Potter had done his best and claimed that the $20,000 he had paid to acquire him had been a mistake. Although Mack's outburst greatly embarrassed him in front of the other players on the bench, Potter took the scolding in silence. He was released on waivers and picked up by the Boston Braves, where he became the top reliever on Billy Southworth's pennant-winning club. The A's bullpen was its Achilles' heel in 1948 and a major cause of the team's fade in the pennant race. Lou Brissie, a player on that team, opined years later that Mack's abrupt and ill-advised dismissal of Potter was a key factor in the A's failure to win the AL title. Jordan, *Athletics of Philadelphia*, 154–55.
19. Kuklick, *To Every Thing a Season*, 114–15.
20. Ibid., 117.
21. William C. Kashatus, *The Philadelphia Athletics* (Charleston, S.C.: Arcadia, 2002), 90.
22. Dykes, *You Can't Steal First Base*, 109.
23. Dick Armstrong, the Athletics' director of public relations when the book was published, acknowledged years later that he was the ghostwriter of Mack's "autobiography." Mack, struggling with mental deterioration by 1950, certainly needed considerable assistance in telling the story of his life. Whether Mack actually uttered these words or they sprung from the fertile mind of Armstrong is open to question. Connie Mack, *My 66 Years in the Big Leagues* (Philadelphia: John C. Winston, 1950), 5–6.
24. Ibid., 6.
25. Multiple authors, including Kuklick, Jordan, and Paxton, identify Earle as Connie's hand-picked successor as manager. See, for example, Jordan, *Athletics of Philadelphia*, 168.
26. Stang, *Athletics Album*, 143.
27. Mack, *My 66 Years*, 5.
28. Lieb, *Grand Old Man*, 263.
29. Ibid.
30. Paxton, *Saturday Evening Post*, 112–13.
31. Mack, *My 66 Years*, 5.
32. Ibid.
33. Paxton, *Saturday Evening Post*, 133.
34. Ibid., 134.
35. Ibid.
36. Ibid., 133.
37. Kuklick, *To Every Thing a Season*, 112–13.
38. Ibid.
39. Paxton, *Saturday Evening Post*, 133–34, 136.
40. Ibid., 134.
41. Ibid.
42. Jordan, *Athletics of Philadelphia*, 168.
43. Paxton, *Saturday Evening Post*, 134.
44. Ibid.
45. Kuklick, *To Every Thing a Season*, 116.
46. Jordan, *Athletics of Philadelphia*, 168.
47. Paxton, *Saturday Evening Post*, 134.
48. Ibid.
49. Jordan, *Athletics of Philadelphia*, 169.
50. Paxton, *Saturday Evening Post*, 134.
51. Ibid.
52. Ibid., 136.
53. Connie Mack Jr. used the money for his stock to open a shrimp business in Florida—far away from his half-brothers and Major League Baseball.
54. Paxton, *Saturday Evening Post*, 136.
55. Ibid., 133.
56. Ibid.
57. Kuklick, *To Every Thing a Season*, 116.
58. Paxton, *Saturday Evening Post*, 133, 136.
59. "Move from Philadelphia?" *Time* 44, no. 7 (16 August 1954): 37.
60. Kuklick, *To Every Thing a Season*, 119–21.
61. Ibid., 120.
62. Paxton, *Saturday Evening Post*, 133, 136.
63. Ibid.
64. Ibid., 133.
65. Ibid.
66. Ibid., 136.
67. "Move from Philadelphia?" *Time*, 16 August 1954, 37.
68. Initial offers to buy the Athletics rested on Roy and Earle agreeing to leave the franchise entirely. Eventually, investors accepted that Roy would have to be retained in some capacity in the club's hierarchy to obtain his acquiescence to the purchase. Ernest Mehl, *The Kansas City Athletics* (New York: Henry Holt, 1956), 67.
69. Investors also may have been put off by Roy's well-known vindictiveness, which is illustrated by a story in Kuklick's book. When Earle and his wife separated, Earle moved into a small suite off the A's clubhouse at Connie Mack Stadium. Roy had the water turned off so that his brother could not bathe or use the toilet. Kuklick, *To Every Thing a Season*, 120.
70. Arnold Johnson's relationship with the Yankees' owners is only mentioned in this story. His business dealings with them, as well as Johnson's well-deserved reputation as a wheeler-dealer, are examined extensively by Jeff Katz in *The Kansas City A's and the Wrong Half of the Yankees* (Hingham, Mass: Maple Street Press, 2007).
71. "Move from Philadelphia?" *Time*, 16 August 1954, 37.
72. In any consideration that Connie was interested in selling his A's stock to Johnson, questions must be raised about the influence his wife had on his thinking. Connie was impaired by the ravages of senility, and newspaper reports from the period often have his wife, Katherine, speaking on his behalf.
73. Attendance figures are taken from www.baseball-almanac.com.

74. Indeed it did. The Athletics drew only 304,666 to Connie Mack Stadium in 1954, their final year in Philadelphia. The 1955 Kansas City Athletics drew 1,393,054 to Municipal Stadium.
75. Mehl, *Kansas City Athletics*, 56.
76. Jordan, *Athletics of Philadelphia*, 184.
77. Ibid.
78. Mehl, *Kansas City Athletics*, 71.
79. Ibid., 61.
80. Ibid., 69.
81. Ibid., 72.
82. Ibid., 71–72.
83. Ibid., 73.
84. Jordan, *Athletics of Philadelphia*, 183.
85. "Philadelphia Keeps A's; $4,000,000 Deal," *Chicago Daily Tribune*, 18 October 1954.
86. The position Roy would hold was not specified, nor was the one that would be held by his son, Connie Mack III.
87. *Chicago Daily Tribune*, 18 October 1954.
88. Ibid.
89. Edward Prell, "Harridge Asks Facts on Sale," *Chicago Daily Tribune*, 18 October 1954.
90. "Johnson Says His Deal Better One for Macks," *Chicago Daily Tribune*, 18 October 1954.
91. *Chicago Daily Tribune*, 18 October 1954.
92. Mehl, *Kansas City Athletics*, 67, 89.
93. The Macks' decision to sell to the Philadelphia syndicate confirmed Roy's realization that he could not buy out his father and brother and could not obtain the A's presidency under new ownership. Roy's exact position in the A's hierarchy once the Philadelphia syndicate would take over was never identified; in newspaper accounts of the deal, it was described only as a "senior position." Clearly implied in these reports, nevertheless, was that the post would not be as club president. Like Earle's aspiration to become Athletics' manager, Roy's dream of being club president was gone.
94. Mehl, *Kansas City Athletics*, 92–93.
95. Ibid., 93.
96. Ibid.
97. Ibid., 94.
98. Although written more than fifty years ago, Mehl's book remains the single most detailed account of the sale and relocation of the Philadelphia Athletics franchise. Mehl, sports editor of the *Kansas City Star*, was an unabashed supporter of moving the A's to Kansas City and incorporated extensive input from Johnson in the book.
99. Mehl, *Kansas City Athletics*, 108.
100. Katz, *Wrong Half of the Yankees*, 109.
101. Jordan, *Athletics of Philadelphia*, 183.
102. "Connie Mack Charges League Is Forcing Athletics to Shift to Kansas City," *New York Times*, 30 October 1954.
103. "Briggs Glad A's Are Not Moving; Most Clubs Silent," *Chicago Daily Tribune*, 18 October 1954.
104. Irving Vaughan, "Did Syndicate Try to Buy A's on Shoestring?" *Chicago Daily Tribune*, 30 October 1954.
105. Ibid.
106. Mehl, *Kansas City Athletics*, 98.
107. Shirley Povich, "Philadelphia Group's Bid Voted Down by League," *Washington Post*, 29 October 1954.
108. "League Rejects Syndicate's Bid for A's," *Chicago Daily Tribune*, 29 October 1954.
109. Ibid.
110. Mehl, *Kansas City Athletics*, 100.
111. "Connie Mack Hits League Run-Around," *Chicago Daily Tribune*, 30 October 1954.
112. Povich, "Philadelphia Group's Bid Voted Down by League," *Washington Post*, 29 October 1954.
113. "Connie Mack Charges League Is Forcing Athletics to Shift to Kansas City," *New York Times*, 30 October 1954.
114. Ibid.
115. Ibid.
116. Joseph M. Sheehan, "American League Rejects Athletics' Sale to the Philadelphia Group," *New York Times*, 29 October 1954.
117. Ibid.
118. Ibid.
119. Ibid.
120. *Chicago Daily Tribune*, 29 October 1954.
121. Kuklick, *To Every Thing a Season*, 125.
122. Jordan, *Athletics of Philadelphia*, 185.
123. "Connie Mack Charges League Is Forcing Athletics to Shift to Kansas City," *New York Times*, 30 October 1954.
124. Ibid.
125. "Angry Connie Mack Says A's Will Go to Kansas City," *Washington Post*, 30 October 1954.
126. "Connie Mack Charges League Is Forcing Athletics to Shift to Kansas City," *New York Times*, 30 October 1954.
127. Ibid.
128. *Washington Post*, 30 October 1954.
129. "Athletics' Status 'Still in the Air,'" *New York Times*, 1 November 1954.
130. Ibid.
131. Mehl, *Kansas City Athletics*, 101–2.
132. According to Mehl, Johnson got an assist from Connie Mack's chauffeur, Chuck Roberts, who supported Johnson's bid to get the club. Roberts took Johnson up the back stairs to the Macks' quarters. While some members of the Philadelphia syndicate still trying to salvage their proposition were waiting in the lobby to see the Macks, Johnson was upstairs closing the deal.
133. Mehl, *Kansas City Athletics*, 110.
134. Ibid., 130.
135. "Phils Forced to Buy," *New York Times*, 9 November 1954.
136. Mehl, *Kansas City Athletics*, 120, 124.
137. Ibid., 123–24. Briggs commented at the time that he decided to vote to approve Johnson because "I finally got sick and tired of all this wrangling and wanted to restore harmony to the American League." In a shot aimed at the Yankees' overtly aggressive support of Johnson's bid, Briggs added, "I also want to prove to some folks I am not so anti-Yankee as I have been pictured." John Drebinger, "Athletics' Transfer to Kansas City Wins Final American League Approval," *New York Times*, 9 November 1954.
138. To gain the owners' approval, Johnson had to agree to "divest myself of all interest in the home of the Yankees [Yankee Stadium] within a period of 90 days." Much of the opposition to Johnson at the November 8 meeting stemmed from concern over "his rather close association with Dan Topping, president and co-owner of the Yankees." Drebinger, *New York Times*, 9 November 1954.
139. Jordan, *Athletics of Philadelphia*, 185.
140. The photo is one of the series of photos that follow page 64 of Mehl's book.
141. Kuklick, *To Every Thing a Season*, 113.
142. Ibid.
143. Kashatus, *Philadelphia Athletics*, 71.
144. Jordan, *Athletics of Philadelphia*, 181.
145. Charles C. Alexander, *Our Game: An American Baseball History* (New York: MJF Books, 1991), chap. 9 and 10.
146. Donald Honig, *The Philadelphia Phillies* (New York: Simon and Schuster, 1992), 121.
147. Rich Westcott and Frank Bilovsky, *The Phillies Encyclopedia*, 3d ed. (Philadelphia: Temple University Press, 2004), 374–77.
148. As evidence of the Phillies' transcendence in Philadelphia, their home attendance figures more than doubled those of the A's in 1953 and 1954.

149. Kuklick, *To Every Thing a Season*, 113.
150. "Griff Loses Fight When Briggs Votes For Move," *Washington Post*, 9 November 1954.
151. Earle Mack used the money he received from selling his A's stock to get into the prefabrication-construction business. He never worked in baseball again. Stang, *Athletics Album*, 202.
152. Kuklick, *To Every Thing a Season*, 125.
153. Mehl, *Kansas City Athletics*, 111.
154. Drebinger, *New York Times*, 9 November 1954.
155. Stang, *Athletics Album*, 202.
156. Ted Taylor, *Philadelphia Athletics by the Numbers* (Bloomington, Ind.: Xlibris, 2009), 19.
157. Jordan, *Athletics of Philadelphia*, 185.
158. Roy Mack was not one of the other shareholders bought out by Finley. So, if Roy had ever had stock in the Kansas City Athletics, he had sold it prior to Finley's acquisition of the franchise in 1960.

159. Donald Dewey and Nicholas Acocella, *Total Ballclubs* (Wilmington, Del.: Sports Media Publishing, 2005), 298–99.
160. Ibid., 297.
161. Katz, Wrong Half of the Yankees, chap. 10–13.
162. Dewey and Acocella, *Total Ballclubs*, 297.
163. Other cities and their states suffered similar fates during this period. In addition to Boston losing the Braves in 1952 and St. Louis losing the Browns in 1953, New York lost both of its National League franchises, the Giants and Dodgers, when they moved west after the 1957 season. The Giants landed in San Francisco, the Dodgers in Los Angeles.
164. John Ford, "The End of an Era," *Baseball Magazine* 91, no.1, (March 1955): 6–9.
165. Ibid., 9.
166. Jordan, *Athletics of Philadelphia*, 183.

Field of Liens

Real-Property Development in Baseball

Robert A. James

Baseball is at one and the same time an idyllic game for children and a gravely serious business for adults. A sport that can be played on a pastoral commons requires, in the world of commerce, space to which some can be admitted and from which others can be excluded—in short, what lawyers call real property. Land must be acquired, grandstands and other improvements must be constructed, and parking and transportation access must be arranged. In these respects, ballparks are like other forms of American urban development.

Yet stadiums are a breed apart from shopping malls, office buildings or municipal centers. They represent the significance of a city, literally as a "major league town," above and beyond their bare economic data. They are founts of media content that create value well past their earnings from in-person attendance. And their reason for being is *baseball*, darn it; even crusty, hard-edged men and women in public life can get misty-eyed and perhaps not entirely rational just thinking about the subject.[1] It remains to be seen whether that peculiar bond between civic leaders and the sport, established by parents and kids entwined over the years in a single pastime, will survive as baseball competes for affection with football, basketball, soccer, skateboarding, and video games.

A number of elements of real-estate law and development can be illustrated by the country's ballparks. To that end, this article examines the two celebrated homes of the Dodgers, Ebbets Field in Brooklyn and Dodger Stadium in Los Angeles. The journey between these venues is one of the most surveyed subjects in all of baseball literature. The story features metaphors of one city's decline and another's ascent, a Homeric struggle between two stubborn men, and a seemingly undying memory of monumental betrayal.[2] Transcending all this baggage, even the stadiums themselves offer lessons for lawyers and developers alike.

ACT I. A BALLPARK GROWS IN BROOKLYN

Assemblage. For urban infill projects, it is critical to employ a strategy of discreet land acquisition. Charles Ebbets, an architect by profession, became president of the team then known as the Brooklyns[3] in 1898, the year that the proudly independent city of Brooklyn merged into New York City.[4] Desiring to escape the all-wood Washington Park, he had nominees set up a shell corporation that anonymously purchased a number of lots along Bedford Avenue in the "Pigtown" district. Though he attempted to maintain secrecy, word leaked out and some of the forty lotholders were able to hike their sales prices.[5] The land assemblage took roughly four years to complete. Ebbets built a $750,000, 35,000-seat stadium bearing his name, which opened amid much local fanfare in 1913.[6]

Design. Commercial and civic projects often emphasize impressive, even awe-inspiring entryways and architecturally striking public areas, and ballparks are true to form. The design of Ebbets Field by the architect Charles Von Buskirk may not be suited to everyone's aesthetic taste, but a description of the opening defies reports of later decay:

> Fans who arrived at the main entrance discovered an ornate rotunda with a soaring domed ceiling, gilded ticket booths, and a white Italian marble floor inlaid with red tiles in the pattern of the stitches on a baseball. Overhead, light came from a chandelier designed to look as if it were made of bats and balls. Valet parking service was offered to the swells who came by car, while businessmen were welcomed to use public phones equipped with desks and chairs.[7]

Maintenance. Even a cathedral requires upkeep; absent ongoing investment, a property can lose its reputation and value. The heirs of Ebbets and his partner Edward McKeever quarreled over the team's direction, while their loans from the Brooklyn Trust Company grew ever more precarious—the ballpark encumbered by its mortgages constituted an early example of a "field of liens." To reduce the likelihood of having to foreclose on those liens, the bank recommended that a lawyer named Walter Francis O'Malley join club management; along with Branch Rickey and others, he ultimately acquired equity interests in the team.[8] As a new executive, O'Malley learned that years of neglect had left

The vacant lots around Ebbets Field accommodated only 700 automobiles. After the Second World War, city-dwellers flocked to outer Long Island and New Jersey, and the lack of vehicle access threatened to cut ties with the longtime Dodger fan base. Attendance languished; for the potential title-clinching Game 6 of the 1952 World Series, there were five thousand empty seats at Ebbets, which was built in the trolley-car era, as Walter O'Malley observed. "There are no trolleys to speak of today," he wrote, "but there are automobiles and intelligently planned parkways."

the stadium both in poor repair and expensive to maintain. Reportedly, only "influence" with an assistant's sister's father-in-law in the New York Fire Department was saving the venue from hazard citations.[9]

Expansion. A developer often has expansions in mind even as the original improvements are being built. Ebbets Field had nowhere to grow, either out or up. While the Yankees could host 67,000 fans and the Giants 54,000, the Dodgers had no means of achieving similar gates for their most popular home games.[10]

Parking and Transportation. Some of the most contentious issues for urban projects revolve around parking and traffic impacts.[11] Unfortunately, the vacant lots around Ebbets Field accommodated only 700 automobiles. Such contraptions were novelties when the park was built. But as World War II ended and city-dwellers flocked to outer Long Island and New Jersey, the lack of vehicle access threatened to cut ties with the longtime Dodger fan base.[12] Attendance languished; for the potential title-clinching Game 6 of the 1952 World Series, there were five thousand empty Ebbets seats.[13] As O'Malley wrote, "Ebbets Field was built in the Trolley car era. There are no trolleys to speak of today but there are automobiles and intelligently planned parkways."[14]

ACT II. CLASH OF THE GOTHAM TITANS

From this point onward, the story of the Dodgers' homes becomes more idiosyncratic. The experience of the club may be in a league of its own, but it nonetheless has applications for other types of real-property development.

By the 1950s, the specter of "community antenna" television haunted the entertainment industry. Still in its infancy, cable TV promised new revenues for baseball game broadcasts and uncertain positive and negative impacts on attendance. Installation of lighting for night games added to most teams' capital and operational expenses. The Dodgers fared better than other clubs with these changes in the short term. But a good investor like O'Malley was more concerned about the future, and he set his sights on a new location.[15]

Contrary to urban legend, O'Malley appears to have made good-faith efforts to relocate within Brooklyn—albeit always with a businessman's eye for profit.[16] Given the vital importance of transportation access, the Dodgers focused on sites adjacent to the Long Island Rail Road and connecting transit lines. Futuristic designs were produced, including a retractable-roof facility planned by Norman Bel Geddes and a translucent geodesic dome conceived by R. Buckminster Fuller.[17]

Astride the path of O'Malley's proposals loomed Robert Moses, the "power broker" of all New York development in the era.[18] Again contrary to urban legend, Moses was no enemy of baseball itself, but he did firmly believe that a stadium should sit on the outskirts of the city, served by highways rather than by surface streets or public transit. Indeed, his early vision for a ballpark near the 1939 World's Fair site, in the Flushing Meadows district of Queens, was finally realized with Shea Stadium.[19] The two men maneuvered themselves into an intractable duel, thrusting and parrying for several years over many sites and mutual accusations.

A bilateral conflict during project development sometimes requires the intervention of a third party. The lawyer in O'Malley seized on the possibility of an external solution to the impasse. Title I of the Federal Housing Act of 1949 (the "FHA") offered federal funds for acquiring lands for "development or redevelopment for predominantly residential uses."[20] The law would soon be used for private developments contributing in some manner to what became known as "urban renewal," and O'Malley suggested to Moses that the Dodgers were worthy recipients of such a program's benefits, courtesy of Uncle Sam. The cities of Baltimore and Milwaukee took advantage of the FHA for similar purposes. And in 1954 the U.S. Supreme Court held, in *Berman v. Parker*, that a District of Columbia law constitutionally allowed non-blighted private property in a blighted area to be taken for private development with a public purpose; the case is best known today as a prologue to the controversial *Kelo v. City of New London* decision.[21]

Moses expressed horror at the prospect of helping O'Malley in such a fashion. In correspondence, he stated flatly that a ballpark could not be included in a "slum-clearance project." In fact, Moses had his sights set on other forms of equally private improvements that would be funded by his FHA grants. (Among them was a project awarded to Fred Trump, a prominent developer who kept a lower profile than does his son Donald.) Mayor Robert Wagner's legal staff came forward with arguments for using public authority to build a stadium, but it was too little and too late. By 1957, Moses had made clear that he would not grant approval to support relocation in any part of Brooklyn that the Dodgers considered acceptable.[22]

The ultimate weapon of any real-estate investor is the threatened alternative—the credible statement of a proponent, lessee, or purchaser to it will go elsewhere if terms cannot be reached with the municipality, lessor, or vendor. The Dodgers played seven games in Jersey City in 1956 and eight in 1957, and sold Ebbets Field, reserving a three-year leaseback. With the fading of efforts by the St. Louis Browns, Washington Senators, and Kansas City Athletics to move to Los Angeles, O'Malley opened up communications with representatives of the California city. He ostentatiously hosted Angelenos, with New York reporters present, at spring training in Vero Beach, Florida, in 1957. He also encouraged Horace Stoneham, the owner of the New York Giants, to explore prospects in San Francisco rather than in Minneapolis. O'Malley rightly reasoned that the other team owners, concerned with travel expenses, would not approve a single West Coast move—but might approve two in tandem.

The Giants proclaimed their relocation to San Francisco in August 1957 and the Dodgers quietly announced their move to Los Angeles in October, whereupon O'Malley entered eternal ignominy in Brooklyn.[23] The last game at Ebbets Field was witnessed by 6,702 souls. A wrecking ball swung into the old ballpark in February 1960. On the site now stands the Ebbets Field Apartments, a high-rise housing development whose grounds feature a sign reading "NO BALL PLAYING."[24]

ACT III. A BALLAD FOR CHÁVEZ RAVINE

The quest for Major League Baseball in Los Angeles pulled the Dodgers into the tortuous story of the Chávez Ravine district—the last vacant downtown sector, lying between the Hollywood and Pasadena

Game 1 of the 1920 World Series at Ebbets Field, October 5, 1920. Ebbets Field opened in 1913. The last game there was witnessed by 6,702 souls in 1957. A wrecking ball swung into the old ballpark in February 1960. O'Malley's efforts to relocate elsewhere in Brooklyn had been opposed by Robert Moses, who thought that a stadium should sit on the outskirts of the city, served by highways rather than by surface streets or public transit. His early vision for a ballpark near the 1939 World's Fair site, in the Flushing Meadows district of Queens, was finally realized with Shea Stadium.

freeways. For decades, the neighborhood had filled with shacks and houses principally of Mexican-American families.[25] The city housing authority used an FHA grant to acquire properties for the express purpose of constructing 3,360 replacement residences, part of the "Elysian Park Heights" development designed by Richard Neutra. Those who sold out were often promised first priority on the planned units. But a 1952 referendum rejected a housing project in the Ravine, and the city acquired the properties in 1953 for a fraction of the acquisition cost, on condition that the land be used for "public purposes only."[26] Eminent domain was used to claim the final properties. In 1959, the last resident was televised being physically carried out of her home, which was quickly bulldozed.[27]

Mayor Norris Poulson, county supervisor Kenneth Hahn, and city councilwoman Rosalind Wyman persistently courted O'Malley. However, the savvy negotiator once disembarked from his airplane at LAX wearing a lapel pin reading "Keep the Dodgers in Brooklyn," and professed a desire for a ballpark not in the Ravine but on the west side of town, the home of the entertainment industry and the wealthier enclaves. Similar strategies have been wielded by many tenants—their current property is a gem when speaking with other owners, and an eyesore when speaking with their current landlord.

In 1957, O'Malley acquired the Los Angeles Angels, formerly the farm club of the Chicago Cubs, and their ballpark. The stage was thus set for a grand exchange between local government and the Dodgers. The real-estate terms (setting aside complex monetary commitments on both sides) were that the team would convey the Angels' "little Wrigley Field" to the city in return for fee simple title to up to three hundred acres in the Ravine, complete with public promises to contract freeway-access improvements.

The economics, wisdom, and legality of the swap were all exposed to intense public scrutiny. After all, the voters in 1955 had rejected a bond proposal to use public funds for a ballpark on the very site. Petitions were circulating calling for a public vote on the Dodgers transaction—though the biggest detractors were owners of the San Diego Padres minor-league club and other competing businesses, not the representatives of the evicted residents. Separate lawsuits alleged that the deal exceeded the city council's authority and was unconstitutional, and two superior courts ruled in the plaintiffs' favor. But the voters narrowly endorsed the exchange in a June 1958 referendum, after a pro-Dodger telethon featuring Debbie Reynolds, Dean Martin, Jerry Lewis, and Ronald Rea-

> Before 1957, New York lawyers chose juries inexpensively and expeditiously by asking just one question: What baseball team do you root for? If the juror answered, "Yankees," the defense exercised a peremptory challenge. If the juror said, "Dodgers," the prosecution exercised the challenge. But Giants fans were eminently acceptable to both sides, under a tacit understanding that they were the only reasonable people in town.
>
> Burt Neuborne
> Letter to the editor, *New York Times*, 17 May 1983

gan. Likewise, in 1959 the California Supreme Court reversed the lower court decisions, and the U.S. Supreme Court declined to review the case.[28]

Many developers find that the entitlements process—the securing of rights to pursue the projects from public authorities and from businesses affected by the development—is the largest challenge for the viability and cost of an urban project. Remaining properties not owned by the city, appraised at $93,000, wound up requiring more than half a million dollars to acquire; the West Coast minor-league clubs demanded and received compensation for the Giants' and Dodgers' entry into their markets. Unexpectedly high rent needed to be paid for the Los Angeles Coliseum while the new stadium was being built. O'Malley found the interest rate and closing fees quoted by Los Angeles banks for the construction loans to be unattractive. The delays and logistical challenges of construction also complicated the financing of the new venue.

Help arrived from an unlikely source, the advertising appetite of Union Oil Company of California. The company's chairman, Reese Taylor, had been instrumental in the success of the "Bring Baseball to Los Angeles" drive. Union Oil became prime lender, advancing $8 million (interest-free and payment-free for the first two years) in return for broadcasting and publicity rights and—a natural in Southern California—a franchise for a Union 76 gasoline service station in the parking lot.[29]

The new "field of liens" was certainly more favorable for the club than was the mortgaged old park in Flatbush. The Union Oil arrangement illustrates the capability of a sports asset to generate revenue far beyond that gleaned from onsite visitors. It bears many characteristic aspects of ballpark development: an enthusiastic booster of civic pride, and of the game itself, had offered above-market value to be affiliated with the ballclub, the venue, and their associated media and transportation rights.

O'Malley's field was touted as the "last privately

built baseball park"[30] until the completion of the San Francisco Giants' new stadium in 2000. It was conceived in a favorable property exchange and nurtured with generous commercial terms, all bestowed on an eagerly coveted market entrant. In any event, the park's design is undeniably classic. Of the facilities built in its era, the colorful Dodger Stadium most retains its appeal for players and spectators.[31]

In the park's inaugural 1962 season, the Dodgers sold a major-league record 2.7 million tickets and continued their position as one of the stronger sports franchises. Walter O'Malley's son Peter became president in 1970; Walter died in 1979 and was inducted into the Hall of Fame in 2008. The O'Malley family sold the team in 1997 to Rupert Murdoch's News Corporation, which justified the acquisition as a source of content for its widespread media outlets, particularly in Asia.[32] The ownership of the club and its stadium is currently in dispute but is generally tied up with the family of Frank McCourt, who is by profession a real-property developer.

———

The Dodgers' move from Brooklyn to Los Angeles had effects in a number of economic, political, and legal dimensions. Scholars have noted that it anticipated the "issues that dominate contemporary stadium politics . . . public versus private development, eminent domain, competing economic development strategies, neighborhood resistance and fragmented local political processes."[33] As illustrated above, many of these issues come up in other forms of high-stakes real-estate development. The signal differences between ballparks and other properties are rather less tangible: the capacity for producing value from afar through media both old and new, and the deeply rooted emotions and memories that connect communities and generations through sport. ■

Notes

This article was published originally in *The 2010 Green Bag Almanac and Reader*, 346–55.

The title of this article pays tribute to an article by Matt Smith in *San Francisco Weekly* (30 October 2002) about an ill-fated minor-league stadium.

1. Several economists have questioned the value of sports clubs to cities and the wisdom of government policies designed to attract or retain them. See Roger G. Noll and Andrew S. Zimbalist, eds., *Sports, Jobs, and Taxes: The Economic Impact of Sports Teams and Stadiums* (Washington, D.C.: Brookings Institution Press, 1997). Such policies have nonetheless proven resilient for decades.

2. See, among many published sources with many more details than are covered here, Michael D'Antonio, *Forever Blue: The True Story of Walter O'Malley, Baseball's Most Controversial Owner, and the Dodgers of Brook-*

lyn and Los Angeles (New York: Riverhead Books, 2009); Michael Shapiro, *The Last Good Season: Brooklyn, the Dodgers, and Their Final Pennant Race Together* (New York: Doubleday, 2003); Doris Kearns Goodwin, *Wait Till Next Year: A Memoir* (New York: Simon and Schuster, 1997); Carl E. Prince, *Brooklyn's Dodgers: The Bums, the Borough, and the Best of Baseball, 1947–1957* (New York: Oxford University Press, 1996); Neil J. Sullivan, *The Dodgers Move West* (New York: Oxford University Press, 1987); Peter Ellsworth, "The Brooklyn Dodgers' Move to Los Angeles: Was Walter O'Malley Solely Responsible?" *Nine* 14, no. 1 (2005): 19–40. For its part, the O'Malley family has sponsored its own web site, www.walteromalley.com, with photographs, audio clips, and documents; D'Antonio was granted access to additional family archives for his work cited above.

3. Also nicknamed the Trolley Dodgers, the Dodgers, the Robins, the Bridegrooms and the Superbas, before they paid homage to their trolley-car environment and settled down as the Dodgers. The name is as inapposite in their adopted city as are those of basketball's Los Angeles Lakers and Utah Jazz.

4. See generally Rita Seiden Miller, ed., *Brooklyn USA: The Fourth Largest City in America* (Brooklyn: Brooklyn College Press, 1979); David McCullough, *The Great Bridge* (New York: Simon and Schuster, 1972).

5. Red Barber, *Rhubarb Patch: The Story of the Modern Brooklyn Dodgers* (New York: Simon and Schuster, 1954), 31.

6. See D'Antonio, supra note 2, at 34.

7. D'Antonio, supra note 2, at 36; see Ellsworth, supra note 2, at 20.

8. See Andy McCue, "Walter O'Malley," Society for American Baseball Research, Baseball Biography Project, available at bioproj.sabr.org (accessed 29 November 2010).

9. D'Antonio, supra note 2, at 90; see Ellsworth, supra note 2, at 20.

10. The cross-town rivals depended to a great degree on their intra-city contests. The Giants' 11 annual home games against the Dodgers generated fully one-third of the team's revenues from all of its 77 home games. Goodwin, supra note 2, at 223.

11. Decades later, the environmental-impact report and analysis for the new Giants ballpark in San Francisco required detailed studies of patterns of traffic on surface streets and highway on-ramps and off-ramps, and justifications for the omission from the project of a new parking garage. The stadium features access by railroad, rapid transit and municipal transit, bicycle racks, and even ferry service. See Metropolitan Transportation Commission, "Bay Area: A Showcase for Public Transit" (September/October 2000), available at www.mtc.ca.gov/news/transactions (accessed 29 November 2010).

12. See Roger Kahn, *The Boys of Summer* (New York: Harper and Row, 1972), xv. "Ebbets Field was located miles away from any expressway and, with insufficient rail facilities and limited parking, did not have the amenities necessary for a thriving ballpark." Ellsworth, supra note 2, at 22. See also Edward G. White, *Creating the National Pastime: Baseball Transforms Itself, 1903–1953* (Princeton: Princeton University Press, 1996), 46.

13. See D'Antonio, supra note 2, at 250. Home attendance during the Dodgers' pennant-winning 1955 and 1956 seasons averaged only 16,000 per game.

14. Quoted in Shapiro, supra note 2, at 73. See also David W. Chen, "Nothing Sub About Us, Suburban Fans Say," *New York Times*, 23 October 2000 (most fans attending the 2000 Mets–Yankees "Subway Series" arrived by car).

15. "Similar profits at that time certainly convinced the large American car companies that they had nothing to worry about. The difference in management foresight was apparent a decade later. . . . O'Malley was basking in higher profits in the Los Angeles sunshine because he had recognized that his 1950s profits cloaked problems that needed to be solved." McCue, supra note 8.

16. "O'Malley was unquestionably a shrewd businessman unaffected by sentiment in his operation of the Dodgers, but he did not scheme to move the Dodgers to Los Angeles. . . . [He] did not move the [team] until it became evident that a stadium was not going to be built in New York."

Ellsworth, supra note 2, at 35. He expected the city to condemn the land and build the stadium, but was prepared to pay significant rentals and gross receipt royalties. See D'Antonio, supra note 2.

17. See Shapiro, supra note 2; Goodwin, supra note 2, at 223. The designs were published in magazines such as *Collier's* and *Mechanix Illustrated*. See Ellsworth, supra note 2, at 24–25. Photographs of a retractable-dome sketch, and of Fuller and O'Malley with geodesic-dome models, are available at walteromalley.com.

18. See generally Robert A. Caro, *The Power Broker: Robert Moses and the Fall of New York* (New York: Knopf, 1974). For fifty years, Moses oversaw almost every major improvement in the city, including the United Nations Headquarters and Lincoln Center, displacing some half-million residents in the process. His official titles included New York Parks commissioner and head of the Triborough Bridge and Tunnel Authority, Construction Commission and Slum Clearance Committee.

19. According to Caro, Moses had envisioned a baseball park in Flushing Meadows "since the 1930s, if not the 1920s." Zack O'Malley Greenburg, "Who Framed Walter O'Malley?" *Forbes*, 14 April 2009. Shea Stadium opened in 1964 as the first permanent home of the New York Mets, bearing the color blue for the departed Dodgers and the color orange for the departed Giants. Shea has been replaced with Citi Field, whose exterior is designed in turn to resemble that of Ebbets.

20. Housing Act of 1949, Pub. L. No. 81-171, tit. I, § 110(c), 63 Stat. 413 (1949).

21. *Berman v. Parker*, 348 U.S. 26 (1954); *Kelo v. City of New London*, 545 U.S. 469 (2005).

22. Sites may have been available in the Bedford-Stuyvesant and Brownsville districts, which O'Malley rejected, possibly on grounds of the neighborhoods' economic and racial makeup. On one of his preferred locations, at Flatbush and Atlantic, the new Barclays Center basketball stadium designed by Ellerbe Becket is being built.

    The recent backlash against Moses rather than O'Malley as the proximate cause of Brooklyn's loss of the Dodgers, see Shapiro, supra note 2, may be overstated. The Dodgers had lukewarm support throughout the city government. "[Moses] may have been right to argue that a privately owned baseball stadium for a privately owned baseball team did not conform to the 'public purpose' and should not have been even partly financed with federal funds." David Nasaw, "Hitler, Stalin, O'Malley and Moses," *New York Times*, 25 May 2003 (review of Shapiro, supra note 2).

23. Reactions expressing betrayal are legion. Three samples will suffice:

    "In the hearts of Brooklyn fans, O'Malley had secured his place in a line of infamy which now crossed the centuries from Judas Iscariot to Benedict Arnold to Walter F. O'Malley. Effigies of the Dodgers owner were burned on the streets of Brooklyn." Goodwin, supra note 2, at 226.

    "O'Malley's reputation only worsens with the passage of time. There is no loss of emotion even in the twenty-first century. Such perpetuation of emotional loss into the next generation suggests just how strong the symbolic relationship between Brooklyn and the Dodgers was." Ellsworth, supra note 2, at 35.

    "The Dodgers were more than a business. They represented a cultural totem, a tangible symbol of the community and its values." Sullivan, supra note 2, at 18.

24. See D'Antonio, supra note 2, at 250; Greenburg, supra note 18.

25. For artists' impressions of the district's social culture, see Don Normark, *Chávez Ravine, 1949* (2003); Ry Cooder, *Chávez Ravine* (Nonesuch Records, 2005); Lynn Becker, ArchitectureChicago Plus (review of Cooder's "ballads of Chavez Ravine"), available at arcchicago.blogspot.com (accessed 29 November 2010).

26. See "Public Housing and the Brooklyn Dodgers: Los Angeles, Double Play by City Hall in the Ravine," *Frontier*, June 1957, available at www.library.ucla.edu/libraries/special/scweb (accessed 29 November 2010).

27. A documentary film narrated by Cheech Marin, *Chávez Ravine: A Los Angeles Story* (Bullfrog Films 2003), includes footage of the evictions. On condemnation for sports facilities generally, see Tyson E. Hubbard, "For the Public's Use? Eminent Domain in Stadium Construction," *Sports Law. J.* 15 (2008): 173.

28. See Cary S. Henderson, "Los Angeles and the Dodger War, 1957–62," *S. Cal. Q.* (fall 1980): 261–86 (detailed description of terms and negotiations); City of Los Angeles v. Superior Court, 51 Cal. 2d 423, 333 P.2d 745, cert. denied, 361 U.S. 30 (1959).

29. See D'Antonio, supra note 2, at 289–90.

30. Steven A. Riess, "Historical Perspectives on Sports and Public Policy," in *The Economics and Politics of Sports Facilities* ed. Wilbur C. Rich (Westport, Conn.: Quorum Books, 2000), 30.

31. "From dugout seats to in-stadium restaurants, to a message board to terraced parking lots removing the need for people to climb stairs or ramps to their seats, Dodger Stadium was full of new ideas. It was the first large baseball stadium built without pillars that blocked the view from some seats." McCue, supra note 8.

32. See Robert V. Bellamy Jr. and James R. Walker, "Whatever Happened to Synergy? MLB as Media Product," *Nine* 13, no. 2 (2005): 19–30; Sallie Hofmeister, "Deal Shows Use of Teams to Build a Global TV Empire," *Los Angeles Times*, 20 March 1998; Sallie Hofmeister, "Murdoch Deal Sets Stage for Fox Challenge to ESPN," *Los Angeles Times*, 24 June 1997.

33. Riess, supra note 30, at 29, citing Charles C. Euchner, *Playing the Field: Why Sports Teams Move and Cities Fight to Keep Them* (Baltimore: Johns Hopkins University Press, 1993), 19.

Brilliant Specialists

David B. Hart

Hub Fans Bid Kid Adieu: John Updike on Ted Williams
by John Updike
The Library of America (2010)
$15.00 (hardcover). 64 pages

John Updike received warm praise from *New Yorker* editor William Shawn for "Hub Fans," but "the compliment that meant most to me," Updike wrote, "came from Williams himself, who through an agent invited me to write his biography. I declined the honor. I had said all I had to say."

IT IS HARD NOT TO BEGIN this review with the phrase "This slender volume." (In fact, I avoided doing so only by pulling the coy trick of beginning it the way I just did.) But this *is*, in fact, a very slender volume, and the few pages it comprises are only sparsely populated by text; it's more an oversized postcard, really. Other than a very brief author's preface and a short coda distilled from a few other of his fragmentary jottings on Williams, the book contains only the text of Updike's celebrated 1960 *New Yorker* essay (with the footnotes he added in 1965), recounting Ted Williams's final game (played at Fenway, against the Orioles) and the splendidly improbable home run he hit in his last at-bat. In the case of this volume, however, the minimalist approach has worked beautifully. A compact and handsome fiftieth-anniversary tribute to what many regard as one of the best baseball essays ever written, it is at the same time a pleasant, slightly accidental commemoration of its author, who died only last year.

Baseball has generated a richer, deeper, and more sustained literary tradition than any other sport. Only cricket has produced books of comparable literary quality, and the best of these—C. L. R. James's masterpiece of social philosophy *Beyond a Boundary*, Hugh de Selincourt's gossamer eclogue *The Cricket Match*—have been slightly eccentric rarities; there is no large continuous school of cricket writing, and the cricket essay has never become a recognized genre all to itself. The literature of baseball, however, is a crowded and distinguished field, and so it really is a considerable achievement for any single short piece of baseball writing to have acquired the sort of mythic luster that attaches to the Updike essay. It is especially impressive, perhaps, in that it is really the only piece of baseball writing Updike ever did.

Of course, according to Updike he was not really writing about baseball at all but rather about Williams, his boyhood hero. Perhaps this is true; but, even so, some of the more famous passages capture the poetry of the game so exquisitely that they have to stir some-

thing in any lover of the game: "Baseball, with its graceful intermittences of action, its immense and tranquil field sparsely settled with poised men in white, its dispassionate mathematics, seems to me best suited to accommodate, and be ornamented by, a loner. It is an essentially lonely game." And, even when reflecting specifically on Williams, Updike occasionally shows what looks like an aficionado's eye for detail, as when he calls attention to the qualitatively peculiar trajectory of some of Williams's low, squarely struck, continuously rising home runs. (My father has often regaled his sons with the golden legend of that trajectory—specifically a home run Williams hit in the old Oriole Park late in his career, a shot that took a foot-long splinter out of one of the wooden seats over the right-field wall, still apparently on the ascent when it did so.)

I suppose the question one ought to ask—since the Library of America has gone to the trouble of producing a single-volume edition of what remains, at the end of the day, only a diverting "occasional" essay—is whether the piece really holds up well fifty years along. In a way—but only in a very impressive way—it does not. The truth is that it's been set apart in a class of its own for so long that it no longer needs to be measured against other specimens of baseball writing to ensure its reputation; one measures it now against itself, and against the memory of it that one has from previous readings. Picking it up again this time around, I couldn't help but notice that it has a somewhat slighter feel about it than I remembered it having. I thought I recalled it as being just a bit longer, more lyrical, more suspenseful in its build-up to that final plate appearance, more saturated with the light and colors of late September. But that in itself is a kind of tribute to the essay: It clearly has an evocative power, and generates a kind of emotional atmosphere, that lingers on and that far exceeds what's immediately evident on the page.

In the end, it really is the nonpareil baseball essay it's reputed to be. Nothing about it seems dated. (Well, almost nothing: It is momentarily arresting to come across a merely anonymous mention of "the Orioles third baseman"—and, really, by late 1960 most serious followers of the game were well aware of who that was.) Only a few sentences seem overly mannered; for the most part, Updike had already, at only twenty-eight years of age, achieved the sparkling ease of his mature style. And all the famous, oft-repeated phrases still ring out with a crystal tone: "the tissue-thin difference between a thing done well and a thing done ill"; or "that intensity of competence that crowds the throat with joy"; or "when a density of expectation hangs in the air and plucks an event out of the future"; or "immortality is nontransferable"; or, of course, "Gods do not answer letters."

And, perhaps most importantly, the high points do not tower over the rest of the essay. It's a model of elegant writing throughout. Even the brief précis of Williams's career with which Updike sets the scene is graceful; only the most interesting and salient statistics are cited, and always in order to cast light on the strangely remote character of the man who amassed them. Then the narrative proper begins, and proceeds at just the right pace; the story almost seems to tell itself. Of course, in a sense it did tell itself. How Updike would have finished the tale if Williams had weakly flied out in the eighth is hard to imagine. He might not have written about the game at all; or he might have dwelled longer on its soft autumnal sadness, and tried to write it with even greater poignancy. Whatever the case, it would have lacked that last, faintly magical moment that draws the whole story—not only the story of that day, but the story of Williams's entire career—to its achingly symbolic dénouement.

In long retrospect, it seems to me that Updike and Williams were oddly suited to one another, and it's something of a fortunate accident that their careers briefly converged in one unexpectedly exquisite magazine article. This may seem like a less than gracious observation, but I mean it as very high praise indeed: Soberly and honestly considered, each man was a brilliant specialist—by which I mean, each was supremely skilled in one vital facet of his craft, and merely better than ordinary at all its other aspects. Williams was a pure hitter of almost uncanny ability, of course, with that fluid, oddly dipping and rising yet perfectly timed swing of his: a dead pull hitter in the live-ball era

After Williams homered in the last at-bat of his career, the crowd, other players, and even the umpires begged him to step out of the dugout and acknowledge the ovation, "but he refused," Updike wrote. "Gods do not answer letters."

who ripped heroically at everything inside and yet who could still post averages with which Ty Cobb or Rogers Hornsby would have been quite contented come the fall. It almost defies belief, frankly. And yet, at everything else in the game he was unexceptional. On the bases or in the field, he discharged his duties well enough, and he kept himself in good athletic trim throughout his playing days; but it was only with the bat that he stood apart from other players.

Similarly Updike was, at his best, an altogether magnificent prose stylist. There are many, many passages in his collected works that rival or surpass the best work of just about any other English-language writer of the twentieth century; there are whole paragraphs and chapters of almost delirious beauty. And yet he never really wrote a great book. Even the very best of his novels (such as *The Centaur*) and the most accomplished of his short stories (such as the early Maples stories) always somehow seemed to add up to less than the sum of their glittering sentences and ingenious metaphors. They were good novels and good stories, diverting and clever, and sometimes astonishingly good in many of their individual parts; but they were never masterpieces.

That, though, is not a criticism. The careers of both Williams and Updike serve as excellent reminders that, in most walks of life, only a very few of us are capable of doing anything as near to perfection as humanly possible. For anyone, though, who does have the ability, concentrating on that one extraordinary skill or gift, even at the price of doing everything else (at most) only a little better than average, is the surest way to achieve genuine greatness. And, having achieved it, such a person should certainly be regarded not only with admiration, but also with a little awe. ■

The Dark Side of a Baseball Dynasty

Ron Kaplan

The Last Boy: Mickey Mantle and the End of America's Childhood
by Jane Leavy
Harper (2010)
$27.99 (hardcover); $12.99 (e-book). 480 pages

Steinbrenner: The Last Lion of Baseball
by Bill Madden
Harper (2010)
$26.99 (hardcover); $12.99 (e-book). 480 pages

Roger Maris: Baseball's Reluctant Hero
by Tom Clavin and Danny Peary
Touchstone (2010)
$26.99 (hardcover); $12.99 (e-book). 422 pages

The Yankee Years
by Joe Torre and Tom Verducci
Anchor (2010)
$16.95 (paperback); $9.89 (e-book). 528 pages

Author's note: The New York Yankees suffered several major losses in 2010, the least of which was their ouster in the American League Championship series by the Texas Rangers. George Steinbrenner, the team's tempestuous owner who brought them back into relevance after several years out of the limelight, passed away, as did Bob Sheppard, their longtime golden-throated public-address announcer. Shortly before he died, Steinbrenner joined a group of Yankee legends who had written or were the subject of recent books, including Joe Torre, Roger Maris, and, most recently, Mickey Mantle.

———

IF SHE'S NOT CAREFUL, Jane Leavy will earn a reputation as the Boswell of the battered ballplayer. In 2002 she published *Sandy Koufax: A Lefty's Legacy*, the definitive biography (to this point) of the role model for Jewish boomers everywhere. In 2010, it's *The Last Boy:*

Mickey Mantle, whose retirement in 1968 rather than his death in 1995 marked what biographer Jane Leavy describes as "the end of America's childhood."

Mickey Mantle and the End of America's Childhood, the much anticipated story of another hero laid low by injury.

Whereas Koufax's arthritic left arm dramatically shortened an amazing career at age 30, the question about Mantle is how much better he might have been had he not exacerbated his numerous injuries with his profligate ways. How many more home runs could he have powered over the outfield walls were it not for the booze and the broads? Surely he would have retired with the .300 batting average he decided was the true mark of a truly great player. Even the book jacket illustrates Mantle's degeneration: The photo of a smiling rookie with unlimited potential is accompanied by that of a broken-down veteran, almost literally on his last legs.

"The end of America's childhood" came not with Mantle's death in 1995 but with his retirement almost thirty years earlier (which I suppose is a kind of death). The Yankees—indeed Boomer America itself—seemed to fall from innocence with the assassination of John F. Kennedy. Since then, the reverence that would have precluded books such as Jim Bouton's *Ball Four* and Jose Canseco's *Juiced*, which take the heroic figure off the pedestal and put him under the microscope, have become the norm, and the heretofore standard reverential tome has flown out the window. It was no longer enough to write about hard work and gumption; now every subject had to overcome some traumatic obstacle, whether it was substance or sexual abuse (or, as it turns out in Mantle's case, both).

Leavy, an award-winning former sports and feature writer for the *Washington Post*, admits to being an unabashed Mantle fan since childhood—and the journalist's objectivism be damned. In that, she shares his fans' adoration and disappointment. But in demonstrating her impressive investigative skills, Leavy goes perhaps a bit overboard as she deconstructs a few of Mantle's tape-measure home runs and provides testimonials for his considerable athletic skills. It is admirable in scope, as she discusses bat velocity, angles, and meteorological conditions with the scientific community, but does it really matter if the ball went 430 feet or 450 or 480? In the Cold War era, when for the American psyche to be the best at everything was so important, this display of power was comforting.

The author interviewed hundreds of people in the course of her research, all to turn out this most in-depth look at the Commerce Comet yet published. But the reader might wonder about the accuracy of her collective memory, as about those questionable tape-measure home runs, or even wonder about the possibility of downright fabrication for the sake of building up the impression of her personal connection to the Mick.

Leavy alternates between some of the biggest events in Mantle's career (for better or worse) and her fateful interview in April 1983, when he was reduced to working as a glad-hander for an Atlantic City casino. Her rose-colored glasses were shattered. Who kidnapped her beloved Mick and replaced him with this boorish drunk with the foul mouth and roaming hands? Still, Leavy managed to retain her composure and professionalism to get the story done . . . which served as the impetus for this book.

There is little joy in *The Last Boy*. Mantle's accomplishments were diminished in his own eyes then and in those of many baseball fans later on when they learned the extent of his boozing and womanizing. That his "live for today" attitude stemmed from his belief that he would die young or from the sexual abuse he suffered as a child (a subject that, despite all the play it got in the media, isn't discussed until the end of the book) makes that outcome all the sadder. The description of his last days, when liver problems and cancer ravaged his once powerful body, defies the ability of even the most sangfroid reader not to get misty-eyed.

JUST A FEW GENERATIONS BACK, many professional clubs were family-run operations that were in business for the long haul. Now there is just one (at least in baseball), and the end of an era is in sight, according to Bill Madden, the award-winning sports columnist and author of *Steinbrenner: The Last Lion of Baseball*.

There were many adjectives used to describe George Michael Steinbrenner III, principal owner and chair of the New York Yankees, and most were not complimentary. Since he took over the team in the early 1970s, there has been no shortage of fodder for the local press, including Madden, who has followed the game for the *New York Daily News*. "Der Boss" (one of Steinbrenner's many nicknames) was famous for his fiery temper; before Joe Torre, the Bronx Bombers went through twenty managerial changes between 1973 and 1995, including several repeat performances, most notably by the late Billy Martin. And that doesn't even take into account front-office personnel. He would order his underlings to handle a task or acquire a certain player, often disregarding the objections of those far more knowledgeable in such matters, and then explode when things didn't work out his way. He would fire, then rehire, at the drop of a pin, often excusing the hasty behavior with "I didn't really mean it" or "I'll let it go, this time."

Yankees fans and haters were well aware of Steinbrenner's mercurial nature. His apologists point to his success while his detractors note the distractions and bad feelings among the team's personnel. Forget the infamous quote from Reggie Jackson about his being "the straw that stirs the drink," that sobriquet should go to Steinbrenner. In fact, one has to wonder: Does such drama like this occur on other clubs (Frank and Jamie McCourt's messy divorce notwithstanding), or did we hear more about Steinbrenner's antics because his team played in the media capital of the world?

Did his megalomania come from some deep-rooted desire to both win the approval of his father—a strict, hardworking, successful businessman—and yet prove himself to be his own man? Hard to say, although Madden certainly pushes the reader in that direction, albeit without the psychological profiling. Citing one example after another, he chronicles the Yankees' chief as a bully and a liar, who could be incalculably mean while at the same time setting up a foundation to make sure that children of deceased New York City police and firefighters were able to go to college. Madden includes the praise as well as the lash, but the former was far-between or generally underreported throughout the years; for all his penchant for being the center of attention, Steinbrenner didn't court the press to promote his good deeds.

A recipient of the Baseball Hall of Fame's annual Spink Award for outstanding career accomplishments as a writer, Madden strives to be even-handed. His role for the New York papers put him in a position to write a first-hand account, but he uses that relationship with a light hand, relying on his skills as a journalist rather than employing his personal observations. While dutifully covering Steinbrenner's rightful banishment from the game in the 1970s because of his illegal campaign contributions to Richard Nixon's presidential campaign, Madden goes to great lengths to show that his subject was unfairly treated by Commissioner Fay Vincent, who kicked him out of the game in 1990 for giving $40,000 to Howard Spira, a two-bit hustler, for his role in digging up dirt on Yankees outfielder Dave Winfield, with whom Steinbrenner was feuding over financial matters. Baseball, it seems, is not a law unto itself, and even Steinbrenner had rights of due process.

Sadly, the last few years were not kind to the Yankees' leader. Ill health rendered him a shell of his former, larger-than-life persona. Madden reports this with a mix of professional objectivity and personal sadness. After all, the two had had a working relationship and had even been fairly close at one point.

Are there elements in the book that might offend the Steinbrenner family? Perhaps. But as Madden relates in the introduction, he undertook the project at their suggestion. And judging by all accounts, he seems to have done a fair and balanced job.

———

IT'S FITTING THAT BOOKS on both of the M&M Boys were published in 2010. While not carrying the same level of notoriety as *The Last Boy*—given the pecking order of the players involved—Tom Clavin and Danny Peary's *Roger Maris: Baseball's Reluctant Hero* is a similarly insightful and welcome profile that looks into the soul of another troubled Yankee great.

Peary has noted in interviews that Maris—who like his buddy Mantle was a small-town boy thrust into the spotlight—was perhaps the least-prepared person to deal with the success and pressure that came when he challenged Babe Ruth's single-season home-run record of 60 in 1961.

It was Maris's misfortune, and obviously not of his own doing, to come along in an era when the schedule had expanded from 154 games to 162, thereby giving "haters" (including baseball commissioner and former Ruth confidant Ford Frick) an opportunity to denigrate the Yankee slugger's accomplishments. Add to that a new generation of iconoclastic journalists who refused to kowtow to athletes as their predecessors did, and you have a confluence of events that turned the loving family man into a taciturn, short-

Roger Maris was, like his teammate Mantle, a small-town boy thrust into the spotlight. His biographers portray the Yankee front office as derelict in not helping him deal with the media crush during the 1961 season, when he chased and eventually broke Ruth's single-season home-run record.

tempered, and uncooperative subject, as he was besieged daily by reporters looking for a fresh story or an original quote.

Peary and Clavin maintain that his employers were derelict in not helping him deal with the media crush. (These days, all the questions would be addressed in pregame and postgame press conferences.) Add to that the team's mishandling of a hand injury Maris suffered and you have a sad situation that was only barely alleviated by his trade in 1967 to the St. Louis Cardinals, a team he helped lead to two National League pennants and a World Series even while on the downside of his career.

———

IN *THE YANKEE YEARS*, former manager Joe Torre teams up with *Sports Illustrated*'s senior baseball writer Tom Verducci for a unique and somewhat baffling presentation.

Although Torre gets star billing, the reader will get the impression that Verducci is telling the story, since the narrative is written in the third person.

Torre was an All-Star and a Most Valuable Player during his 18-year career. He also managed the New York Mets, Atlanta Braves, and St. Louis Cardinals before taking over the Yankee reins. His considerable lack of success in those previous go-arounds made him a curious candidate in the eyes of the press and the fans.

For the most part, this is a standard baseball tale of hard work, success, and frustration. The last element is especially salient when you consider that Torre's employer, George Steinbrenner, was one of the most hands-on (or meddlesome, depending on your point of view) owners in the history of the game, going through managers like a cold-sufferer going through boxes of tissues.

But Torre gave the club a stability it hadn't known since Casey Stengel led the Yankees to a constant stream of pennants and world championships from 1949 through 1960. From the very beginning, he took control over a mix of veterans and rookies and molded them into a team, as trite as that might sound: The Yankees ran off a string of three consecutive World Series titles and four in five years.

Ultimately, *The Yankee Years* is a sad tale on the natural order of things in the sports world. Athletes grow older, their skills diminish, and they are replaced by others who may be better or worse, with different drives and agendas. That was part of Torre's downfall. In his first few seasons he was surrounded by the likes of Paul O'Neill, Bernie Williams, Derek Jeter, Jorge Posada, and others who meshed so well together, working for that common goal. But the ones who followed seemed less interested in Yankee tradition and more in individual performances. Some—David Wells, Kyle Farnsworth, Carl Pavano, and Kevin Brown, to name a few—were a constant source of disappointment. The Yankees kept winning, but for Torre the spark and joy were missing.

Working for Steinbrenner and his front-office minions presented its own set of difficulties, constant scrutiny and job insecurity being two of them. Despite thirteen consecutive postseason appearances, someone was always looking over Torre's shoulder, quick to criticize if some bit of strategy backfired or if things weren't running smoothly. After an initial euphoria, the tone of the book becomes more forlorn with every chapter. Baseball fans know the inevitable outcome—Torre was not retained following the 2007 season and was named manager of the Los Angeles Dodgers (which he led to the postseason in his first season)—but Verducci hammers the point home anyway: "It was," he writes, "the 1,294th win with the Yankees for Torre, including postseason play, over 12 seasons. It would be the last." And: "He showered, dressed and left his office and the clubhouse believing this would be the final time he would do so as manager of the New York Yankees. He did not look back." It is fitting that the book jacket features a picture of Torre walking away from the camera.

There was a great gnashing of teeth in the run-up to the publication of *The Yankee Years*, with promises of dirt to be dished and secrets to be revealed, but Torre's autobiography/memoir can be summed up with a title from Shakespeare: *Much Ado About Nothing*. Like the trailer of a two-star movie, the media—many members of which admitted to not having read the book in its entirety when they made their com-

ments—cherry-picked parts for maximum bang. In particular, they focused on Torre's remarks about Alex Rodriguez, whom he characterized as high-maintenance, more concerned with how he looked and performed than with his contributions to the team's success. They failed to mention that Torre also praised Rodriguez: "Nobody has ever worked harder in my memory than this guy," he wrote.

Torre also expressed disappointment in his deteriorating relationship with Brian Cashman, the Yankees' general manager, whom he accused of not supporting him when the chips were down.

Taken as a whole, *The Yankee Years* is a standard bit of baseball memoir, no worse and perhaps better than others that have been published in recent years. Too bad it couldn't have had a happier ending.

Charlie Finley

Steve Weingarden

Charlie Finley: The Outrageous Story of Baseball's Super Showman
by G. Michael Green and Roger D. Launius
Walker and Company (2010)
$27 (hardcover); $14.85 (e-book). 368 pages

WITH ITS WEALTH OF FIRST-HAND interviews and archival resources, Charlie Finley: The Outrageous Story of Baseball's Super Showman provides insights from those who dealt with Charlie Finley. In fact, this book arguably is more about the reflections of his players, staff, media, and family than about the icon himself. The in-depth investigation by the authors, their *sweat* and *sacrifice*, is the key to making this book a *success*—as in Finley's own formula of S + S = S.

Much of the book's focus is on Finley's need for control and how it led him to alienate others. Examples are multiplied throughout. He insisted on having the ultimate authority and the ability to override the decisions of general manager Frank Lane and field manager Joe Gordon. There were his late-night phone calls to his cousin Carl and others who worked in the front office. To Reggie Jackson and Mike Andrews he presented prewritten statements for them to sign. No doubt, Finley had issues with control, and like many MLB owners, apparently (this may be nearly a requirement for battling one's way into the exclusive club), he demonstrated behavioral evidence of high levels of narcissism—there were his feelings of self-importance, his pronounced angry reactions to criticism, his unreasonable expectations of favorable treatment, his extreme lack of concern for others.

I took a look back at some research I completed with colleagues several years ago. Consistent with one of the central premises of Green and Launius, our study of approximately one hundred team presidents and owners found that Finley had the lowest ranking on measures of providing individualized support, defined as behaving in a manner that demonstrates both respect for members of the organization and concern about their personal feelings and needs.[1]

One wonders, given other details the authors provide, if the character of Finley's involvement in baseball would have been different had he entered the fray at a more mature time in his life. His insurance office and the American League office were in the same building when, all of 36 years old, he first tried to buy the A's. The ensuing negative experience taught him some lessons about the ownership clique. It may also have activated and amplified his narcissist tendencies. He was 42, still perhaps with opportunity for personal leadership growth (age tends to be a factor but is not the only determinant for leadership growth), when he finally succeeded in his bid to purchase the A's and was thrust into the spotlight. My suspicion is that the authors would argue that Finley's personality would have been susceptible to the same leadership derailers regardless of his maturity at the time of purchase, but they offer such extensive detail that readers can choose their own customized paths of inquiry.

The book moves quickly and the authors write well. The stories and quotes are rich and enjoyable. Joe Rudi reflects on an emotional-whirlwind phone call from Finley about Rudi's 1974 contract; Martin Finley recounts a picture taken of his mother, Shirley Finley, at Charlie's funeral. And there is Hank Peters summing up Finley's qualifications to lead the front office: "Charlie Finley didn't know beans about baseball."[2]

That said, I did nonetheless feel anger over the treatment—the misguided and Machiavellian processes and hard-to-fathom decisions he suffered through—that Finley suffered at the hands of other owners and Bowie Kuhn. It is interesting to note that Green and Launius indirectly (and at certain points more directly) do a nice job fleshing out, perhaps, the baseball establishment's real problems with Charlie Finley. Ford Frick's autobiography does not mention Finley even once and barely mentions the Kansas City Athletics.[3]

One concern I did have is that the book may not

Charlie Finley, Steve Weingarden found, ranked exceptionally low among club owners and presidents on measures of demonstrating respect for members of the organization. He was 42 when he bought the A's. Would the character of his ownership had been better had he been more mature when he entered the "owners' clique"?

have been consistently critical enough of the media treatment Finley received. The criticism leveled by reporter Ernie Mehl was less than objective and almost swaggering, and the potential conflict of interest in his coverage was given something of a pass, while Red Smith received only a glancing light knock when he failed to include the World Series in his coverage, although Shirley Povich, by contrast, received strong pushback for his unsupported personal attacks on Finley.

A related concern is the occasional overstatement. For example, I wasn't convinced by the logic and evidence for the claim that Finley's three-ball-walk rule, which he proposed as a measure to increase offense, was similar to "the decision made by owners in the 1990s to turn a blind eye to the players' bulking up through steroid use." Foremost, the statement wasn't incorporated naturally into the text and I was unclear, in multiple ways, as to the true similarity of the three-ball-walk rule and steroid usage—pitchers were just as likely to use steroids as were power hitters, suggesting that increased offense was not a goal pursued by owners when they addressed steroid usage, and I am unaware of public statements by owners that they would turn a blind eye to steroids to increase offense. Another example is the claim that, "Kansas Citians simply wanted stability and harmony in their Major League Baseball team." That could be true, but I wasn't fully convinced, by the evidence, that for Kansas Citians a winning team wasn't actually a priority.

The book is written in chronological order but does jump around within any given year. So the sequence of events can sometimes be difficult for the reader to juggle, leading to a stoppage and review of the previous page or two to determine what event happened first. For example, in a discussion of the A's, a Beatles concert, and the Kansas City market for baseball, I became a little bit lost between 1963, 1964, and 1965. Fully understanding the need to complete a portion of a story or theme before moving on to the next item, I considered this a minor issue, but I would recommend that important events be included on a timeline as part of an appendix, to help ground readers as to what was happening when.

From my perspective, there are four key takeaways from this book:

Charlie Finley had unusual demands for control.

Charlie Finley mistreated others—most others.

Charlie Finley was mistreated by most members of the owners' clique, the commissioner, and some unprofessional members of the media (aka anyone who clung onto the owners' clique).

This book has new details on most of the fantastic Charlie Finley stories told over the years.

For the fourth point, alone, *Charlie Finley: The Outrageous Story of Baseball's Super Showman* is a worthwhile read. Compared to other books on Charlie Finley or other MLB owners, this one fares well, making a contribution through original interviews and a nice table-turning focus on the reactions that others had to Finley's behavior and on the interpretation of how that behavior reflects Finley's personality.

One last note of importance is the authors' acknowledgment of SABR conferences and several SABR members as being important in their writing of this book. It's good to know that SABR is fostering research for its members and through its members, events, and publications. ∎

Notes

1. See, for example, Steve Weingarden, Christian J. Resick, and Daniel S. Whitman, "Why Is That Executive a Hall of Famer? Have You Seen His Leadership Stats?" *Outside the Lines* 12, no. 2 (2006): 1–4. Finley ranked lower than such famously self-centered owners as Marge Schott, Jerry Reinsdorf, and George Steinbrenner. He was rated at 1.42 on a 7-point scale, making him the only executive in the study to receive a rating under 2.0 for providing individualized support. The average rating was 4.86. Finley's graciousness, examples of which are highlighted in the book, was overshadowed by the rage and disrespect he demonstrated to the same individuals over time.

2. Marvin Miller suggests something perhaps in contradiction to Peters, calling Finley "the finest judge of baseball talent I ever saw at the head of a team. See Miller, *A Whole Different Ball Game: The Inside Story of the Baseball Revolution* (Chicago: Ivan R. Dee, 2004). Peters's quote stood out to me, as it made the emotional connection, especially when combined with player reminisces of their dealings with Finley. If you have ever suffered a boss who not only lacks the necessary technical knowledge, skills, and abilities for his position—something that to some degree he can correct over time—but also lacks the ability to lead, insists on overinvolvement, and is prone to be cruel when protecting his own hollow status, your stomach can only turn when reading what it must have been like for the individuals who worked in the A's organization during Finley's tenure. This fact, the infliction of unnecessary suffering on others on a daily basis for an extended period of time and the lack of sensitivity toward others, made it difficult for me to feel any affection for Finley or much pity for him in his suffering.

3. Ford C. Frick, *Games, Asterisks, and People: Memoirs of a Lucky Fan* (New York: Crown, 1973). In turn, the authors of *Charlie Finley: The Outrageous Story of Baseball's Super Showman* mention Frick only a couple of times and don't mention short-termer Spike Eckert at all. It wasn't until Finley moved the A's to Oakland and the team started winning that the vicious and uneven treatment of Finley picked up steam, led by Commissioner Kuhn, who was serving in a role in which, theoretically, he should have protected and affirmed Finley's equal standing with the other owners. It's difficult to find a hero in an assassin's guild. Even though I knew how many of the stories were going to end, I found myself needing someone to root for and, in many instances, landing on Marvin Miller, a side character in this particular book.

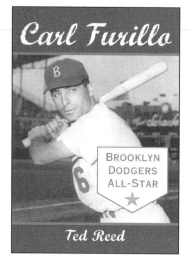
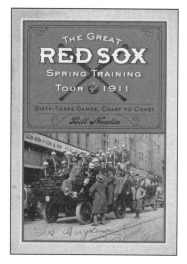
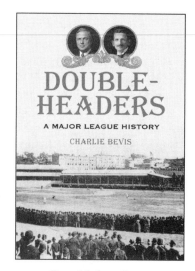
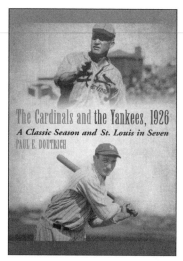
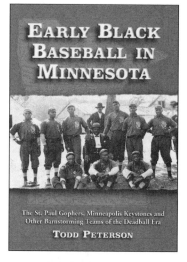
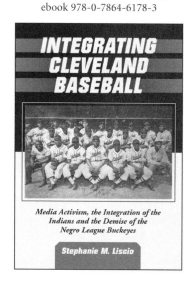

Contributors

JIM ALBERT is professor of mathematical statistics at Bowling Green State University.

DAN BASCO is a graduate student and teaching assistant in the statistics department at the University of Akron.

ROBERT C. BERRING is Walter Perry Johnson Professor of Law at the University of California, Berkeley, School of Law.

PHIL BIRNBAUM is editor of *By the Numbers*, the newsletter of SABR's Statistical Analysis Committee. A native of Toronto, he now lives in Ottawa, where he works as a software developer.

MICHAEL DAVIES is a student at Sidwell Friends School in Washington, D.C.

ROSS E. DAVIES, editor in chief of the *Green Bag Almanac and Reader*, is a law professor at George Mason University.

KEN FENSTER is professor of history at Georgia Perimeter College, Clarkston Campus. His baseball writing has appeared in *Nine*, *The New Georgia Encyclopedia*, *The African American National Biography*, and *The Baseball Research Journal*.

GLENN P. GREENBERG is a former collegiate baseball pitcher who has always been interested in the use of statistics in baseball.

DAVID B. HART is the author of five books, including *Atheist Delusions: The Christian Revolution and Its Fashionable Enemies* (Yale, 2009), and of the article "A Perfect Game: The Metaphysical Meaning of Baseball" in *First Things* (August/September 2010).

RYAN HUTZLER, who has received academic awards for his scholarship on baseball and Chinese culture and society, works for a law firm in Washington, D.C.

MARCUS JAICLIN, assistant professor of mathematics at Westfield State University, is coauthoring a book on the application of statistics to measure performance in sports and wellness.

ROBERT A. JAMES is a partner in the San Francisco and Houston offices of Pillsbury Winthrop Shaw Pittman LLP and a lecturer at the University of California, Berkeley, School of Law.

RON KAPLAN, editor of SABR's Bibliography Committee newsletter, blogs about baseball literature and other media at ronkaplansbaseballbookshelf.com.

HERM KRABBENHOFT, a retired research chemist, is a lifelong Tigers fan. His current baseball research is focused on establishing accurate runs-scored and runs-batted-in statistics on a game-by-game basis for each Tigers player— in order to ascertain their longest consecutive-games streaks for scoring or batting in at least one run.

JOSEPH McCOLLUM is assistant professor of quantitative business analysis in the school of business, Siena College, where he teaches math primarily to future teachers. He has published in pure mathematics and random-walk theory.

TRENT McCOTTER is a law student at the University of North Carolina at Chapel Hill.

BOB MOTLEY, the only living Negro Leagues umpire, lives in Kansas City, Missouri.

BYRON MOTLEY, the son of Bob Motley, is a historian of the Negro Leagues.

JUSTIN MURPHY is a reporter for *The Citizen* newspaper in Auburn, New York. He also contributes to the website Seamheads.

C. PAUL ROGERS III is the coauthor, with boyhood hero Robin Roberts, of *The Whiz Kids and the 1950 Pennant* (Temple, 1996) and, with Eddie Robinson, of Robinson's memoir *Lucky Me: My Sixty-Five Years in Baseball* (Southern Methodist University Press, forthcoming). He is president of the Hall-Ruggles (Dallas–Ft. Worth) chapter of SABR, but his real job is as a law professor at Southern Methodist University.

BRYAN SODERHOLM-DIFATTE, who lives and works in the Washington, D.C., area, is devoted to the study of Major League Baseball history.

BOB WARRINGTON, a member of the Philadelphia Athletics Historical Society, has written extensively about the history of baseball in Philadelphia.

STEVE WEINGARDEN is an organizational psychologist. He has researched MLB team owners and presidents for nearly a decade. He currently cochairs SABR's Business of Baseball Committee.

Corrections

The National Pastme: Baseball in the Peach State, SABR convention journal, 2010

    Cover: In the team photo, the player IDs of (Zeke) Wilson and (George) Leidy, written in vintage ink, should actually be transposed. Who would have guessed? Mark Fimoff. For details, see Fimoff, *Pictorial History Newsletter Supplement*, October 2010, 10.

The Baseball Research Journal, volume 39, number 1, spring 2010

    "Stealing First Base" by Jim Kreuz, 35–38.

        Page 37: The correct spelling of the players' names are Dontrelle Willis and Don Newcombe.

    "Larry Doby's 'The Catch'" by Ken Saulter, 103.

        Page 103: The correct spelling of the pitcher's name is Art Houtteman.

    Henry Chadwick Award, David S. Neft, 127.

        Page 127: David S. Neft was born in 1937 (and currently lives in New York City).
He did not interview for a job at Information Concepts Incorporated but was a founding member and chief financial officer. Gannett owned the polling company Louis Harris and Associates when Neft returned to work for them in 1976. He retired from Gannett as vice president for research in 2002.

Update: Emile H. Rothe, in "Fielding Feats" (*The Baseball Research Journal* 7 [1978]: 22–28), identifies three players as sharing a record of committing four errors in a single inning:

    Jimmy Burke, third base, Milwaukee (AL), 1901; **Ray Chapman**, shortstop, Indians, 1914; **Lenny Merullo**, shortstop, Cubs, 1942. To that list, add **Bob Brenly**, third base, Giants, 1986. Brenly committed four errors in one inning in a game against the Braves on September 14, 1986, at Candlestick Park.